D1002619

How do we determine whether an action is right or wrong? Until recently, philosophers assumed that this question could be answered by means of a theory of morality, which set forth clearly established rules for moral behavior. More recently, however, a number of philosophers have questioned whether a theory of morality can be postulated in quite this sense. Jean Porter is sympathetic to their critiques of moral theories, but questions whether these go far enough in offering a positive alternative to the accepted view of the moral act. Such an alternative she finds in the work of Thomas Aquinas, whose account of moral rationality is placed in a wider context of ethical thought, and whose moral reasoning is understood as dialectical rather than deductive. The Thomist account of the moral virtues is seen to offer unexpected insights into the relationship between moral rules and the practice of the virtues. For the author, this account can contribute to our own moral reflection, even for those who do not share the religious beliefs of Aquinas.

MORAL ACTION AND CHRISTIAN ETHICS

NEW STUDIES IN CHRISTIAN ETHICS

General editor: Robin Gill

Editorial board: Stephen R. L. Clark, Antony O. Dyson,
Stanley Hauerwas and Robin W. Lovin

In recent years the study of Christian ethics has become an integral part of mainstream theological studies. The reasons for this are not hard to detect. It has become a more widely held view that Christian ethics is actually central to Christian theology as a whole. Theologians increasingly have had to ask what contemporary relevance their discipline has in a context where religious belief is on the wane, and whether Christian ethics (that is, an ethics based on the Gospel of Jesus Christ) has anything to say in a multi-faceted and complex secular society. There is now no shortage of books on most substantive moral issues, written from a wide variety of theological positions. However, what is lacking are books within Christian ethics which are taken at all seriously by those engaged in the wider secular debate. Too few are methodologically substantial; too few have an informed knowledge of parallel discussions in philosophy or the social sciences. This series attempts to remedy the situation. The aims of New Studies in Christian Ethics will therefore be twofold. First, to engage centrally with the secular moral debate at the highest possible intellectual level; second, to demonstrate that Christian ethics can make a distinctive contribution to this debate – either in moral substance, or in terms of underlying moral justifications. It is hoped that the series as a whole will make a substantial contribution to the discipline.

A list of titles in the series is provided at the end of the book.

MORAL ACTION
AND CHRISTIAN ETHICS

JEAN PORTER

Associate Professor of Moral Theology,
University of Notre Dame

CAMBRIDGE
UNIVERSITY PRESS

Published by the Press Syndicate of the University of Cambridge
The Pitt Building, Trumpington Street, Cambridge CB2 IRP
40 West 20th Street, New York, NY 10011–4211, USA
10 Stamford Road, Oakleigh, Melbourne 3166, Australia

© Cambridge University Press 1995

First published 1995
Reprinted 1997
First paperback edition 1999

Printed in the United Kingdom at the University Press, Cambridge

A catalogue record for this book is available from the British Library

Library of Congress cataloguing in publication data

Porter, Jean, 1955–
Moral action and Christian ethics / Jean Porter.
p.   cm. – (New studies in Christian ethics)
Includes bibliographical references.
ISBN 0 521 44329 6 (hardback)
1. Christian ethics.   I. Title.   II. Series.
BJ1190.P67   1995
241–dc20 94–18230   CIP

ISBN 0 521 44329 6 hardback
ISBN 0 521 65710 5 paperback

For Joseph Blenkinsopp

Contents

General editor's preface

Jean Porter's new book is the fifth in the series New Studies in Christian Ethics. Like the first book, Kieran Cronin's well received *Rights and Christian Ethics*, it is more distinctly philosophical than others in the series. Yet it is written with a minimum of jargon and in elegant, pellucid prose. It offers, I believe, a very serious theological challenge to much recent moral philosophy.

As I had hoped, a distinctive shape is beginning to emerge in the series. Not only are contributors well versed in one of the humanities, science, or social science disciplines, they are also prepared to challenge some of the secularist assumptions that often underpin them in the modern university. Kieran Cronin saw considerable areas of overlap between Christians and secularists in the debate about "rights." However, he concluded that Christians (and many others with religious faith) do have deeper "justifying reasons for acting morally" than secularists, precisely because moral behavior for Christians is a part of their relationship to God.

James Mackey's *Power and Christian Ethics* also offered a theological challenge to much secular thought. He argued that, in a world that frequently equates power with force, religious communities (despite their many failures) can have real significance. At best such communities offer a "radical and encompassing sense of life as grace" which "enlightens and empowers people to imagine and create an ever better life, and also to overcome the forces of destruction which one could otherwise only join and increase, but never beat."

Ian Markham's *Plurality and Christian Ethics* also offered a

distinctive theological challenge. In arguing for a position of
what he termed "constructive plurality," he maintained that
secularism as a basis for rational dialogue in the modern world
is surprisingly weak. He argued that theism offers "a more
coherent description of life than any alternative world perspective." He was in the end convinced by those who argue that it
is theism which "makes sense of the objectivity of value and the
intelligibility of the universe."

Others have made similar claims in the debate that is currently raging between modernists and postmodernists.
However, none of the writers in this series relies upon hyper-
bole or engages in dramatic end-of-the-Enlightenment discourse. Ian Markham was quite critical of such discourse,
reminding his readers of some of the positive features of the
Enlightenment, as well as its inherent weaknesses. The dominant discourse in this series is that of a sustained dialogue with
secular disciplines, albeit a critical and non-subservient dialogue. Jean Porter's stance is exactly that. She offers a very
significant theological challenge to much secular moral philosophy, albeit a challenge couched in her sympathetic and
gentle delivery.

Jean Porter is finally unconvinced by what she regards as the
false security of modern moral theories "with their promise of
certainties that we cannot attain." With great skill she undermines a position based simplistically upon moral rules. For her
they pay insufficient attention to the difficulties inherent in
applying notions (whether moral or not), and ignore the analogical nature of moral reasoning. She is sympathetic to the
critiques of modern moral theories that have been offered
recently by philosophers such as Alasdair MacIntyre, Bernard
Williams, and Martha Nussbaum. However, she questions
whether these critiques go far enough in offering a positive
alternative to a modern view of the moral act.

Jean Porter returns to Aquinas and seeks to reclaim his
understanding of the moral act as a product of interdependent
moral virtues. For her the moral life is shaped by subtle
interplay between a healthy self-regard grounded in restraint
and forthrightness, kindliness and decency built out of caring,

and fairness and responsibility forming a basis for justice. These virtues are interdependent and become, so she argues, seriously distorted if adopted in isolation. In combination they suggest that to live justly is also to live well. By way of contrast, she regards Kant's single-minded call to duty as inadequate.

Jean Porter offers a sustained and well-rounded account of the moral act which is both theologically grounded and distinct from many of the products of moral philosophy.

ROBIN GILL

Preface

Scholarship is by its nature a collaborative enterprise, and I cannot even identify, much less thank, everyone who has contributed in some way to the development of my thought on the subject of this book. None the less, I would like to thank those who have contributed more directly to its completion.

In the first place, I wish to thank the administration of the University of Notre Dame, and my department chair, Professor Lawrence Cunningham, for allowing me a sabbatical during the fall semester, 1993, during which I completed a good part of this book. The Association of Theological Schools and the Notre Dame Institute for Scholarship in the Liberal Arts generously provided funding for my research on this project. David Baer offered invaluable help in preparing the final draft of the manuscript, and he also prepared the bibliography.

A number of colleagues have commented on some portion of this manuscript, including Harlan Beckley, Martin Cook, Margaret Farley, William French, James Gustafson, Stephen Pope, and Diane Yeager. My patient and indefatigable editor, Alex Wright, the editor for the series, Robin Gill, and an anonymous reader for Cambridge University Press also offered invaluable suggestions on subsequent drafts of this project. My copy editor, Gillian Maude, offered many helpful stylistic suggestions. David Baer, Laurel Jordan, Louise Prochaska, and Gerald Schlabach prepared extensive bibliographies on some of the subjects that are discussed in this book. Alasdair MacIntyre reviewed and commented on an early draft of a proposal for this project, and offered me considerable help at an early stage of my research. This book should make my continued debt to him abundantly clear.

Portions of the third chapter were read at the Dominican School of Philosophy and Theology, and I received many helpful suggestions from those present. Portions of chapter 4 are taken from two previously published articles, "The Unity of the Virtues and the Ambiguity of Goodness: A Reappraisal of Aquinas' Theory of the Virtues," *The Journal of Religious Ethics* (published by Religious Ethics, Incorporated), 21, 1 (Spring, 1993), 137–163, and "The Subversion of Virtue: Acquired and Infused Virtue in the *Summa theologiae*," *The Annual of the Society of Christian Ethics* (1992), 19–41. Both articles are used with the kind permission of the editors of the journals in which they appeared.

Finally, I want to add a special word of thanks to my husband, Joseph Blenkinsopp. He read most of this manuscript in several drafts, and offered many suggestions for improvement. He also reviewed my translations of Aquinas and saved me from many infelicities and outright mistakes; I take full responsibility for any remaining errors. I am deeply appreciative of this practical assistance, but my greatest debts to him are on another level. It is hard to know how to express my gratitude for all that he has brought into my life without sounding banal. This book is dedicated to him as a small token of my gratitude and love.

Introduction

This book is offered as a contribution to the series, New Studies in Christian Ethics, which has as its aims "1. To engage centrally with the secular moral debate ... 2. To demonstrate that Christian ethics can make a distinctive contribution to this debate – either in moral substance or in terms of underlying moral justification." It brings together two fields of inquiry which are generally kept distinct, often with considerable energy. Yet the distinctions between philosophy and either theology or Christian ethics are not all that obvious. It may be helpful to the reader to have some indication of the aims and assumptions which underlie this project.

In its original form, the distinction between theology and philosophy was grounded in a more fundamental distinction between two disparate sources of knowledge, the one given by divine revelation and received through faith, the other grounded in ordinary human observation, experience, and reflection. Theology was therefore seen as an enterprise for the few, the privileged recipients of revelation, whereas philosophy was seen as an undertaking in which the whole human race could share. Eventually, with the gradual emergence of a secular society, the value judgements associated with this distinction were reversed, but it persisted in more or less the same form right up to the modern period.

At this point, however, the fundamental assumptions which undergirded this division have themselves been called into question. While I am not prepared to say that critical biblical scholarship has discredited any sort of claim to a special revelation, it certainly calls for a serious rethinking of what such a claim could mean. More recently, the collapse of foundation-alism, at least in its more robust modern forms, has similarly undermined our confidence in the powers of a universally valid reason to establish timeless truths. The boundaries between theology, grounded in a privileged revelation, and philosophy, which stands on reason alone, have begun to break down from both sides of this classical divide.

I do not intend to take on the general question of the nature of philosophy and theology as disciplines, or, much less, to attempt to determine their proper interrelationship. At any rate, I have not attempted to draw sharp distinctions between the theological and philosophical components of my own work. In the light of the developments mentioned above, it is not clear, to me at any rate, how the line between these two disciplines should now be drawn. Moreover, it does not seem to me that there is much to be gained, in the way of clarity or persuasiveness, by making an effort to be theological as opposed to philosophical in one's own arguments, or vice-versa. The distinction between theology and philosophy was not originally a distinction of methodology anyway.

Is there any distinction at all, therefore, between Christian ethics and moral philosophy? More to the point, is there any justification for writing a book such as this, or attempting to develop a series such as the one in which it appears? There are, at least, two distinct bodies of literature, within which we find parallel discussions of similar questions, developed more or less in isolation from each other. This fact alone would suggest that it would be a good idea to compare these two literatures, so as to see how the insights of each might contribute to the work of the other. I do attempt this sort of comparison, bringing together discussions of the moral act from philosophical and Christian sources. However, because my aim is to develop a constructive argument, I do not attempt the sort of com-prehensive survey and comparison that would be appropriate to another sort of study.

There is a more fundamental distinction between Christian ethics and moral philosophy, which is reflected in the distinc-tive literatures of each discipline. That is, the Christian author inevitably brings a set of concerns, and a sense of what is problematic, that is different from the concerns and presuppositions of someone who is not committed to Christianity. The Christian ethicist will see different problems, and will construe familiar problems in different ways, than does her counterpart from another tradition. These different perspectives, in turn, can lead to distinctive insights, which can be recognized as such, and appropriated, even by those who do not share one another's starting-points.

The development of this project is a case in point. It would be unusual to find a treatise in moral philosophy on the moral act *per se* in contrast to moral rules or, more recently, virtues and character. On the other hand, this subject would naturally suggest itself to someone within the Christian tradition, especially a Catholic of a certain age, who would have been brought up in the atmosphere of the confessional and the examination of conscience.

Certainly, my own interest in the moral act, which goes back to my days as a graduate student, first arose in the context of studying Catholic moral theology. I am well aware that a focus on the moral act *per se* appears somewhat odd, seen from within the context of contemporary moral philosophy. Yet, for that very reason, this focus has opened up a fruitful line of approach to contemporary philosophical questions on the nature of moral reasoning and the relation of the virtues to moral discernment. By focusing on the question of the criteria by which actions are described in moral terms, I have been able to bring together what would have seemed to be disparate approaches to moral judgement, that is, roughly, rule-oriented and virtue-oriented approaches. Furthermore, once these approaches have been brought together, it becomes apparent that each is incomplete and distorted without the other.

At the same time, I do not want to give the impression that the valuable insights run in only one direction. I am as interested in the possible contributions of moral philosophy to Christian ethics as in the contributions of the latter to the former, and it would be disingenuous to pretend otherwise. Specifically, moral philosophy offers Christian ethics, with respect to the question of the moral act, a possibility of refor-mulating the question in such a way as to escape the unhelpful dichotomy set up by deontological and consequentialist theories of morality.

Since the heady days of Vatican II and the publication of Joseph Fletcher's *Situation Ethics*, there has been a debate within Christian circles over the question of whether some kinds of actions are never morally justifiable, or, as Catholics would say, intrinsically evil.[1] (The emphasis on kinds of actions is important; no one has ever denied that some specific actions are morally evil.) For most of its history, this debate has been construed as a debate between deontologists, who hold that some kinds of actions are never morally justified, and con-sequentialists, who insist that the morality of a specific action is determined by the overall balance of good versus bad con-sequences that it produces.

This debate has been extremely frustrating, and, seen from the perspective of developments in the philosophy of language in this century, it is easy to see why. Consequentialism cuts across the grain of our ordinary usage of generic moral terms, such as "murder," so much so that it is impossible to offer it as an account of the moral language that we actually do use. Yet, seen in this context, the deontological claim that some kinds of actions are never morally justified is revealed to be trivial and unhelpful. Of course some *kinds* of actions are never morally justified; the question is, how do we move from that observa-tion, which concerns the way in which generic moral concepts function, to conclusions about specific actions, which might or might not fall under the relevant moral descriptions?

Moral philosophy offers to this specifically Christian debate a new and more fruitful question: "how are we to move from concepts of generic kinds of actions to correct descriptions of specific actions?" There have been some within the theological debate who have attempted to move it in this direction, most notably Paul Ramsey and Richard McCormick, and, follow-ing McCormick, those Catholics who are commonly described as proportionalists.[2] They did not provide, however, a cogent account of the way in which generic concepts do function, including, critically, an account of the way in which these concepts constrain moral judgement in particular cases. Without some such account, they left themselves open to the charge of being consequentialists, even though they made it clear that that was not their intent. Here, too, contemporary work in philosophy can supply a much-needed perspective, by offering an alternative way of understanding rule-guided judgement.

My own approach in this book has been to start on the philosophical side, with the work of those men and women collectively known as the moral anti-theorists. As will become obvious, I am in sympathy with their approach, and agree entirely with their rejection of the modern theoretical approach to morality, as exemplified by the work of Immanuel Kant. Yet this conclusion still leaves the question, "how do we arrive at moral judgements?" which, as it turns out, is equivalent to asking for an account of moral rationality. It is here that the resources of Christian ethics can offer an alternative and more satisfactory account of moral reasoning that functions analogically rather than apodictically, and of ideals of virtues that are integrally connected to moral rules without being reducible to them. That, at least, will be my thesis. In developing it, I hope to make a contribution both to moral philosophy and to Christian ethics, by bringing to each discipline some of the resources and the questions that have come to typify the other.

There are two other issues that I want to address briefly, before turning to the book itself. First, I want to say something about my use of the work of Thomas Aquinas, who plays a central role in what follows. Secondly, I should comment on the relation of my thesis to the recently promulgated encyclical, *Veritatis Splendor.*[3]

First, then, a word about my use of Aquinas. In spite of the considerable recent interest in the virtues, there has been very little examination of Aquinas' extensive account of the virtues by either philosophers or theologians. Among philosophers, it would appear that this neglect is due, at least in part, to a lingering prejudice against religious thought. It is true that

Aquinas is not a modern thinker; his modes of thought and expression are strange to us, and call for a certain effort in order to be appreciated; and he holds some quite unpalatable views. But all these observations are even more true of Aristotle, and yet Aristotle's thought has received considerable attention among moral philosophers. If it is possible to engage with Aristotle, to appropriate his insights without burdening oneself with all the details of his overall world-view, the same approach should be possible with Aquinas.

It is also the case that Aquinas is often thought, by theologians as well as philosophers, to have adopted Aristotle's ethic more or less intact, simply adding Christian content to certain of Aristotle's key concepts, for example, replacing the Aristotelian concept of happiness with the Christian notion of the beatific vision. Given this assumption, it may well seem that it is hardly worthwhile to study Aquinas' discussions of virtue and the moral life, since he would not be expected to contribute anything of more than parochial interest to what we could already learn in Aristotle.

There is a grain of truth in this assumption. Aquinas' moral theory is deeply indebted to Aristotle's *Nicomachean Ethics*. At the same time, however, Aquinas' reading of Aristotle is a critical appropriation, involving a synthesis with other very different approaches and a rethinking in the light of different commitments and concerns; it is not a simple adaptation of Aristotle's structure to theological purposes. The creativity of Aquinas' own account of the moral life is nowhere more in evidence than with respect to the subjects that concern us here, namely, his treatment of the virtues and their relation to the moral law. While it is true that Aquinas takes much of his discussion of the virtues from Aristotle, it is also the case that he goes beyond Aristotle's account to offer a detailed analysis of specific virtues, the actions that typify them, and the manifold ways in which the language of virtues and vices, moral law and moral failure, can be employed. And this is precisely the point at which his analysis can be helpful to us, helpful to a degree, and in specific ways, that Aristotle's analysis is not.

My aim in this book is constructive, and not primarily

exegetical. Thus, I will not attempt to argue in detail against interpretations of Aquinas that are contrary to my own, or to undertake all of the historical and exegetical work that would be called for in a different kind of study. My aim is rather to present Aquinas' account of the moral act, as I understand it, in such a way as to indicate its relevance for contemporary thought on the moral act, moral rules, and the virtues. I do not think that Aquinas offers the last word that needs to be said on these matters, but I do claim that he brings a distinctive, cogent, and illuminating perspective to our own discussions.

Finally, I should say something about the relationship of this study to the encyclical, *Veritatis Splendor*. This encyclical appeared after my work on this project was more than half completed, and the main lines of my arguments were already in place. For this reason, and because I felt that the document deserves a more considered response than I am now in a position to offer, I have not attempted to incorporate an extensive commentary on this encyclical into my account of the moral act.

In any case, it would be difficult for me to know how to respond to *Veritatis Splendor* within the traditional categories of Catholic theological praxis. Those who are familiar with the document will recognize that it presupposes that the relevant alternatives are deontological and consequentialist theories of morality. As I have already indicated, I take this to be an unhelpful approach to the issues raised by a consideration of the moral act. It is difficult for me even to say whether or not I am in dissent from this document, as the technical language would have it. How is it possible either to concur or to dissent, when one is convinced that the questions being asked are the wrong questions? To the extent that what follows is directed to my fellow Catholics, my aim is not to intervene in the current debate over intrinsically evil acts, but to suggest that we might make more progress by changing the terms in which that debate is conducted.

CHAPTER I

The moral act, moral theory, and the logical limits of rules

Moral philosophy in the modern period has been dominated by an ideal of rationality which takes mathematical reasoning as its paradigm. Consider, for one illustration of this view, the remarks of Immanuel Kant, offered as a defense of *The Groundwork of the Metaphysics of Morals*, in a footnote to *The Critique of Practical Reason*:

A critic who wished to say something against that work really did better than he intended when he said that there was no new principle of morality in it but only a new formula. Who would want to introduce a new principle of morality and, as it were, be its inventor, as if the world had hitherto been ignorant of what duty is or had been thoroughly wrong about it? Those who know what a formula means to a mathematician, in determining what is to be done in solving a problem without letting him go astray, will not regard a formula which will do this for all duties as something insignificant and unnecessary.[1]

Although Kant was not the first or the last philosopher to express this high ideal of moral reasoning, he gave it its most powerful expression and defense. Let us, therefore, call it the Kantian ideal of moral reasoning. On this view, moral rules are to be understood as functioning, in the realm of practical reason, in the same way as mathematical functions work in the realm of speculative reason. If correctly applied, they determine the uniquely correct answer to any moral question that may arise, in a way that is compelling to any impartial, rational individual. This conception of moral rules is connected, moreover, with the further claim that the diverse rules of morality are grounded in one principle which is universally knowable. Thus, Kant offers a theory of morality in the strong sense. That is, he offers an account which both brings coherence to moral judgement by showing the relation of diverse moral norms to one foundational principle, and provides a decision procedure by means of which it is possible to arrive at the uniquely correct solution to every moral problem.[2]

It has been apparent for some time that the Kantian understanding of moral rules presents difficulties. The most notorious of these is generated by the realities of moral pluralism and the persistence of moral debates, which seem to go on interminably without ever reaching a generally satisfactory resolution. Debates in mathematics do not proceed in this way. Once a mathematical function is applied to a problem, it is resolved for good and all, in a way that everyone can see to be rationally compelling. Even scientific disputes, which involve the messy realities of the empirical world, appear to allow for a generally satisfactory resolution, once the necessary experimental data have been gathered. Yet there is no guarantee that any amount of new factual evidence will resolve any moral dispute; men and women may agree on the facts relevant to a particular issue, and still disagree morally. How can it be said, then, that moral rules function in a way that is (somehow) analogous to mathematical functions? More generally, how can it be said that moral discourse is rational at all?

Much of the history of modern moral philosophy in Europe and the United States can be seen as a history of repeated attempts to answer this question. Kant's own work is largely motivated by a desire to show that morality has a central place in rational discourse.[3] Jeremy Bentham also attempted to place moral discourse on the same footing as scientific inquiry, albeit in a very different way than did Kant.[4] As the difficulties generated by moral pluralism became more acute, more refined versions of utilitarianism were put forward as systematic ways of analyzing and resolving moral disputes.[5] Later, in the early and middle decades of this century, a growing number of philosophers took up the view that moral claims are neither true nor false, but are either expressions of the speaker's feelings about a particular action, as A. J. Ayer and Charles Stevenson claimed, or disguised statements of policy with respect to an action, as R. M. Hare argued.[6] Still more recently, some philosophers, following the lead of Bernard Williams, have argued that morality is not the sort of thing about which we should attempt to develop a theory at all, at least not in the strong modern sense of "theory" that Kant exemplifies.[7] This position, which is sometimes described as moral anti-theory, is frequently associated with an appeal to concepts of virtues and an Aristotelian notion of practical wisdom as more adequate alternatives to a Kantian or utilitarian system of moral rules.

These debates have been paralleled among moral thinkers who identify themselves explicitly with some strand of the Christian tradition. It is possible to read both Søren Kierkegaard and Karl Barth as holding that the Christian can find herself obliged to act, at least in some situations, without any reference to moral rules at all, in response to what Kierkegaard describes as a "teleological suspension of the ethical."[8] This position has understandably caused a certain amount of dismay, but other theologians have argued for less radical positions that none the less imply that there are no exceptionless moral rules. In 1927, the notable Anglican scholar, Kenneth Kirk, argued that the possibility of conflicts between moral rules implies that there can be at most one such rule which cannot be broken in any circumstances whatever.[9] Almost forty years later, Joseph Fletcher argued that the Christian is obligated to do the most loving act in any given situation, and, therefore, no specific moral rule could be taken to be an absolute. Thus, he argued, the Christian is committed to a version of act-utilitarianism, with love substituted for happiness as the criterion for utility.[10] This view was contested by Paul Ramsey, who argued that the norm of Christian love cannot be understood apart from certain more specific rules, which the fulfillment of love always prescribes.[11] A number of notable scholars within the Reformed tradition, beginning with H. Richard Niebuhr and including, most recently, James Gustafson, have argued that moral choice must be guided by the particularities of specific situations, as those are interpreted within the framework of broadly Christian commitments.[12] Among Catholics, the past thirty years have seen an extensive and sometimes acrimonious debate over an account of morality known as proportionalism, which in its earlier versions appeared to be a form of mixed consequentialism, and which is opposed by a stringent theory of absolute rules that originated with Germain Grisez and John Finnis.[13] More recently still, the turn to virtue theory as an alternative to moral rules has found enthusiastic defenders in Stanley Hauerwas and James Keenan.[14]

So far, this very brief survey may suggest that the debate over the nature and scope of moral rules has been long and complex, or it may suggest that there is nothing more to say on the subject. The former conclusion is certainly correct, but the latter would be too quick. The debates over the philosophical and theological significance of moral rules, and the kinds of actions forbidden or enjoined by them, raised real and important issues that still merit close examination.

It might also be thought that Christian ethics would have nothing distinctive to contribute to our understanding of the basis and scope of moral rules, given the similarity of the debates on this question as they have emerged in philosophical and theological circles. That conclusion also would be too quick. While the boundaries between sacred and secular moralities, and correlatively, between moral philosophy and Christian ethics, are disconcertingly permeable, none the less Christianity as a moral tradition, and the body of disciplined reflection generated by that tradition, do potentially offer a distinctive and illuminating perspective on moral rules and moral actions. However, the best way to vindicate this claim is not to offer a more extensive survey, but to develop a constructive account of the moral act that draws on the resources of Christian moral thought, as well as on moral philosophy.

In a widely influential essay, "Modern Moral Philosophy," Elizabeth Anscombe contrasts the Christian moral tradition with contemporary moral philosophy on precisely the point at issue, arguing forcefully that her contemporaries in philosophy have broken with the Christian tradition over the question of whether there are some kinds of actions that are never permissible.[15] While I will not ultimately defend her analysis, she none the less provides one of the best brief statements of what is at issue in debates over the status of moral rules, together with a powerful and influential interpretation of the religious significance of these debates.

THE INTERMINABILITY OF MORAL ARGUMENTS

In "Modern Moral Philosophy," Elizabeth Anscombe begins by setting out three theses. The first two of these need not concern us, but the third will lead us immediately to the issue at hand: "the differences between the well-known English writers on moral philosophy from Sidgwick to the present day are of little importance."[16]

What does Anscombe mean when she says that the differences among English moral philosophers are much less significant than their similarities? According to her, every English philosopher since Sidgwick has argued against a conception of morality that, in her view, is central to the Hebrew-Christian moral tradition:

> every one of the best known English moral philosophers has put out a philosophy according to which, e.g., it is not possible to hold that it cannot be right to kill the innocent as a means to any end whatsoever and that someone who thinks otherwise is in error ... Now this is a significant thing: for it means that all these philosophies are quite incompatible with the Hebrew-Christian ethic. For it has been characteristic of that ethic to teach that there are certain things forbidden whatever *consequences* threaten, such as: choosing to kill the innocent, for any purpose, however good; vicarious punishment; treachery (by which I mean obtaining a man's confidence in a grave matter by promises of trustworthy friendship and then betraying him to his enemies); idolatry; sodomy; adultery; making a false profession of faith. The prohibition of certain things simply in virtue of their description as such- and such- identifiable kinds of action, regardless of any further consequences, is certainly not the whole of the Hebrew-Christian ethic; but it is a noteworthy feature of it.[17]

In other words, according to Anscombe, what is distinctive about Christianity as a moral tradition, and what is rejected by her philosophical contemporaries, is the claim that some kinds of actions are always morally wrong, whatever extenuating circumstances there may be in a specific case. Let us put aside the claims that Anscombe makes in this passage about her own contemporaries, and, for the moment, let us also bracket her historical and interpretative judgement about the Hebrew-Christian moral tradition.[18] What are we to make of the substantive claim that there are some kinds of actions that are always morally prohibited, whatever the circumstances or the foreseeable consequences of acting otherwise?

Firstly, Anscombe is right to say that this claim is controversial. Not only is it widely debated among theologians as well as philosophers, but, in some form, it is debated in the wider community as well. However, when this claim arises in practical discussions, it does not generally take the theoretical form that Anscombe gives it, at least not initially. Rather, the questions that engage men and women who are faced with practical dilemmas are far more likely, at least initially, to take the form of questions about the scope and force of particular prohibitions. "Is it always wrong to kill the innocent – even to spare them irremediable suffering?" Or again, "Is it necessarily wrong to insinuate oneself into the confidence of another? Suppose the other is the leader of a drug cartel and you are an undercover agent; is it morally wrong to attempt to discover his plans by pretending friendship and alliance to him?" Questions like these are not easy to resolve in a generally satisfactory way. Why should this be so?

Surely, the question whether some kinds of actions are always morally wrong is difficult to resolve, in part, because the moral life is sometimes hard to live. We are weak creatures, but the difficulties that face us as moral agents are not confined to the failures of vision and will that we experience as a result of our deficiencies. Some of these difficulties are generated by the logic of the moral life itself, or so it seems. It is not difficult to imagine instances in which conflicts of moral duties would seem to force an individual to choose which of two morally problematic actions to perform. We can also readily imagine a situation in which it would seem to be both pointless and destructive to observe even a very serious moral prohibition. The current debate over euthanasia is rich with examples of both kinds of dilemmas. After all, euthanasia, as the term is now generally understood, involves killing a human being, who is neither a dangerous assailant, nor a soldier on the battlefield, nor a duly convicted criminal. Killing a human being, in the absence of one of these qualifications, is understood by most of us to be murder, and murder, as Anscombe reminds us, is always wrong. Yet in the case of someone who is dying in extreme, intractable pain, a doctor or caregiver may well begin to question whether the prohibition against murder might conflict with her obligation to relieve suffering, particularly extreme and pointless suffering. Perhaps, also, the physician is faced with the possibility that her obligation not to kill has come into conflict with her duty to respect the wishes of her patient, who, at an earlier time perhaps, requested euthanasia once his illness had progressed to a certain point. Furthermore, it may well seem to her that the prohibition against murder, which is designed to protect persons, loses its point and becomes destructive rather than protective when life has ceased to be a benefit, when everyone agrees that death, as it is said, would be a blessed release. In fine, she may conclude that the general prohibition against killing has come into conflict with other obligations, which may be equally exigent, or she may conclude that, in the particular situation that she faces, this prohibition has no point. Either consideration is powerful by itself, and if they come together, as they very often do in these situations, the case for euthanasia may seem very strong indeed, even though it can also be described as killing an innocent human being.

While this line of reasoning may seem persuasive, and it has been persuasive to many, it has seemed to others to raise a troubling set of possibilities. If the prohibition against killing the innocent can be overridden, even for the best humane motives, then who is to say that the whole structure of prohibitions against killing will not eventually unravel under the pressures of hard cases, helped along by the ubiquitous human tendency towards self-deception? If we allow a doctor to kill a patient who is dying in intractable pain, then why should not we allow her also to kill a patient who is not dying, but who is none the less irremediably miserable, say, from an incurable psychosis? Why insist that euthanasia be limited to medical contexts, rather than allowing for the possibility that suicide, and perhaps even a merciful homicide, might be justified in other situations of irremediable human misery? Why not allow anyone to kill anyone else who seems to be too sick, or too unhappy, or too mean to live? Once we begin asking questions like these, we may well find ourselves wondering whether we would want to be the kind of persons who would do anything if the circumstances seem to call for it, living in a community of others who are prepared to do the same. Yet once we have reached this conclusion, we are once again confronted with a hard case, in which it seems inevitable or even morally exigent that we do something that our best judgements had led us to say we should never do. And so we continue, living in uneasy truce with ambiguities that we cannot resolve.

This is not a comfortable situation, either for individuals or for a society, and naturally we would like to find some way out of it. Anscombe's essay suggests one solution, namely, a return to the Hebrew-Christian tradition, which identifies some kinds of actions as morally wrong, thereby putting an end to debates like the one described above. However, it must be noted that Anscombe was writing in the context of academic debates, and her primary targets are the moral theories of professional philosophers, chiefly consequentialism and moral non-cognitivism. It is not so clear that her arguments would apply straightforwardly to the ordinary, non-academic moral discourse in which practical questions about the scope of the traditional moral rules are continually being raised. If either consequentialism or moral non-cognitivism really were regnant in our society, we would not experience widespread intractable moral disagreement. To the extent that matters of morality were debated at all, they would be debated under the rubric of difficult technical questions about the best way to maximize utility and to minimize pain, or else they would be treated as exercises in value clarification, along the lines proposed by R. M. Hare.[19] And even a slight acquaintance with public debates on euthanasia, or abortion, or sexual morality is enough to demonstrate that, for most of us, these are not questions of utilitarian policy or individual value choices.

Yet even granting that the moral disputes in our society cannot be traced to the triumph of utilitarianism and non-cognitivism, might it not still be the case that Anscombe's essay offers a means to resolve our own issues, different though they may be from the issues that were of central concern to her? That is, whatever the ultimate sources of the breakdown of moral consensus in our society, does not it seem plausible, at least, that a return to the Hebrew-Christian moral tradition, with its clear moral boundaries reinforced by divine sanctions, would offer a way to restore a socially viable moral consensus? Anscombe lends support to this suggestion by her remark that our concepts of morality and obligation are survivals from an earlier intellectual framework, that is, the Hebrew-Christian world-view, that is no longer widely held. The claim that the interminable nature of moral discourse is a symptom of the breakdown of a sustaining moral tradition has since been developed forcibly by Alasdair MacIntyre.[20]

If Anscombe and MacIntyre are right, and the interminable nature of our moral disputes can be traced to the fragmentary nature of moral discourse in our society, then why not return to the Hebrew-Christian tradition in which our fundamental moral convictions were shaped? Or, if that seems unlikely, or too costly, in the context of modern liberal democracies, why not attempt to build sustaining communities of moral discourse within the churches, which continue to be informed by that tradition? This alternative is hinted at by MacIntyre at the end of *After Virtue*, and it is developed at length by some theologians, most notably, Stanley Hauerwas.[21]

There can be little doubt that MacIntyre is right to say that moral discourse in modern industrialized societies has come to incorporate a number of diverse and sometimes competing traditions. Nor is there much reason to doubt that, to some extent, this diversity has contributed to the extensive moral debates within these societies. Yet it is not obvious that our widespread moral disagreements can be explained exclusively in terms of a pluralism of moral traditions.

This suggestion presupposes, first of all, that the Hebrew-Christian moral tradition, unlike the dominant ethos in modern liberal democracies, *is* a unified tradition, in which moral arguments can be settled by an appeal to its definite boundaries. It is far from clear that this is the case, however. For one thing, we have already seen that there are a number of theologians who would take issue with Anscombe's claim that Christianity is committed to the view that some kinds of actions are always wrong, whatever the consequences. Of course, these theologians could just be wrong about their own tradition. More importantly, however, the supposedly unified Christian tradition does not provide unanimity for the communities that live by it. The Christian churches today are not generally models of unanimity and concord on the difficult issues of the day, and it does not seem that this is a new situation.[22]

The same observation can be made more generally about the pre-modern moral traditions to which MacIntyre looks back as examples of unified traditions of moral discourse. Pre-modern societies do give the impression that they provided a framework for normative judgements in which any ambiguities were resolved in a way that was rationally compelling to every member of the community. But the more recent research of classicists, scholars of the Bible, and historians suggests that this appearance of unanimity is illusory.[23] As far as can be determined, even very early societies were characterized by some degree of internal tension and indeterminacy with respect to what we would characterize as moral matters, and, as these societies developed through the institutional and economic transitions that mark every community's history, the internal tensions that they experienced with respect to these matters grew more pronounced. To some extent, these tensions were resolved by the coercive fiat of religious or political authorities, and since much of our documentary evidence comes from these authorities (directly or indirectly), the realities of continuing moral ambiguity in pre-modern societies have tended to be obscured.

Nor is it clear that a unified moral tradition would really serve to bring closure to moral arguments within our society. MacIntyre himself raises a doubt on this point by his remark that "when a tradition is in good order it is always partially constituted by an argument about the goods the pursuit of which gives to that tradition its particular point and purpose ... Traditions, when vital, embody continuities of conflict. Indeed when a tradition becomes Burkean [therefore, closed to internal conflict], it is always dying or dead."[24] These remarks suggest that even a unified tradition, if it were possible actually to achieve such a thing, might not serve to eliminate moral conflict. If this is the case, however, then we cannot simply conclude that our moral disagreements are grounded in conflicts of competing traditions. It may well be that our most intense conflicts are generated among persons who largely share the same moral traditions and presuppositions. We will subsequently see reason to conclude that this is the case.

It would appear that we need to examine the contours of our moral arguments more closely, in order to see why they proceed in the frustrating, interminable way that they do. Let us return, therefore, to the question, "Are there some kinds of actions that are never morally justifiable, whatever the circumstances, the foreseeable consequences, or the intention of the agent?"

A CASE IN POINT: MURDER AND LEGITIMATE FORMS OF KILLING

How are we to go about attempting to answer the question whether some kinds of actions are always morally wrong? As was noted above, moral reflection does not typically begin at this level. Rather, this sort of question is more likely to emerge from reflection on more specific questions, out of which larger issues then emerge.

Let us begin with a more specific question. The prohibition against murder would seem to be one of the best candidates for an exceptionless moral rule, at least within our culture. The very idea of killing another human being (fortunately) fills most people with horror, and both legal sanction and social opinion are directed with full force against anyone who violates this sanction.

Yet, further reflection indicates that the question, "is murder always wrong?" is not as wrong-headed as it appears at first to be. After all, there are some forms of homicide that are generally acknowledged to be legitimate, in particular, killing in self-defense, killing in warfare, and capital punishment (although doubts about the legitimacy of the latter two, especially capital punishment, have increased recently).[25] Other sorts of actions, which resemble murder in some respects, are defended as morally legitimate options by many, while others consider these kinds of actions to be forms of outright murder. We mentioned the example of euthanasia above, and both suicide and abortion would also fall into this category.

Not only do these instances of seemingly legitimate homicide call into question the scope of the concept of murder, they also suggest disturbing analogies between cases that would typically be described as murder and cases that would be described as legitimate homicide. For example, if it is legitimate for at least some persons to kill in the line of duty, why should it be illegitimate for the physician to kill as an expression of her duty to relieve intractable suffering? The circumstances in which she would do so are likely to be extreme, painful, and difficult, but the same can be said (or should be said) of the circumstances in which the police-officer or the soldier kills in the line of duty.

Considerations of these sorts have led some to conclude that "murder" simply means "wrongful killing."[26] On this view, the claim, "murder is always wrong," can be rephrased to read, "wrongful killing, i.e. killing that is wrong, is always wrong," which is analytically true. On the other hand, if a particular instance of killing is not wrong, then it does not count as murder.

But matters are more complex than that. Since W. V. O. Quine first challenged the analytic/synthetic distinction in "Two Dogmas of Empiricism," philosophers have become increasingly skeptical of the notion of analytic truth.[27] Concepts as they emerge and function within natural languages do not have the neat, precisely defined boundaries that this conception of truth presupposes. To the contrary, as Werner Heisenberg once observed, it is always to some degree an empirical question how far our concepts should apply.[28] It is always possible to *stipulate* that "murder" means "wrongful killing" and nothing else, but an argument that must be won by stipulation is hardly worth winning. Nor is this sort of move illuminating. What is of interest to us is the insight or principle that is implied by the concept of murder as it is actually used.

The richness and ambiguity of the concept of murder is apparent, first of all, when we consider the way in which this concept is linked with allied notions of other sorts of homicides and even acts of killing animals. Traditionally, we have drawn two lines in evaluating acts of killing. In the first place, the act of killing an animal has generally been seen as morally neutral in itself, or very nearly so, in a way that the act of killing a human being never can be. But, secondly, while homicide as such has never been considered to be without moral weight, a distinction has been drawn between acts of justifiable homicide and outright murder. As we have already observed, the killing of enemy soldiers in wartime, capital punishment, and killing in self-defense have traditionally fallen on the permissible side of the line, and just about everything else has fallen under the heading of murder.

It may seem that this observation reinforces the strategy of simply defining murder as wrongful killing. And in one sense it does, but only if it is recognized that "wrongful killing" in this context has a substantive meaning, given it by the sorts of cases that we have come to place under the heading of murder. That is to say, if we are to respect common usage at all, we cannot just stipulate that murder means any sort of killing that is wrong; the term has come to include certain specific kinds of killing, which we are generally agreed in condemning. Moreover, this consensus has a history that can be traced. Each of the three kinds of killing that we would now generally regard as permissible was once widely considered to be at least problematic, if not outright murder. On the other hand, there are other kinds of killings that were once widely regarded as acceptable, but are now generally condemned, for example, infanticide and killing in the course of a duel. The concept of murder, as we now employ it, is a distillation of an extended, rich process of reflection by which we have progressively drawn a line between permissible and impermissible forms of killing.

This process of reflection is still going on. It is probably no longer the case that the majority opinion would hold that capital punishment is legitimate, certainly not in Europe or Canada, and probably not in the United States either. There is a significant division over whether war can be morally justified at all, given the conditions of our nuclear world, and even the killing of animals is increasingly being called into question. On the other hand, there are extensive debates over whether some sorts of killing that have been generally condemned might not be legitimate in some circumstances, particularly active euthanasia and, still within medical contexts, some forms of infanticide. And we continue to debate kinds of killing that have always been ambiguous, most notably, suicide and abortion.

By now it is apparent that once we attempt to address the question, "is murder always wrong?" in any textured detail, it becomes very difficult to sustain a clear sense of just what it is that we are asking. If a defender of the legitimacy of (say) active euthanasia is told that she is arguing that murder is not always wrong, she *might* agree with the charge, asserting that her view is indeed that murder is sometimes justified. But this sort of response is unlikely, unless perhaps someone is making a rhetorical point. It is much more likely that a defender of euthanasia would respond, to the contrary, that she has as much abhorrence of murder as anyone, but, on her view, euthanasia should not count as a form of murder. This sort of response suggests, in turn, that the question, "is murder always wrong?" is the wrong question to ask, if we want to get at the issues involved in moral conflict. It would be better to ask whether a specific kind of killing, such as euthanasia, should *count* as murder, and if not, why not.

When we are considering whether a particular action or kind of action should count as murder, we will be very conscious of any ambiguities that appear as we attempt to apply the concept, because the issues at stake are of such importance. For this reason, it would be easy to assume that these ambiguities are inherent in the concept of murder *per se*. From this point, it is only a short step to the claim that they are inherent in murder as a moral concept, and from there it is a further short step to the conclusion that there is something peculiar about *moral* concepts.

There is a grain of truth in this conclusion. As I will argue in the next section, our generic concepts of morally significant kinds of actions are indeterminate, in the sense that we can never eliminate the possibility that a *real* doubt may arise with respect to the scope of their application. That is, it is always possible that discerning and sincere persons may find themselves faced with intractable disagreements with respect to the application of a moral concept, *even though* they agree with respect to the facts of the case, and, even more importantly, agree on the fundamental validity of the disputed concept and the range of its application to a central core of cases. To continue with our initial example, sincere persons may well disagree on whether an act of euthanasia counts as murder or not, even though they share the same factual knowledge, and even though they agree about the proper description of a wide range of other acts of homicide.

At the same time, those philosophers who have called attention to the oddness of moral concepts have generally made one mistake, in that they have assumed that moral concepts are *uniquely* problematic. To the contrary, the indeterminacy built into the application of moral concepts is also to be found in most, if not all, of the generic concepts that find their context in empirical description of the world around us. Not only "murder," "theft," and "adultery," but also "man" and "gold," for example, are indeterminate in this way. To adopt the terminology of Friedrich Waismann, to whose analysis of concepts I am indebted here, generic moral concepts, like most generic empirical concepts, are open-textured.[29]

J. M. Brennan, in his unjustly neglected *The Open-Texture of Moral Concepts*, has already applied Waismann's analysis of generic concepts to moral questions, and other philosophers, most notably Julius Kovesi, have arrived at a similar analysis of moral concepts by other routes.[30] In spite of this, however, the implications of Waismann's analysis for moral theory are still not fully appreciated. It would seem to be worthwhile, therefore, to examine the implications of Waismann's analysis as applied to moral concepts in more detail.

THE OPEN-TEXTURE OF EMPIRICAL CONCEPTS

In its original context, Waismann's analysis of empirical concepts was developed as a part of a response to the claim, which is central to empiricism in at least some of its forms, that the meaning of a statement is exhaustively given by an account of the observational evidence that verifies it, or would verify it if it happened to be true. Waismann responds to this claim by arguing that it presupposes that our observations always lead ineluctably to one, uniquely correct description of an object or event; such, he insists, is not the case. Most of our empirical concepts are open-ended, in the sense that we can never exhaustively determine, in advance, the specific cases to which they will apply or not apply. It is always possible that, under some combination of circumstances, we might be genuinely in doubt whether or not to apply what had previously been a straightforward, well-behaved empirical concept. For this reason, we can never say for certain that a descriptive statement has been verified by our observations, since it is always possible that some further observation might call into question the validity of the description that we have attached to what we have observed. As Waismann says:

The fact that in many cases, there is no such thing as a conclusive verification is connected with the fact that most of our empirical concepts are not delimited in all possible directions. Suppose I come across a being that looks like a man, speaks like a man, behaves like a man, and is only one span tall – shall I say it *is* a man? . . . "But are there not exact definitions at least in science?" Let's see. The notion of gold seems to be defined with absolute precision, say by the spectrum of gold with its characteristic lines. Now what would you say if a substance was discovered that looked like gold, satisfied all the chemical tests for gold, while it emitted a new sort of radiation? "But such things do not happen." Quite so; but they *might* happen, and that is enough to show that we can never exclude altogether the possibility of some unforeseen situation arising in which we shall have to modify our definition.[31]

This quality of empirical concepts, in turn, is grounded in what Waismann calls "the *essential incompleteness* of an empirical description."[32] That is, no empirical description can exhaustively render all the details that are relevant to determining the correct concept under which to subsume an actual object or event. When dealing with an actual reality, as opposed to the abstract constructions of mathematics or highly structured games (for example), it is always possible to add another detail, and this further detail might call into question the appropriateness of the conceptual structure that we have applied so far. To quote Waismann again:

A term is defined when the sort of situation is described in which it is to be used. Suppose for a moment that we were able to describe situations completely without omitting anything (as in chess), then we could produce an exhaustive list of all the circumstances in which the term is to be used so that nothing is left to doubt; in other words, we could construct a *complete definition*, i.e., a thought model which anticipates and settles once for all every possible question of usage. As in fact, we can never eliminate the possibility of some unforeseen factor emerging, we can never be quite sure that we have included in our definition everything that should be included, and thus the process of defining and refining an idea will go on without ever reaching a final stage . . . no definition of an empirical term will cover all possibilities. Thus the result is that the incompleteness of our verification is rooted in the incompleteness of the definition of the terms involved, and the incompleteness of the definition is rooted in the incompleteness of empirical description.[33]

If Waismann is correct, as I believe him to be, then there will always be a lack of precise fit, so to speak, between our observations of the world and the concepts that we bring to bear on those observations. It is crucial, in order to understand the significance of this point for moral theory, not to misunderstand Waismann here in either of two tempting ways.

In the first place, as Waismann points out, the open-texture of most empirical concepts should not be confused with the quality of vagueness that attaches to certain sorts of concepts, including those attached to color-words and deliberately general descriptive terms like "heap."[34] Such terms are vague and indefinite in their normal usage. It might almost be said that these sorts of terms are designed to be indefinite, in order to fit the kinds of situations to which they apply, situations in which the realities themselves are not particularly clear-cut (what is the difference, *really*, between salmon pink and peachy pink?), or else, we don't want to be bothered to arrive at a more definite description ("just put it on that heap over there"). As such, these terms contrast with terms like "man," or "gold," which are clear-cut and definite in normal usage, and only become indeterminate when some unforeseen aspect of a particular situation leads us to call into question the appropriateness of their application.

It would be possible to misread Waismann in a second way, which would obscure the nature of the interpretative judgement that is in question. It might be said that, after all, Waismann is simply calling our attention to the fact that it can sometimes be difficult to apply general concepts. But this is not an *interesting* difficulty, as it were; it simply reflects the limitations of our everyday use of language and our ordinary observations of the external world. Difficult as it may be in practice to arrive at an exact fit between empirical concepts and the world that they describe, it is none the less possible to do so, if we are willing to invest enough thought in our concepts and enough care in our observations. A well-formulated concept will contain within itself, implicitly, all that is needed for an adequate and correct application of that concept to external realities. Therefore, if someone really understands a concept thoroughly and exhaustively, and has the means and the time to establish all the facts that are relevant to a correct description of a given particular, she will be able to fit the concept to the world without any ambiguity or dubiety. The phenomenon that Waismann identifies, which has been described here as judgement in the application of concepts to the world, is actually the result of the imprecision of our ordinary thought and observation, not something that is necessarily given with the nature of language itself.

This interpretation presupposes, however, a model of language that can no longer be sustained after the work of Wittgenstein in his *Philosophical Investigations*.[35] Specifically, Waismann's interlocutor presupposes an assumption that the meaning of concepts resides primarily in the mind of the individual whose concepts they are. On this account, if someone really understands a concept, she knows enough, on this view, to determine all of its applications, which are contained, so to speak, within the concept. It may be that she does not know that she knows all this; the knowledge may be implicit, until it is elicited by a situation of ambiguity, such as Waismann describes. None the less, someone who really understands a concept does know enough to be able to apply it, even if she cannot say in advance of doing so exactly what it is that she knows. At this point, one might think, for example, of Socrates' slave boy, deriving geometrical theorems under his master's guidance.

The difficulty with this model, as Wittgenstein has shown, is that the whole idea of meanings "in the head" is untenable. Under close examination, it is seen to be unintelligible (as the oddness of the metaphor should suggest). When we say that some concept is meaningful, at least a part of what we are saying is that that concept serves to set guidelines for, or parameters around, speech and action, in some way that is appropriate to the domain of the concept. If I understand what it means to be a man, I will not exhort my dog to be a man when it cringes behind the furniture (unless I am being cute, in which case it would be essential to my use of the term "man" that I am deliberately using it in an odd way). In this sense, every concept (and not just moral concepts) is correlated with rules for speech and action.

Now, if a concept is to set parameters around speech and action in this way, it is necessary that there be some criteria for correct usage and performance attached to the concept, and, correlatively, some way to identify incorrect uses of the concept. Yet, if meanings were really located "in the head," that is, if they were internal to the individual making use of the concept, there would be no way to distinguish between correct and incorrect applications of the concept. As Wittgenstein says, "This was our paradox: no course of action could be determined by a rule, because every course of action can be made out to accord with a rule."[36] Whatever bizarre application of a concept an individual may propose, she can always reformulate the relevant rules for usage in such a way as to accommodate her application. There need be no question of insincerity or intent to deceive, in order to imagine such a reformulation taking place. Since, by hypothesis, the individual's grasp of the meaning of a concept is partially implicit, she will not be able to appeal to her own prior *articulate* understandings to test her current application of the concept; even if she could do so, her memory, her past understandings themselves, all could be faulty. It follows that no application of a concept, including ordinary unproblematic applications, could be validated: "if everything can be made out to accord with the rule, then it can also be made out to conflict with it. And so there would be neither accord nor conflict here."[37]

Wittgenstein's point is that the criteria for correctness in following a rule, and, correlatively, the criteria for understanding a concept, must be grounded in intersubjective structures of meaning and usage. The practices of the community provide the *immediate* and *necessary* context for the individual's comprehension and use of a concept: "And hence also 'obeying a rule' is a practice. And to *think* one is obeying a rule is not to obey a rule. Hence it is not possible to obey a rule 'privately': otherwise thinking one was obeying a rule would be the same thing as obeying it."[38] It does not necessarily follow that the practices of the community are themselves *ultimate*, that there is no sense at all in which we could say that a given community, or even the human race as a whole, has misunderstood the nature of something.[39] Whatever may ultimately be said on the topic of realism, however, the fact remains that we cannot cogently appeal to an implicit understanding of the meaning of a concept as a way of eliminating the ambiguity of application that Waismann has described.

Even so, might it not be possible to eliminate the ambiguity that Waismann sees as built into open-textured concepts, without appealing to some implicit or tacit mental understanding of a given concept? That is, would it be possible to arrive at an *explicit*, socially shared formulation of a concept of sufficient completeness to eliminate all ambiguity from its application? There is nothing in Waismann's analysis that strictly rules out this possibility. However, it is important to be clear on just what would be involved in formulating a concept to this degree of explicitness. In the first place, it should be noted that no concept can be understood in isolation from other concepts. It is misleading to speak of a completely defined concept, when what would be called for, in order to resolve all possible ambiguities, would be a completely elaborated *framework* of concepts.

Consider, for example, the way in which we have developed the concepts of living and non-living beings, and, within the former class, concepts of animals and plants, and the various divisions within each category. These concepts comprise a framework of classification that, in its general outlines, seems to be ubiquitous. Every society divides living things from non-living things, and plants from animals, and within these broad categories there is furthermore a considerable overlap among basic categories such as dog, cat, fish, horse, bird, and so on.

And yet, even within a particular community, among persons who share the same broad framework of concepts of kinds of living creatures, there will almost certainly be ambiguous cases, about which there may well be interminable disagreement concerning the proper classification of some odd kind of thing. In our own society, we have an elaborate and subtle system of concepts, which has evolved over the two centuries since the pioneering work of Linnaeus. Yet even this framework is not sufficient to settle every question that might arise about the status of some odd creature or other. Is a virus a living creature, or not? Are certain kinds of bacteria plants or animals? Is a fungus a plant, or (as has recently been suggested) a very simple kind of animal? The difficulty, in each case, is not that we lack factual data about the functioning of

viruses, bacteria, and fungi. Nor is it the case that the conceptual framework within which we approach these questions does
not allow us to say anything about the facts of these cases. The
difficulty is that we can say *too much* about these cases within the
framework of modern biology. Viruses, some kinds of bacteria,
and fungi are ambiguous because they contain elements in
virtue of which they can reasonably be placed in more than one
category, among categories which are generally taken as not
only distinct, but mutually exclusive. In each case, a knowledge of the facts is not sufficient to resolve the question of
classification, since our difficulty lies precisely in determining
what significance we ought to give to the facts that we know.

It would seem that there is ultimately no way to settle
interpretative disputes of this sort except through a decision to
count certain features of a particular case, rather than others,
as being decisive for the classification of that particular kind of
creature. This decision need not be a sheer ungrounded choice
for one alternative over another. It may well be that the
individual proposing a given determination of an ambiguous
case will be convinced that she can give reasons for her determination, overwhelmingly cogent reasons. And yet, even she
may have to admit that those reasons do not apodictically
determine her, or any other specific determination of the
ambiguity at hand, since it is always possible that someone else,
offering reasons drawn from within the same conceptual framework, may argue for taking a different configuration of features
of the same case as decisive for its classification. In other words,
in such a case the reasons for a given application of a concept
underdetermine the conclusion that they support.

At the same time, it should be noted that the process of
attempting to resolve ambiguous cases within a conceptual
framework will tend to reduce the scope for further ambiguity
within that framework. The decisions that we make to construe
ambiguous cases in one way, rather than another, have implications for our construal of other cases, and, ultimately, for the
elaboration of the overall conceptual framework within which
our reflections and observations alike take place. As this conceptual framework develops, observational data can become

relevant, if not decisive, in a way that they did not seem to be relevant to the resolution of a particular ambiguity taken in itself. The question that arises at this point is not just how the data support this or that particular classification. Rather, we will ask how a whole body of observed data, together with what we take to be established theoretical judgements, that jointly ground the framework of concepts within which we move, is better explained, more persuasively interpreted, more cogently systematized, by elaborating that framework in this way rather than another. Moreover, subsequent observations may serve to reinforce, or else to challenge, a particular resolution of an ambiguous case. For example (to go back to a much earlier instance of conceptual ambiguity), there was a time when it was unclear whether a whale should be counted as a fish, or a mammal. It is certainly relevant to our classification of whales as mammals that they have turned out to be much smarter than the average fish, given the fact that in the vast majority of undisputed cases, mammals are smarter than other kinds of animals.

These observations suggest that it might be possible, in theory, to arrive at an elaboration of our generic concepts in their relations to, and distinctions from, one another, that is so subtle, so responsive to the messy data of observation, and withal so logically elegant and cogent, that every ambiguous case could be resolved in such a way as to be rationally compelling to all. It has sometimes been suggested that this would be possible; in that case, a given body of knowledge would comprise a perfected or a completed science, in which the theoretical system relevant to a given body of data would be capable of resolving any question that might arise with respect to that data.[40]

This claim raises difficult issues, and I for one am agnostic about whether the ideal of a perfected science could ever be met, "in principle" or otherwise. The significance of this claim for Waismann's thesis is that it is only within the framework of this sort of perfected science that the ambiguity that he sees to be inherent in most empirical concepts could be resolved. Yet, even if it were possible to develop a perfected science, it is clear

that few, if any, of our actual theoretical frameworks are perfected sciences in this sense, although some have claimed that
physics is approaching that point of development. Moreover,
even if it were possible to bring a natural science to the level of a
perfected science, it is not clear that it would be possible to do
the same for the framework of moral concepts that structure our
lives.[41] At any rate, so long as a given conceptual framework
falls short of the level of completeness proper to a perfected
science, it will fall short of the adequacy and completeness
necessary to ensure that any ambiguity that it generates can be
resolved in a way that will be satisfactory to all.

Our analysis suggests two points. The first is that, even if it
were possible to arrive at a perfected science, there will be an
irreducible element of discretion and judgement involved in the
application of concepts so long as we are moving within a
framework that is not (yet?) a perfected science. And no system
of normative concepts, such as our framework of moral concepts, would seem to be even close to approaching the status of
a perfected science, if any normative system could be developed
in this direction. Secondly, however, the kind of discretion that
must be exercised in order to apply concepts within an incom-
pletely developed framework should not be understood as if it
were an exercise of sheer fiat. So long as an individual has a
stake in remaining within a particular conceptual system, she
will try, as far as possible, to justify the judgements that she
makes by appeal to reasons that are drawn from within that
system. Yet judgement will be called for none the less, because,
within any conceptual framework that falls short of the ideal of
a perfected science, there will always be at least some ambiguous cases in which the reasons that are given for one judgement
or another, while genuinely persuasive, are not sufficient to
determine the judgement in one direction or another.

THE OPEN-TEXTURE OF MORAL CONCEPTS

At this point, the patient reader may be wondering what all this
has to do with the use of generic moral concepts such as
"murder," "theft," "adultery," and the like. Whatever may be

said about the merits of Waismann's analysis of empirical concepts, it will be said, surely we are not justified in applying that
analysis to generic moral concepts, without some consideration
of the special features of moral concepts. This objection presupposes that moral concepts are in some way logically odd, that
they have special characteristics that must be addressed in any
moral theory. Yet this is not the case. It is true that moral concepts will have some special features because of the particular
character of their subject matter. None the less, the special
logical difficulties that were supposed to be inherent in moral
notions are inherent in most, if not all, empirical concepts.[42] Is
there a logical gap between "is" and "ought," that is to say,
between description and moral evaluation? Indeed there is,
but, as Waismann points out, there is also a gap between a
description of sensory observations, and the application of a
general term such as "man" to the object of those observations.
Do moral debates continue indefinitely, even in the presence of
agreement on the facts of the case at hand? Sometimes they do,
but there are also debates over the proper application of concepts in the sciences or natural history which cannot be
resolved simply by an appeal to the facts at hand, precisely
because they are disputes about how to characterize the facts.

Again, a number of philosophers, of whom R. M. Hare is the
best representative, have dwelt on the fact that there is an ineluctable element of choice in the application of moral concepts.[43] Waismann reminds us, however, that a knowledge of
the facts is not sufficient to resolve every possible question concerning the application of most empirical concepts either. With
respect to these concepts, too, it is always possible that we may
confront a problem with respect to their proper application
that can only be resolved, if at all, by means of a decision to
count certain features of a particular case, rather than others,
as being decisive for the classification of that particular. If it is
formed within the framework of the accepted conceptual
scheme within which the problem has arisen, a decision of this
sort will be rational, in the sense that it can be supported by
reasons in terms of the accepted framework; yet, those reasons
will underdetermine the decision that they support.

There is no reason to deny that moral concepts like "murder" *are* empirical concepts, just as "man" and "gold" are empirical concepts. "Murder," just as much as "man," is used to describe something that is observed in the world around us, an action rather than an object, but none the less a reality that is observed through the senses and understood in the mind. It is true that a moral concept, like "murder," is integrally connected to action, and in that sense is a practical, rather than a theoretical, concept. This distinction should not be overplayed, however. It is possible to apply a description like "murder" even in situations in which we have no immediate intention of taking any action at all, because (for example) the case we are considering took place a long time ago. More importantly, any generic concept will have some normative implications, at least in the pedestrian sense of governing the activities of recognition, description, and classification.

The best argument for counting moral concepts as empirical concepts, understood along the lines set forth by Waismann's analysis, lies in the fact that moral disagreements do typically go in the way that his analysis would lead us to expect. Recall the discussion of debates over murder and other forms of homicide. As we saw, these debates are not generally couched in the terms of a fundamental disagreement over whether it is a good or a bad thing to kill people. Killing people is bad, and most forms of killing, anyway, are morally wrong, that is, they are murders; that much is generally agreed upon. Moreover, there would be widespread agreement concerning the proper characterization of a wide range of cases, even though we would expect to find a substantial overlap of agreements, rather than complete unanimity with respect to all the cases that might be suggested. Most men and women in our societies would agree that it would be murder to poison one's aunt in order to get her inheritance, or to shoot the lover of one's wife, or to drown the only witness to one's robbery. Most would also agree that it would not be murder to shoot an attacker who comes at one in a dark alley with blood in her eye and a knife in her hand, and who cannot be stopped in any other way. Similar sorts of cases, on which there would be extensive agreement one way or the other, could be brought forth indefinitely, particularly with the aid of a good library of true crime and mystery stories. In spite of this impressive range of agreed-upon cases, there is still considerable dispute within our societies about whether certain kinds of killing should count as murders, or not. Yet these disputes do not call into question the wide-ranging consensus that exists with respect to murder and homicide; they presuppose that consensus, and could not occur without it.

Even if this line of argument is accepted, the reader might wonder why it is necessary to belabor it. If sound, it does serve the useful purpose of establishing that moral concepts are not distinctively problematic, although some would add, we must pay for this conclusion with the further conclusion that all (or nearly all) empirical concepts are potentially problematic.

Weismann's analysis has at least one further, critical implication, namely, that moral rules logically cannot function in the way that the Kantian account would suggest. That is, we cannot equate a moral rule with a decision procedure by which we can apodictically determine a unique and correct solution to every moral dilemma, or (to put the same point in a different way) determine the uniquely correct description (from a moral standpoint) of every real or contemplated action. It does not follow that there are no such things as moral rules, or that they have no force; but we must revise our understanding of what it means to understand and to follow a moral rule.

Consider again just what is involved in a typical moral argument. As we have already seen, moral disputes do not necessarily presuppose that the interlocutors disagree about the relevance and force of certain basic moral concepts. To the contrary, such disputes normally take place against the background of a consensus, at least a partial and overlapping consensus, with respect to the moral concepts that are in dispute. Those who are in dispute about the legitimacy of some form of killing, for example, euthanasia, cannot be said to disagree radically about the prohibition against murder. Not only do they agree that murder is a bad thing, they are also able to reach agreement on the application of the concept of murder over a wide range of cases.

This implies that the understanding of a moral rule (or any sort of rule) is not logically prior to some comprehension of the cases to which it does, or does not, apply. We do not begin with a general rule, which is grasped in some mysterious analytic way and then applied to particular cases. To the contrary, if one is to understand a rule at all, it is necessary to begin with a set of cases that are recognized as unproblematic instances of that rule, together with a set of cases in which it is generally recognized that the rule does not apply. In order to follow a rule, one applies it to relevantly similar cases, unless there is some reason to call its application to a given case into question. If there is some such reason, then the case is a borderline or ambiguous case, and (if it is important enough) it may well become the focus for moral dispute. But in the majority of cases, there will be sufficient warrant, based on analogies with non-problematic cases, to either apply the rule in question or to decide that it does not apply in this situation.

One other point should be noted. It is natural to equate moral rules and the correlative moral concepts with their linguistic formulations. This tendency should be resisted. The primary criterion for understanding a concept is the ability to *act intelligently* with respect to the object or the domain of the concept. This ability will include a capacity to form propositions using the concept, to determine the truth-conditions for those propositions, and more generally to formulate the rules which govern the linguistic use of the concept. But, as Wittgenstein reminds us, linguistic interpretations of a rule do not determine the meaning of the rule; rather, they are *approximations* of that meaning, which is adequately expressed *only* in intelligent action.[44] To return to the example at hand, someone's understanding of the concept of murder does not find its only expression in an ability to formulate a rule, or a set of rules, about murder. Rather, it is expressed in a whole set of abilities, including the ability to recognize that certain kinds of killing do count as murder and others do not, to anticipate and comprehend the reactions that others have to instances of murder, and other similar practical capacities.

This example raises one last point. It is possible that someone might have sufficient linguistic capacity to use the term, "murder," in appropriate ways, and yet lack the ability fully to understand the concept. It would seem that there are such persons, and they are dangerous people indeed. At the same time, however, it is no part of my argument that anyone who really understands a moral concept will necessarily act in accordance with it. It is possible really to understand what it means to murder, and yet to be a murderer; difficult, I suspect, but possible.

THE MORAL ACT AND MORAL JUDGEMENT: REFORMULATING THE QUESTION

"Are there some kinds of actions that are never morally justifiable, whatever the circumstances, the foreseeable consequences, or the intention of the agent?" We are now in a position to answer this question. The answer is yes. There are some kinds of actions that are never morally justifiable. Anscombe is right in her general characterization of the moral tradition that we have inherited; right, that is, to insist that it is structured around beliefs that there are some kinds of actions that are always wrong.

Yet she is mistaken to claim that our inherited tradition is structured in this way because it was originally *Christian*, or more generally, because it is grounded in religious convictions. Our traditional concept of morality rests on the conviction that there are some kinds of actions that always exemplify immorality, because it is a part of our conception of these kinds of actions that they are never morally justifiable. It does not follow, as we have already observed, that the meaning of these kinds of actions can be reduced to the judgement that they are wrongful. Rather, we have come to judge, over centuries, that certain kinds of actions, which are understood in terms of paradigmatic cases, are themselves paradigmatic examples (albeit, in this case, negative ones) of the still more generic concept of morality. Morality itself, in turn, is understood in this way, not because it is originally a religious conception, but because it is a *generic* conception. And, as we have already observed, we cannot form a generic concept of any sort without appealing to a set of paradigmatic exemplifications of that concept, even when, in this case, those exemplifications are themselves generic concepts, and even when, again in this case, they are negative rather than positive. Anscombe's characterization of the "Hebrew-Christian moral tradition" owes more, at this point, to her allegiance to Wittgenstein, than to her theological commitments.

Moreover, a positive answer to the question, whether some kinds of actions are always wrong, does not establish as much as some would like. It is important to recall that Anscombe herself insisted on this claim in the context of an argument with her philosophical contemporaries, who were mostly non-cognitivists or utilitarians. And I believe it is fair to say that, with respect to these positions, Anscombe's analysis of moral language is quite relevant. We have already seen that the distinction between description and evaluation, which is central to moral non-cognitivism, is seen to be a misplaced distinction, once the functioning of moral concepts is correctly understood. Moreover, Anscombe is right to insist that any reductive strategy, which attempts to replace moral concepts as they emerge in use with supposedly more basic concepts of goodness or value, will inevitably omit or distort much that is central to our actual lived understanding of those concepts. While that point is not a decisive refutation of utilitarianism and other forms of consequentialism, it is a telling point none the less, and has not yet received an adequate response.[45]

However, when men and women find it necessary to remind one another, and themselves, that some kinds of actions are always wrong, their motivation in doing so is not generally to correct utilitarians or non-cognitivists. Rather, the usual point of a remark such as, "murder is always wrong," or "that would be murder!" is to rule out some course of action that involves (for example) killing someone, in such a way as not to fall within the parameters of a form of killing that is generally acknowledged to be legitimate. More generally, this sort of appeal is intended to cut off debate, to end consideration of a proposed course of action as a morally legitimate option. Yet this sort of appeal cannot work, either as a cogent argument or as a piece of rhetorical strategy. If a serious question has been raised about the legitimacy of a given kind of action, then what is at issue is precisely whether this kind of action should count as (for example) murder. Someone who believes that there are cogent reasons for allowing the practice of euthanasia, suicide, or abortion will not be persuaded of anything by being told that murder is wrong (much less, by someone's shouting that murder is wrong), because, if she has come to conclude that euthanasia, say, is justified, then she has already concluded *ipso facto* that euthanasia is *not* murder. Moreover, if the analysis of moral concepts offered above is correct, then there is nothing in the logic or the practice of moral judgement to rule out such a conclusion. It is always possible that some ambiguity will arise in the application of even the most central and well-formulated moral concepts.

This point has not always been appreciated. It has sometimes been assumed that one of the implications of Wittgenstein's understanding of language, as applied to moral discourse, is that fundamental moral judgements cannot be questioned. For example, R. W. Beardsmore, writing in reference to an event in Graham Greene's novel, *The Heart of the Matter*, remarks that

Mrs. Scobie and Father Rank agree in regarding Scobie's killing himself as sufficient grounds for condemning him, because they share the same viewpoint – that of a Catholic morality. Within this viewpoint no reference to an element of evaluation or to the end of morality is required. To draw attention to the fact that Scobie took an overdose of drugs commits one to the moral judgment that what he did was wrong.[46]

Given that moral discourse takes its starting-point from generic concepts of kinds of actions that are always morally wrong (or morally right), then it is true that within *any* moral community (not just among the Catholics) an action that falls under the rubric of one of these generic action concepts can be said, for that very reason, to be wrong (or right) *in the absence of some particular reason to question the aptness of that description.* It is precisely at this point, however, that the difficulty raised above makes itself felt. For, if Waismann is correct, there is no way that we can describe a particular (actual or contemplated) action so exhaustively that we can say that we have taken account of all the morally relevant details, and, therefore, have certainly arrived at the correct description of this action from the moral point of view. It is true that in many, perhaps most, cases, this sort of doubt will be purely hypothetical, or even contrived. But there is still a sufficiently large number of cases in which this sort of doubt is not at all hypothetical to give us pause, and the sort of analysis that Beardsmore offers does not help in these cases.

Anscombe herself is aware, as Beardsmore apparently is not, that we cannot always move directly from a description of a specific action to a moral evaluation of that act. Yet she does not acknowledge the extent of the doubts that can arise with respect to the application of generic moral concepts; on her view, difficulties arise only with respect to "borderline" cases, that is to say, specific situations that are in some way unusual.[47] Similarly, Paul Ramsey, in his essay, "The Case of the Curious Exception," not only acknowledges, but insists upon, the fact that generic moral concepts can only be applied through the exercise of a kind of judgement that cannot be expressed exhaustively in formulae.[48] Yet he, too, apparently assumes that this sort of judgement is exercised only with respect to individual cases, and only causes difficulty in situations that are unusual in some way.

Neither Anscombe nor Ramsey acknowledges the fact that, for most of us today, the most serious difficulties that arise with respect to the application of generic moral concepts are generated by *kinds* of actions that are seen as problematic for some reason. We do not often have occasion to worry about whether a particular individual in some unheard-of, really awful situation should be held to be guilty of murder or not, but we do have occasion to worry, a great deal, about how we as individuals and as a society should respond to certain *kinds* of killing, such as euthanasia, suicide, or abortion. I do not mean to say that the exercise of judgement with respect to difficult individual cases is either unimportant or uninteresting, but the moral worries that preoccupy us as a society have more to do with the re-evaluation of kinds of actions.

This should not be surprising. As industrialized societies continue to go through the extensive changes that have characterized this century, it is inevitable that the basic moral concepts, which express and help to sustain the boundaries of the society, should be called into question as those boundaries are challenged and redrawn. The resultant processes of re-examination, debate, and renegotiation, by which the meaning of a concept such as "murder" is called into question and reformulated, are not expressions of a weakened moral fiber or the wholesale collapse of moral discourse. They are the inevitable products of processes of social change that we cannot evade, and can only partially control.

CHAPTER 2

The meaning of morality

Perhaps there is something unsatisfactory about the analysis of the previous chapter. It may seem that I have placed too much emphasis on the role of judgement in moral discourse and action, and, as a result, I have left the impression that moral reasoning is a matter of individual discretion. Yet it is dangerous, at best, to hold that moral judgement is *merely* a matter of individual discretion. To quote Hilary Putnam:

Someone who thinks that torture is morally impermissible, and who is *serious* about this view, will not suggest torture (or go along when someone else makes the suggestion) even if it is a case of finding where a bomb is going to go off before many innocent lives are lost ... If the idea of tricking the terrorist rather than torturing him does not occur to one; if, at worst, one does not consider sodium pentothal rather than torture; if one is not too scrupulous about whether one is *sure* one has caught a terrorist and that the explosion is imminent – then one's "principle" of nontorture is just *talk* ...

The problem with thinking in terms of "values" and "conflicts" rather than in terms of "rules" and "exceptions" (and rules to prevent the exceptions from becoming rules) is that the metaphor of *balancing* quickly gets the upper hand. To think of all moral problems in terms of "trade-offs" is precisely not to think morally at all.[1]

I have quoted Putnam at some length because he offers a clear and forceful statement of the issues that will be addressed in this chapter. Just what *does* it mean "to think morally?" The preceding chapter offered a negative answer, as it were, to this question, by establishing that moral rules cannot function in such a way as apodictically to resolve all moral dilemmas. None the less, as Putnam's remarks remind us, a negative answer to this question is not sufficient. It is a part of our understanding of morality that moral rules have a special stringency, in that they override conflicting norms and considerations. For this reason, the conclusion of the preceding chapter, that there is an ineliminable element of judgement in the application of moral rules, may well generate some uneasiness in those who share Putnam's views on the meaning of moral thinking. How is it possible to offer an account of moral judgement that does not finally reduce that elusive capacity to a "balancing" of competing considerations? More generally, how are we to account for, and respect, the special stringency of moral rules?

It would not do to respond to this question by claiming that Putnam's insight is just mistaken, that moral considerations do not have the stringency that he insists on, or, alternatively, that we have no stake in "thinking morally," at least as he understands moral thinking. To the contrary, Putnam is quite right to insist that we *do* have a stake, very much so, in "thinking morally" and in maintaining the distinctive quality of moral thinking. This distinctive quality is a reflection of the multiple functions that moral rules play in our individual and social lives. As Putnam goes on to observe, "Rules ... are important because they are the main mechanism we have for challenging (and, if we are successful, shaping) one another's consciences."[2] He might have added that they are one of the main mechanisms that we have for challenging our own consciences, for erecting barriers against the self-deception and callousness to which we are all prone. Moreover, they can offer an indispensable mechanism for challenging the mores and the practices of our communities, if they are appropriated in a critical, reflective way.

Any account of moral judgement that does not respect the distinctive functioning of moral rules will be seriously deficient. Yet it would also be a mistake to attempt to account for these functions in terms of the operations of moral rules considered *as rules*. As we saw in the previous chapter, rules as such logically cannot bear the whole weight of the special stringency of moral concepts.

Putnam's remarks about hedging exceptions reflect, again,

the difficulties inherent in the Kantian conception of rules. He calls for exceptions to be hedged with further rules. Yet, as Paul Ramsey has pointed out, this sort of interpretative hedging is better understood as a process of deepening our understanding of the rationale of a rule, and applying it accordingly, than as a process of justifying an exception: "The so-called exception disappears in the very process of trying to find warrants for it . . . The effort to locate a *justifiable* exception can only have the effect of utterly destroying its exceptional character."[3] Moreover, as we have seen, this sort of iterative interpretation cannot go on forever. Sooner or later, there will come a point at which further explanations fail, and it is necessary simply to act on one's best judgement. To quote Ramsey again: "If the breadth and depth and flexibility of good moral reason is lost from view, then all that once passed for rationality is bound to seem a cruel master."[4]

How, then, are we to do justice to Putnam's concern to preserve the distinctive character of moral thinking, without falling once again under the sway of the "cruel master" of a fallacious understanding of moral reasoning? In order to do so successfully, it will be necessary to locate the distinctive stringency of moral rules in something other than their character *as rules*. It is certainly not a mistake to insist that moral rules, and the generic concepts correlated with them, do function in certain distinctive ways. Only, we have tended in the past to confuse what is distinctive about moral concepts with certain logical features attaching to the functioning of almost *any* generic concept. In order to understand what is distinctive about moral concepts, it is necessary to look at their *substantive content*, and to analyze their correlative rules in terms of the rationale specific to that content.

Accordingly, one aim of this chapter will be to examine the concept of morality. This examination will begin with the question of what we mean by "moral," and the related and fundamental question of whether this notion is either cogent or useful. I will next consider how substantive features of our basic moral notions inform moral judgement and give it its distinctive character, both at the level of reflection on norms and social structures, and at the level of concrete judgement of individual cases. What will emerge is an account of moral thinking that does justice to its distinctive character and its importance in our lives.

Moreover, this account will begin to address a question that was left implicit by the last chapter. If moral thinking does not function in accordance with the model of modern moral theories, can it be said to be rational at all? As we will see, it is the case that good moral thinking is rational in its character. And, since rationality in any domain of thought implies the possibility of error, I will conclude this chapter with a discussion of some of the forms of moral error and moral wrongdoing.

MORALITY AS AN ANALOGICAL CONCEPT

So far, I have proceeded as if the meaning of expressions such as "moral rules," together with related expressions such as "obligation," "ought," and the like, was clear and unproblematic. Of course, this is not the case. As early as 1958, Elizabeth Anscombe called the cogency of such expressions into question: "the concepts of obligation, and duty – *moral* obligation and *moral* duty, that is to say – and of what is *morally* right and wrong, and of the *moral* sense of 'ought,' ought to be jettisoned if this is psychologically possible; because they are survivals, or derivatives from survivals, from an earlier conception of ethics which no longer generally survives, and are only harmful without it."[5] At first, Anscombe's objections to the cogency of our notions of morality, obligation, and the like, were not widely accepted. But, in recent years, a growing number of philosophers have come to share Anscombe's reservations about these notions, albeit not always for her reasons.

In the previous chapter, we noted that Alasdair MacIntyre agrees with Anscombe that contemporary moral discourse is fragmentary, in the sense of incorporating survivals from traditions that are no longer vital, and, he would add, incompatible traditions at that.[6] A number of other scholars have likewise concluded that moral discourse in contemporary societies incorporates survivals from traditions that are no longer vital, and are, moreover, incompatible – although they disagree among themselves about whether this state of affairs is a good or a bad thing, on the whole.[7] Others have observed that the sorts of considerations that we include under the heading of morality, or, more generally, that we incorporate in our judgements of persons and their actions, are more heterogeneous than we have previously realized, without necessarily offering a historical explanation for that fact.[8] Finally, there are some, Bernard Williams foremost among them, who argue that the modern conception of "the moral" is a distinctive social construct, which in Williams' view is characterized by a tendency to reduce all evaluative considerations to a notion of obligation.[9] Williams, like Anscombe (but again, for somewhat different reasons), would prefer to drop notions such as morality altogether – which is not at all to say that he is not interested in reflection on normative evaluation more broadly construed, which he calls the realm of the ethical.

According to Williams, once we recognize the institutional and conventional nature of morality, we will see that it is a mistake to attempt to develop a theory of morality of the sort that both Kant and Bentham, and any number of their followers, have attempted to develop since.[10] That is, it is a mistake to attempt to determine what is essential to morality *per se*, and to offer an analytic account of morality on that basis, by which we can determine what does or does not count as a valid moral claim, extend the scope of our moral judgements, and so forth. There is no such thing as an "essence of morality," because morality is a complex social institution with a long history behind it. That, at least, is the basic argument offered by Williams. Similar arguments are developed by others who, like Williams, have come to be known as moral anti-theorists.[11] And, as far as it goes, this argument is quite correct.

None the less, for better or for worse, concepts of "the moral" and related concepts are still central to evaluation and related practices throughout much of the world. In spite of the philosophical difficulties that these concepts generate, there is no real reason to expect that they will lose their place in our lives. That fact alone would justify giving some attention to the ways in which these concepts function, even if it were not also the case that our notions of morality and related concepts contain important insights and commitments, which we would do well to preserve. Moreover, the historical and social contingency of our notions of morality, obligation, and the like does not prevent us from reflecting on the meaning of these concepts, so long as we keep in mind that we are reflecting on concepts that have a particular history and serve more than one purpose in a complex social environment. Almost no one, including the moral anti-theorists, rejects the possibility of this sort of contextualized reflection on the meaning of our (as opposed to *the*) concept of morality and its related notions.

How are we to undertake this sort of reflection, if the analytic approaches of Kantian or utilitarian theories will not work? The answer to this question is suggested by Julius Kovesi's observation that our concepts of moral goodness and moral obligation, which are themselves generic concepts formed at a very high level of generality, can only be understood through some apprehension of the sorts of cases which we take to exemplify this concept.[12] In this respect, the concept of morality is similar to specific moral concepts like "murder," which, as we have seen, must also be understood in the context of a consensus on cases which count, unproblematically, as murder. Because the concept, "the moral," is formulated at a high level of generality, however, it is exemplified by, and understood in terms of, lower-order generic concepts, primarily concepts of kinds of actions that exemplify moral wrongness in some way or other.

The meaning of our concept of the moral must, therefore, be given first of all in terms of the concepts of kinds of actions that exemplify immoral behavior, for example, murder, theft, lying, adultery, fraud. What can we say, at the outset, about these kinds of actions?

It is worth noting, first of all, just what a conventional list this is; "conventional," not only in the sense that these concepts mark social conventions (which they do), but also conventional in the more ordinary sense of general acceptability. I do not mean to say that there would be universal agreement that any item on this list represents a real violation of morality. None the less, there is clearly a *widespread overlapping* consensus about the kinds of actions that should count as immoral actions. That is, there would be nearly universal agreement that some kinds of actions are morally wrong, and there would be substantial, although not universal, agreement on many other kinds of actions. Furthermore, there would be few, if any, disjunctive lists; that is to say, anyone who shares the concept of morality, if asked to list examples of immoral actions, would almost certainly include at least some of the standard ways of going wrong.

Yet, even though it would be easy to generate a standard list of immoral actions, it is not so clear what all these concepts would have in common, beyond all counting, for us, as negative exemplifications of the concept of morality. Murder, theft, and adultery are all ways of harming someone, but it is not so clear that lying always is. And what are we to say about fornication or homosexual behavior, which many would count as immoral, even though they do not involve any obvious harms at all?

The heterogeneity of our basic moral concepts may suggest that they have nothing in common, beyond all counting, for us, as moral concepts. If this were the case, then we would have to give up any hope of making sense of the concept of morality, at least on the basis of the moral concepts that we do actually share. There would be, so to speak, no sense to make, and nothing to be learned from moral concepts beyond the sheer fact that we do count these and those particular kinds of notions as moral concepts.[13]

However, this conclusion would be too quick. There are some unifying threads which run through most of what we would count as the basic moral concepts. While these strands of unity do not comprise a moral theory in the Kantian sense, they do offer a basis for the more limited claim that we do have a coherent concept of morality.

We must recognize this: the unity proper to the concept of morality is that mode of unity that is proper to concepts, especially very general concepts, as they actually emerge and function in natural languages. That is to say, it is analogical, rather than analytical.[14] As such, the unity of the concept of morality cannot be derived from *a priori* analysis. Rather, it must be discovered through inspection, in this case, inspection of the basic moral notions, on the basis of which we can arrive at a grasp of the formal element, or the focal meaning, in virtue of which all these count as exemplifications of one, more general concept. Correlatively, the formal notion underlying the concept of morality can be articulated (I am about to do just that), but it cannot be stated in the form of an exhaustive definition, understood as a definitive statement of the necessary and sufficient conditions for something to count as a moral claim. Any articulation of "the meaning of morality" will be nothing more than an interpretation of the concept, and, as Wittgenstein reminds us, no interpretation of a concept can be more basic or foundational than the concept itself.[15]

Thus, our interpretation of the concept of morality must be guided by inspection and reflection on the actual usage of the concept, and not used to determine in advance what counts as a moral concept, and what does not. Whatever is said about our present concept of morality may or may not apply to past versions of it, and the relationships between past and present versions (of this or any concept) will have to be established historically, not analytically. Similarly, we should not be surprised to find that there are some usages of the concept of morality, and related notions, that do not fit well with our interpretation, particularly in the light of what MacIntyre and others have shown about the history of our moral discourse. It should be sufficient, it will have to be sufficient, to offer an interpretation of the concept of morality that accounts for most of our applications of the concept, and illuminates the ways in which these diverse applications are related to one another. The complexities of our most important concepts will generally outstrip our efforts at interpretation. That is not surprising, and it does not mean that an analogical interpretation of the concept of morality (in this case), is not possible at all.

NON-MALEFICENCE, EQUALITY, AND THE FOCAL
MEANING OF MORALITY

The task of this section is to locate the meaning of our concept of morality in terms of a focal meaning, which is instantiated in a variety of ways in the different notions which exemplify morality for us. It is important to note at the outset that the analogous character of the concept of morality is not a peculiar feature of this concept. Most, if not all, empirical concepts are analogical, in the sense that they can only be understood in terms of a formal element that is revealed through reflection on paradigmatic examples of a given concept.

This is a further implication of Waismann's account of the open-texture of empirical concepts. That is, because empirical concepts do not generally have precise boundaries, they cannot be understood analytically; they can only be understood in and through a grasp of some formal element, in virtue of which the various instantiations of the concept can be recognized for what they are, that is, instantiations of *this* concept. The most ordinary empirical concepts, such as "plant," "animal," "living creature," "inanimate creature," and the like, are none of them simply given by the world as it presents itself to us. They are all descriptions that are given unity and point by some formal character, the character of being vegetable or animal life, of being living or non-living, or whatever. These formal qualities are displayed in and through the paradigmatic examples that give content to the concepts in question, without which those concepts could not be understood. Yet these formal qualities convey more than could be gathered from an iterative list of the relevant paradigmatic examples alone. They indicate the *point* of the description in question, as conveyed by the relevant general concept. That is why it is possible, and perfectly comprehensible, to exemplify two different concepts by the same set of examples; as I might offer "maples, pines, oaks," as examples of kinds of trees, or of kinds of plants, or of kinds of living creatures.

It is important to recall that conceptual knowledge is not exclusively verbal in form. The capacity to use the relevant language in appropriate ways is only one of the capacities for intelligent action that go to make up comprehension of a concept. I have only a vague idea of what the correct definition of "tree" would be, even for lay use, much less for scientific purposes. Yet I understand perfectly well what a tree is. My knowledge is manifested in my ability to make statements about trees, and to determine the truth or falsity of those statements (or, at least, to determine what it would mean for some such statement to be true or false). But it is also manifested by the fact that I know how to act in appropriate ways with reference to trees. I recognize trees and I distinguish them from other sorts of plants, I do not talk to them (or, at least, I do not talk to them with the expectation of a response), I water and fertilize them, rake their leaves, and so on. All of this presupposes a grasp of the concept of a tree that is not exclusively verbal. Indeed, without some non-verbal grasp of what a tree is, it is highly doubtful whether I could talk about trees in the appropriate ways at all, except in the most simple and imitative of ways.[16]

This much can be said about any concept within a natural language, including our moral concepts. Moral understanding is imbedded in, presupposes, and informs those fundamental capacities for action which are brought to bear in our relations to other people and, reflexively, to ourselves.

A number of authors have emphasized the deep connection between fundamental moral concepts and our most basic attitudes towards other human beings, considered as fellow agents and as potential participants in a community of shared meanings.[17] They sometimes give the impression that the concept of morality is an essential component or expression of the fundamental concept of a human person.[18] So expressed, this claim is too strong. No society fails to distinguish between human beings and other sorts of living creatures, and this distinction is signaled by practices that are to be found in all human societies; we name our children, we speak with one another and expect responses, we bury, or otherwise honor, our dead.[19] Moreover, we place expectations on ourselves and others, which go beyond, and can cut across, calculations of individual or social well-being. Yet these practices of human recognition can apparently exist quite well in a society which is informed by radically different normative commitments, so much so that it does not make sense to say that it has anything like our concept of morality.

None the less, the concept of morality is deeply intertwined *for us* with the fundamental concept of a human person, that is to say, for all those of us who have been shaped in traditions informed by this concept. Whatever may be the case in other societies, for us the whole range of attitudes and responses that inform our behavior towards others *qua* human persons is inextricably informed by the basic moral concepts, even as these attitudes and responses provide these basic concepts with the necessary contexts for intelligibility.

This connection would not be readily apparent to those who defend one important position on the meaning of the concept of morality and related concepts. On this view, a notion of obligatoriness or "oughtness" is fundamental to that concept. No one would deny that the idea of obligation is an important component of our moral concepts. Yet it does not seem that a notion of obligatoriness provides the focal meaning for our concept of morality. So long as we attempt to make sense of the concept of morality in terms of a general notion of obligatoriness, we will find ourselves puzzled by what, taken in the abstract, is a very odd notion.

The difficulty with this approach is not that it is difficult to make sense of the idea of a moral law, if we do not believe in a divine lawgiver, as Anscombe claims; the Stoics did so, and, contrary to Anscombe, I think Kant succeeded in doing so, as well.[20] The more fundamental difficulty is that it is very difficult to understand obligatoriness, apart from some context in which to speak of relations of obligations, which have a history and a point. For this reason, it is very easy to move from a free-floating notion of obligation to Prichard's peculiar view, that moral duties have neither foundation, nor point, nor rationale, and, if they did, they would cease to be moral obligations![21]

A better suggestion for the focal meaning of the concept of

morality is offered by Thomas Aquinas, who explicitly rejects
the claim that some kinds of actions are wrong *because* they are
forbidden by God, arguing to the contrary that certain kinds of
actions are forbidden by God because they are harmful in some
way: "We do not offend God except by doing something
contrary to our own good, as has been said."[22] This suggestion
is attractive, because it opens up a way of linking our understanding of the concept of morality with still more fundamental
concepts of what it is to be a human being. On this view, our
concept of morality is grounded in a sense that there is something fundamentally *wrong* (for lack of a better term!) with
inflicting pain or loss on another human being; this sort of
action is at odds with our deepest sense of appropriate action
with respect to other human beings.

Moreover, this interpretation of the concept of morality
would appear to be borne out by the notions which exemplify
this concept. When we examine our notions of the kinds of
actions that exemplify moral wrong doing, we find that, by and
large, they are notions of harms. It is true that some would
include on this list kinds of actions, such as fornication or
homosexual intercourse, which do not involve any obvious
harm to anyone. However, many, albeit not all, of those who
would include actions of these kinds on a list of immoral actions
would argue that the sort of behavior in question really is
harmful.

Moreover, if we take non-maleficence rather than obligatoriness to be the focal meaning for the concept of morality, we
can more easily make sense of the notions of obligation and
"oughtness." These notions express the special stringency of
the basic moral prohibitions, and their status as overriding
other sorts of considerations. Why should this be the case? Why
do not we generally take the norms of etiquette, for example, to
be similarly overriding? The answer surely lies in the fact that
the basic moral concepts express our sense of the importance of
refraining from certain kinds of harms to others (and perhaps
ourselves), even in the face of considerable inducements or
provocations. Thus, someone who *assumes* (as opposed to
arguing) that the moral rules are merely presumptive, in such a

way that they can be overridden by any sort of competing claim whatever, has failed to understand the concepts involved.[23] That is why Putnam is right to insist that we cannot think exclusively in terms of "trade-offs" if we are to think morally.

The point of moral concepts such as murder is precisely that these concepts identify certain kinds of harms that ought not to be inflicted on others, even for good reason; or, to put it another way, they point to considerations that fall outside of the realm of relative advantages and costs. Concepts of serious offenses, including, for example, theft and rape, as well as murder, have a kind of stringency that expresses the overriding importance of the boundaries that they set. Other moral concepts do not concern matters that are ordinarily so grave: lying, cheating, and gossiping, for example, do not normally involve inflicting injuries that would affect the whole course of a human life, although in some circumstances, each of these could do so. The sort of stringency that is appropriate to the application of concepts of murder, for example, would not be appropriate to concepts such as lying or cheating. Yet concepts like these latter do have their own stringency, and, within a limited range, their own quality of overridingness, that is appropriate to their usual areas of concern.

It would be misleading to identify non-maleficence as the focal meaning for moral concepts, without any further qualification. For one thing, we cannot assume that because most of our central moral concepts are concepts of kinds of harms, therefore our concept of morality implies that it is always wrong to inflict harm. This conclusion is not logically valid, and furthermore, it is not true; we do recognize that there are situations in which it is legitimate to harm another. It is difficult to see how our common life could be sustained unless we acknowledged the legitimacy of at least some kinds of harms; otherwise there would be no police, no military forces, no law-courts, no property or commerce, no schools, none of the institutional forms that sustain human life. The question that arises, in the face of this melancholy fact, is whether there is some rationale for the distinctions that we draw between legitimate and illegitimate forms of harming.

A second consideration should lead us to qualify the claim that a commitment to non-maleficence is central to our concept of morality. So far, we have proceeded as if all our moral concepts were negative concepts, correlated with prohibitions. Yet there are surely at least some positive moral concepts, that is to say, concepts of kinds of actions that are morally praiseworthy or even obligatory. Moreover, we have any number of concepts of admirable qualities of character or disposition, for example, bravery, kindness, patience. It is true that these sorts of positive concepts stand in an ambiguous relationship to what we might describe as standard moral concepts, such as murder, adultery, or theft.[24] Some of them, including all of those just listed, would probably be counted as moral notions by many people, but other, similar qualities would not be widely considered to be moral qualities, even though they would be widely admired, for example, intelligence, grace, wittiness, or charm. Moreover, it would probably be more difficult to generate a list of generally agreed upon positive qualities, than a list of generally agreed upon prohibitions. None the less, there is enough of an overlap between our positive ideals for action and character on the one hand, and our concept of morality on the other, to call for some qualification of the claim that non-maleficence provides the focal meaning for our concept of morality.

Granting the need for some qualification, I would still argue that a commitment to non-maleficence is central to our concept of morality. Only it must be realized that the concept of harm is itself a generic concept which must be understood analogically. Our moral concepts are informed by our concerns with a number of different kinds of harms, and the differences, as well as the similarities, among them must be taken into account, if we are to be capable of moral thinking that is really sensitive to the whole range of human needs and concerns. Even more importantly, it must be remembered that our commitment to non-maleficence, and the concept of morality that this commitment generates, are for us essential qualifications of the fundamental concept of a human being, which serve to indicate parameters on the ways in which persons can behave to one another. We believe that we ought to refrain from certain kinds of harms to others, because these sorts of harms are inconsistent with an acknowledgment of the value and worth of the human person.

Why not simply say, then, that the focal meaning for our concept of morality is best articulated by the notion of respect for persons, which should be taken as the fundamental moral commitment? This claim would not be false, but it could easily be misunderstood. It is certainly the case that our moral judgements presuppose and express a certain understanding of what it means to acknowledge and respect the humanity of another. On this understanding, certain kinds of harms are more serious than others, because they appear as direct assaults on human life and dignity. Moreover, this understanding reflexively conditions what we take to be a harm (justified or not). Thus, we think that it is harmful to do something to another against her will, to violate her autonomy, because we take a capacity for reasoned choice to be an essential part of normal human life. This sort of harm may be justified, but it calls for a very serious justification indeed, and, on the other hand, there are those who would argue that *only* a violation of autonomy counts as a harm (understandably, but wrongly).

None of this is problematic. What is problematic, however, is the further conclusion that respect for persons (or alternatively, respect for rational nature or for autonomy) is central to morality, in the sense that all moral norms worthy of the name can be *derived* from a commitment to respect for persons, or shown to be versions or specifications of such a commitment.[25] Any number of moral theorists, philosophers and theologians alike, have tried to do just that. The difficulty with this approach becomes evident, however, as soon as we consider the question of our moral obligations to all those fellow-sufferers who do not have the capacities necessary to function as rational, autonomous agents: fetuses, infants, children, those whose mental abilities are damaged or destroyed by illness, injury, or extreme age, and non-human animals. So long as respect for persons, interpreted as respect for rationality or autonomy, is taken to be the *foundational* moral commitment, it is necessary either to deny that we have moral obligations to any of these sorts of creatures, or else, to contrive a notion of rationality or autonomy that will somehow fit the situation of at least some of them.[26]

It is certainly the case that our concept of morality would have no point or application, and therefore no meaning, outside of the context of a community of persons, who are normally and normatively capable of rational, autonomous action. This context, in turn, qualifies the notion of harm that is central to our concept of morality, so much so that the commitments to non-maleficence and to some version of equal regard can be taken as two mutually qualifying normative ideals at the core of that concept. Yet, precisely because these are mutually qualifying ideals, the meaning of morality cannot be reduced to respect for those qualities of rationality and free choice that are central to contemporary interpretations of equal regard.

At any rate, it would be a mistake to assume that the central or focal meaning for a concept must necessarily be foundational for all the applications of that concept, in the sense that the latter can be analytically or deductively derived from the former. Again, it should be noted that the unity of the concept of morality is analogical, rather than analytical. It is possible to identify a focal meaning for this concept, but that does not mean that all of the correct applications of the concept of morality can be analytically derived from this focal meaning. Rather, these applications stand to the focal meaning of the concept as exemplifications which are related by relevant similarities to that focal meaning, and to each other, yet in diverse ways.

My point will be clearer if I say what I take the focal meaning of the concept of morality to be, and how I take its various instantiations to be related to one another. In brief, then, I take the focal meaning of our concept of morality to lie in a commitment to non-maleficence, understood in the context of, and as a fundamental expression of, our basic attitudes towards other human persons. Thus, I take our basic concepts of wrongful kinds of actions, such as murder, theft, adultery, rape and the like, to be paradigmatic moral concepts. What is significant about these kinds of actions is that they all outrage human dignity in some fundamental way, by assaulting the forms of life that are essential to human existence in some clear way, or by violating human freedom with respect to the basic goods of human existence. For this reason, these kinds of actions can be understood to exemplify violations of respect for persons, as well as exemplifying maleficence *tout court*.

The paradigmatic moral concepts bring together our commitments to non-maleficence and to respect for persons. At the same time, however, the concept of morality may also be said to include concepts of other kinds of actions, and of attitudes, characteristics, or ideals, which are related to the paradigmatic moral concepts in a variety of ways. Thus, it is at least intelligible to claim that the harms that we inflict on non-human creatures are of moral significance. On the other hand, we may also give moral significance to kinds of actions, characteristics, and ideals which are in some way expressive of, or contrary to, human dignity, without necessarily involving any obvious harm to anyone. It is again intelligible to give moral significance to forms of behavior that do not obviously harm anyone, and yet appear to be contrary to human dignity, as, for example, certain kinds of sexual behavior, or certain forms of intemperance with respect to eating and drinking. Similarly, it is intelligible to count the ideals associated with the traditional virtues as moral concepts, since these also can be construed as expressions of a fundamental commitment to human dignity.

In each of these cases it is also possible intelligibly to deny that the concepts in question are moral concepts, or that the relevant concerns are moral concerns, because, in each case, the concepts in question lack some feature of what we take to be the paradigmatic moral concepts. Harms to non-human creatures do not appear to involve violations of respect, and actions that are just inconsistent with human dignity do not appear to involve harms. Here, again, there is scope for judgement, which may defensibly come down on either side of a question. It would not be intelligible, however, to deny that concepts such as murder or theft are moral concepts. Someone who tried to deny the moral significance of these paradigmatic moral concepts would be rejecting the very concept of morality itself, refusing to think or speak morally.

At this point, a terminological note is in order. As I interpret it, the concept of morality is a general concept which is exemplified by notions of kinds of moral or immoral actions. These paradigmatic moral notions are themselves concepts, at a lower level of generality. To avoid confusion, however, I will speak of these latter as paradigmatic or basic moral notions, in contrast to the more general concept of morality which they exemplify.[27] Moreover, I have so far spoken, and will continue to speak, of the traditional rules of morality, meaning by that the set of prohibitions associated with the paradigmatic moral notions. I do not mean to imply that other sorts of evaluative norms, whether moral or not, are not also rules. None the less, references to the norms associated with concepts such as murder, theft, and adultery, as *the* rules of morality, are so deeply embedded in our discourse, both within and outside the academy, that any other usage would be confusing and stilted.

MORAL JUDGEMENT AND KINDS OF ACTIONS

In this section and the next, I will offer some considerations in illustration and defense of the claim that moral thinking is essentially analogical. In this section, I will focus on the sorts of thinking that are most in evidence when we are considering whether some general kind of action should be brought under the scope of a still more general prohibition, or not. In other words, I will be looking at the issues that arise in connection with questions such as: "Does euthanasia count as murder? Does suicide count as murder? Does abortion count as murder? Does capital punishment count as murder?" In the next section, I will focus on the sorts of considerations that are more evident when we are considering particular cases in which the application of a moral rule is in doubt for some reason. There is a considerable degree of overlap between these two sets of considerations, but it seems desirable, in the interests of clarity, to consider them separately.

In both sections, it will be necessary to go through complex issues very quickly. Each of the particular questions mentioned here could be the subject of its own book, and a number of them have generated many books. I do not claim to offer anything like a comprehensive treatment of any of these issues. I only hope to be able to say enough to support the claim that our concept of morality is an analogical concept, with its own proper coherence in diversity.

I begin, therefore, with a consideration of moral thinking as it is displayed at the level of social reflection. This is a level at which conflict is especially evident in today's modern societies, and that fact should come as no surprise. Widely accepted norms are such, that is, widely accepted, because they play a number of different and overlapping social functions. It might seem that this fact counts against the claim that our concept of morality displays an analogical unity, focused on a commitment to non-maleficence and respect for the humanity of others. But this is not the case. Our general commitment to non-maleficence expresses itself through the prohibition of different sorts of harms, which, moreover, can come together, and come into conflict, even with reference to one general rule. It should not be surprising that when we are brought to the margins of this consensus, by the pace of social change or for some other reason, these divergent purposes should be articulated and debated, sometimes for the first time.

For example: the prohibition of murder serves a number of functions. It protects individuals, not only from the basic harm of loss of life, but also from a fundamental kind of violation of freedom, from suffering, and from insecurity. At the same time, it also serves to promote public security and order. It embodies and conveys fundamental values, including, for us, respect for life, individualism, and equality. Which of these purposes is central, and which are secondary or peripheral? How are we to resolve the dilemmas that arise when two or more of these purposes come into conflict, for example, respect for life versus the general obligation to relieve suffering? Many of the debates over just what should count as murder can be analyzed as debates over questions such as these.

There is a second context within which debates over the applicability of moral norms can arise, and that is the context set by questions of conflicts of claims, duties, and social commitments. It is sometimes difficult to see how far this sort of reflection has already been incorporated into our fund of generally accepted moral judgements, because these judgements tend to take on the status of formulaic truisms, and these truisms, in turn, develop the patina of non-negotiable, absolute prohibitions. But a closer examination will reveal that there is almost no norm or value that is institutionalized in our society as a non-negotiable absolute prohibition which must never be made to give way to other norms or values. Closely related to these are the considerations that arise from a sense of human limitations. While it is not strictly true that there is no point in formulating a norm of morality that is so stringent that most persons could not live up to it (it could serve as an expression of an ideal, or as a means of social control through the inducement of perpetual guilt), a system of morality that persistently ignores the limitations of what persons can do and sustain is doomed to collapse. For this reason, the norms of morality are generally formulated in such a way as to take account of what we can expect of most persons (ourselves included) as we try to live up to the ideals of a given society. Very often, these judgements are intertwined with judgements about what we *ought* to expect of persons, and in this way, they are interlinked with adjudications of conflicts of claims or duties.

For this reason, our shared sense of what we can expect of persons is generally not amenable to expression simply in terms of what persons can or cannot be asked to do or to forbear doing, but reflects a more complicated set of judgements as to the degree of sacrifice that it is reasonable to expect under varying conditions and for varying aims. So, for example, we do not expect persons to sacrifice their own lives in order to shield an attacker, but we *do* generally expect someone to do so, if she can only save herself by killing someone who is not intentionally threatening or attacking her in any way.

How are we to negotiate these complexities in our examination of the basic moral notions? The analysis of the previous chapter suggests a strategy. We will examine the different classes of ambiguities that arise in the course of our efforts to apply moral concepts, in order to draw out the different kinds of reasoned considerations that generate ambiguity in each sort of case.

Let us return to the notion of murder, and the lower-order concepts of actions that might or might not count as kinds of murders.[28] The starting consensus for any discussion of the ethics of homicide might be described as follows: it is very bad to kill another human being, and we should expect ourselves and others to make almost any sacrifice, rather than to do so. None the less, there are situations in which we do not ask persons to sacrifice their most basic interests in order to refrain from killing another, specifically, those situations in which the victim has put herself at risk by attacking the life, or (some, not all, would add) the bodily integrity or the property of another. That is, we do acknowledge that homicide can sometimes be justified if the costs of refraining are very great (for example, someone who kills another in self-defence will herself be killed otherwise), but such an appeal is not sufficient, taken alone. It is also necessary to be able to point to special circumstances, in virtue of which the notion of murder should not be applied to a given class of cases (for example, the person who is killed by another in self-defense may be said to have brought her death on herself by deliberately threatening another).

When we turn to questions as to whether a given kind of homicide should count as murder, we find that the same twofold consideration appears again and again. That is, these kinds of homicides typically involve some situation in which the human costs of refraining from killing are considerable, and, at the same time, there seems to be no point, or insufficient point, in applying the prohibition against killing in this situation.

For example, many would want to distinguish between murder and euthanasia, on the grounds that the latter describes a significantly different kind of action from murder as it is generally understood. When we examine the arguments offered for this distinction, we find that they regularly combine the same two sorts of appeals that underlie the judgement that killing in self-defense is legitimate. On the one hand, we are reminded that the sick and the dying are often subject to extreme physical suffering, which must be endured with no hope of relief or compensating benefit. On the other hand, it is argued that the usual reasons for prohibiting homicide often do not obtain in the case of gravely ill persons, either because they prefer to die rather than to endure a life of suffering (thus, this would not be a case of depriving a person of life against her will), or because they no longer have, or never did have, the capacities to enjoy those things that make human life valuable to us, or simply because they are going to die shortly anyway. In a second class of cases, we are again faced with circumstances in which the costs of sustaining a prohibition against killing may be very high, and the relevance of the traditional prohibition against killing is unclear. But, in this class of cases, the relevance of the concept of murder is unclear, not so much because the prohibition seems to have no point, as because it is unclear whether the criteria for applying the prohibition obtain. This sort of argument is frequently made with respect to abortion. Of course, arguments for the legitimacy of abortion can be developed that are analogous to the arguments offered for the legitimacy of euthanasia; for example, it is sometimes said that, because the fetus has no awareness of itself as a subject, and no desire to go on living, abortion does not deprive it of something that it values, in the way that murder deprives a self-reflective agent of her valued life. But a different sort of argument for the moral legitimacy of abortion is also offered, namely, that the prohibition against homicide should not apply in the case of abortion, because the fetus is not a human *person*, even though it is clearly a human *life* in the sense that it is biologically human (it is not going to develop into a puppy) and it is alive (it would not be a stillborn baby, if carried to term). Thus, it is said, the essential criterion for applying the concept of murder to an action, namely, the status of the victim as a human person, is lacking in the case of abortion.

It is important to note that the processes of judgement by which we apply the basic moral notions are not consequentialist in form. That is to say, they do not involve an attempt to weigh all the advantages and disadvantages of each possible course of action, in order to pursue the one which seems to promise the greatest possible balance of benefits over harms. Rather, these sorts of judgements involve assessing one's options in terms of the considerations which underlie the prohibition against killing (for example), in an effort to determine whether they apply to the situation at hand. It is true that this sort of assessment is very often motivated by a sense that the cost of applying a traditional prohibition would be intolerably high in a given situation. None the less, if we are to assess a situation in terms of the basic moral concepts, the cost of applying a traditional rule cannot be the only, or even the decisive criterion for judgement. Moreover, certain considerations which a consequentialist would factor into her deliberations are ruled out of consideration in the process of applying the basic moral notions; all those, that is to say, which cannot be described in terms of the considerations which inform the basic moral notions themselves.

Because of the central importance of the harms and the goods that are at stake, the notion of murder, and our related notions of other legitimate or dubious forms of killing, provide good examples of the ways in which moral notions are formed, applied, and debated. The relevant distinctions are drawn fairly sharply, and the corresponding rationales have been articulated through centuries of debate. Yet the very significance of murder and related notions of kinds of killing make them less helpful examples in other respects. With reference to moral notions that concern less significant actions, both the boundaries and the rationale are likely to be less sharply drawn. Moreover, the stringency and overridingness that we readily associate with the prohibition of murder are less likely to be found, or to be found in modified or clearly derivative ways, with respect to less serious moral notions, such as lying or promise-keeping. It is possible to conceive of a trivial lie, an unimportant broken promise, or even a minor theft, in a way that it is not possible to conceive of a trivial or unimportant murder.[29] And, while a purist might insist that the prohibitions against lying, promise-breaking, and theft are overriding in just the same way as the prohibition against murder, most of us, when we are not in the grip of a theory, would not agree. We regularly judge and act as if at least some lies, for example, can be justified by relatively limited aims, such as the avoidance of social embarrassment. In general, the more serious a kind of harm, the more its infliction would tend to damage or destroy a whole human life, the more nearly the moral notions associated with it tend to function in the same ways as does murder and its associated notions.

At the same time, however, it is possible to imagine how someone might be justified in killing another human being, or might do so out of admirable motives. The same cannot be said for every other basic moral notion. For example, it is exceedingly difficult to imagine either a plausible justification, or an admirable motive, for the act of rape, and even harder to imagine a justification or a good motive for rape that would recur frequently enough to generate the concept of a distinctive kind of action, to be distinguished from rape as euthanasia and abortion are (arguably) distinguished from murder. While we are currently engaged in a heated debate over exactly what should count as rape, this debate is almost entirely focused on the difficult question of what counts as consent in the context of sexual relations. Almost no one is prepared to argue that one might sometimes be justified in forcing another to have sex.

When we turn to the realm of sexual ethics more generally, we are faced with some distinctive issues. On the one hand, at least some kinds of sexual actions involve inflicting harms on others (rape, adultery, seduction, sexual harassment). On the other hand, a number of kinds of sexual behavior that once carried a negative moral connotation are now viewed as neutral or positive by large segments of the population, while continuing to carry a negative connotation for others (fornication/premarital sexual activity, homosexual activity, masturbation). It is still the case that these kinds of actions are analogically related to paradigmatic moral concepts, in that they are seen by some as inconsistent with human dignity. This negative claim would be widely challenged, of course, but the significance of sexuality for human life is so pervasive and deep that it is difficult to believe that sexual acts could ever become matters of widespread indifference, calling for no special ideals for action at all.

One's evaluation of sexual behavior will depend, more than any other genus of human activity, on one's understanding of the capabilities and limitations of the human agent, and of the possibilities for human flourishing and harm. Those who are inclined towards a more Kantian view of human capabilities, which tends to drive a wedge between human volition and the affective and physical life of the person, will be more inclined to construe abuses of the sexual function as being exactly parallel to clear-cut acts of maleficence such as murder or theft (whatever specific kinds of actions are considered to be abuses). On the other hand, those who are inclined to a more psycho-dynamically oriented view of the human psyche will also be more inclined to view moral conceptions of sexual behavior as forming a continuum from ideal forms of sexual expression on the one hand, to kinds of actions that are altogether prohibited, on the other. For example, a growing number of Catholic and Anglican theologians, who want to remain in continuity with their church's traditional views on sexuality without committing themselves to the full range of traditional prohibitions, have argued that sexual behavior ought to be evaluated in terms of the nearness of its approach to the ideal of lifelong, faithful heterosexual marriage, while admitting that forms of behavior that do not fit this ideal are not necessarily to be prohibited on that account.[30] It might be said that this approach amounts to waffling, but I would not agree. To the contrary, it seems to me to reflect the flexibility and the analogical character of moral concepts as they are actually used, rather than trying to impose an abstract conception of morality in contexts in which it may not fit.

There is one other category of moral notions that calls for special comment. That is the category set by the notion of rights, and the kinds of actions that we take to be violations of

rights.[31] It is not my intent to enter here into the extensive
debate over human rights; I simply want to observe that,
within most modern industrialized societies, concepts of kinds
of actions that count as violations of rights have a special place
among those concepts of kinds of actions that we would be
inclined to say are never justifiable. What is significant about
rights notions, and what gives them their distinctive quality of
overridingness, is the fact that these notions have historically
emerged in the context of debates over the extent and the limits
of the power of the modern nation-state.[32] That is, they set
boundaries of an especially important sort, because they place
constraints on political authorities which have far more power
than most individuals. For this reason, it is central to the idea
of a right that it cannot be overridden for the sake of general
expediency. The very point of rights claims is that they protect
the individual from being compromised in certain ways in the
name of general expediency, and do so, moreover, in contexts
in which there are often considerable temptations to do so. It
does not follow that rights claims can *never* be overridden; none
the less, the most serious rights claims cannot be overridden
except in highly unusual and painful circumstances.

At this point, I believe that enough has been said to indicate
that the concept of morality, as instantiated by our basic moral
notions, is coherent, even though it is not univocal. So long as
we are conscious of the analogical character of the concept of
morality and the basic moral notions that exemplify it, it is
possible to "think morally," as Putnam would rightly have us
do, without committing ourselves to the strait-jacket of a
narrow and reductionistic concept of morality.

Moreover, we have seen that the inevitable ambiguities that
arise when we attempt to apply the concept of morality, or any
of the moral rules, do not call the rationality of moral discourse
into question. These ambiguities are not simply random breaks
in the structured interactions of that discourse. To the contrary, they are themselves generated by the commitments that
give structure and direction to that discourse. So, for example,
our difficulties with respect to the extension of the notion of
murder are generated by our reflections on what seems, at least

initially, to be the rationale of the rule itself. As we reflect on the point of a prohibition on most forms of killing, it seems that at least a part of the rationale for this prohibition is not met in certain kinds of situations, or else, circumstances are such that it seems somehow inappropriate to place the full onus of "murder" on a desperate act. Yet, in other respects, these kinds of actions do appear to fall within the rationale for the general prohibition against killing, and, in any case, they do meet the standard criteria for counting an act as murder. Our difficulty, therefore, is not simply that we do not know how to describe a particular action or class of actions. We can appeal to criteria grounded in past usage for describing an action in more than one way.

If this line of analysis is correct, it suggests further that the inability of moral rules to provide one unique resolution to every case need not be taken as evidence that there can be no objective standards for moral discourse. So long as we keep our reflections focused at the middle level of moral abstraction, that is, at the level of basic moral notions such as murder or lying and the typical situations in which these concepts apply, we will have no difficulty in identifying any number of considerations that must be taken into account if we are to judge well in particular cases.[33] Our awareness of moral considerations will not always enable us to resolve every moral dilemma, but it will offer us criteria by which to judge whether we ourselves, and those around us, are acting as rational and responsible moral agents. On the basis of those criteria, we will be able to discriminate among more and less satisfactory examples of moral judgement, and, therefore, to avoid self-deception and the insensibility of vice in ourselves, and to determine where best to place our trust in others. Even if we cannot always come to agreement, or even arrive at individual certainty, with respect to the solution of moral dilemmas, we can at least have reason to trust that we and those around us have tried in good faith, and in a reasonable way, to resolve these dilemmas.

So far, we have been considering questions that arise when we have some reason to question whether a notion of a kind of action should be brought under a still more general moral concept. There are also times when we do not know what to say about a specific action, and these situations raise some distinctive issues.

MORAL JUDGEMENT AND SPECIFIC ACTS

At the level of individual cases, we are frequently at a loss to determine the proper application of the basic moral notions because we find ourselves faced with what seems, at least, to be a conflict of duties. We have already noted that many of our disputes over the proper classification of kinds of actions such as euthanasia are initially generated by a recurrence of certain kinds of conflicts of duties, in a context which permits ready generalization. In this section, however, we will change our focus, from a consideration of the ways in which perceived conflicts of duties can lead to a reformulation of generally accepted moral norms, to a consideration of the ways in which we attempt to negotiate these conflicts at the level of individual judgement.

Conflict of duty situations, as they may be called, arise continually, sometimes with tragic consequences, sometimes trivially, usually with a seriousness that is somewhere in between these two poles. What characterizes these sorts of situations is the fact that they seem to present the agent with a dilemma: whatever I do in this situation, I will be forced to violate a moral rule. Often, it will be the case that I am in this unfortunate situation because of some past act of immorality, either my own or someone else's, but this will not always be the case, and, even if it is, that fact will not be of much comfort to me now.

It has seemed to many that the very possibility of finding oneself in this sort of dilemma presents an intolerable affront, either to the justice of God or to the rational character of morality.[34] For this reason, there has been until recently a pervasive tendency to deny the very existence of moral dilemmas, or else to argue that they can only arise for someone who has already put herself in a bad position by violating a moral obligation on a previous occasion. In order to sustain this view, an appeal is made to a general rule of casuistry which, it is claimed, will eliminate all putative moral conflicts by indicating which of two obligations, seemingly in conflict, really is incumbent on the agent, and which is not.

This principle, sometimes called the Pauline principle, may be stated in general terms as follows: do not do what is evil in order to bring about a good result. Or we may state it in this way: when faced with a choice between doing something evil, and allowing some evil to come about, do nothing. A number of moral thinkers, including traditional Catholics, would further specify this general principle in terms of what is referred to as the doctrine of double effect, according to which a person may do something that has an evil effect as one of its side consequences, if the good aimed at is proportional to the evil incurred, but she may not directly cause an evil effect in order to bring about a good result.[35]

It would seem at first that the Pauline principle would indeed serve to eliminate the possibility of moral conflict. It offers a general decision procedure for resolving all dilemmas: when all one's options are bad, do nothing. And, since it is always possible, at least logically possible, to do nothing, it would seem that this principle offers a morally acceptable way out of any and all dilemmas, hard though it may be to endure the results of inaction in practice.

On closer examination, however, it is not so clear that the Pauline principle, in either its more general or its more specific versions, can provide the unambiguous decision procedure that its advocates want. The difficulty is that this principle depends on a distinction between a direct action, in which the agent's action is the immediate cause of the outcome, and indirect actions, in which the agent simply allows certain things to take place. This distinction presupposes that the causal relationship between what an agent does and what occurs is a matter of straightforward, objective fact, which can be determined prior to passing any moral judgement on what occurs. This assumption, in turn, further presupposes a particular understanding of causality, according to which effects follow causes in invariant sequence. Yet, as Hart and Honore point out in their extensive analysis of the concept of causation in legal contexts, we cannot expect to be able to ascertain the *individual* causes of *individual* effects with that degree of certainty, even if it is the case that this model of causation is valid at the level of descriptions of classes of events. As they argue in some detail, our judgements to the effect that someone has caused an event to occur always presuppose assumptions about the conditions that are usually present, the normal course of a particular kind of event, and the like, and they frequently embody normative assumptions as well.[36]

In any case, what we are looking for, when faced with a moral dilemma, is not a logically possible course of action, but a morally justifiable course of action. Yet, even if it were possible to sustain and apply a distinction between direct and indirect causation, it is difficult to know why this distinction alone should be decisive in *every* situation in which we are faced with a conflict of duties. As was noted above, almost no one calls for an absolute prohibition of all actions that involve harming someone. Moreover, we do not always judge an instance of deliberate inaction to be morally neutral. Someone who has a special responsibility to do something can be judged both legally liable and morally guilty for the consequences of her inaction; for example, a doctor who fails to clean a wound properly after surgery may be morally responsible for her patient's subsequent death. More generally, anyone is responsible for taking certain kinds of actions in some sorts of situations, and is guilty for the outcome if she fails to act; consider how we would judge someone who walks past a child drowning in a barrel, and knowingly lets the child drown.

Our moral concepts have emerged, and continue to develop, against a background of assumptions about the extent and the limits of human capabilities. These assumptions reflect our beliefs about what human persons are capable of doing, in the sense of sheer physical and psychological possibility; more importantly, they also reflect a complex tissue of assumptions about what it is reasonable to expect of persons, given the significance of certain harms on the one hand, and the limitations of human capacities, on the other. These assumptions include, centrally, judgements about the limits of our responsibilities to one another, and our need to draw certain boundaries around those responsibilities. If we were all committed to doing the greatest possible good to everyone, all the time, we would have no leisure left over to pursue our own interests, our own affairs, or even our own recreation. Moreover, we would not be morally justified in singling out certain persons – our parents, children, spouses, or friends – for special attention and concern. Indeed, it is not clear that any sort of special relationships could be morally justified. These would be the costs of a relentless commitment to maximization, and they have seemed, for most of us, too high to pay.

It is possible to argue that the assumption of limited responsibility is mistaken, and we do have far greater positive obligations to promote the good than we generally acknowledge. I will not attempt to defend the assumption of limited responsibility against these arguments. My point is simply that the insight expressed by the Pauline principle, or the doctrine of double effect, is better understood as a reflection of these general assumptions about the limits and the extent of human responsibility, than as a decision procedure, based on an analysis of causality, for resolving any and all moral dilemmas. Understood in this way, the Pauline principle makes sense as a general expression of the limits and the conditions of our responsibilities. We do generally consider our responsibilities to refrain from harming one another to be more exigent than our duties to help one another, and that is why it is usually true that, when faced with the possibility of helping one person by harming another, we conclude that such an action would be wrong. Moreover, there are contexts in which it is both difficult and yet supremely important to sustain a distinction between the kinds of harms that we may or must do, and the kinds of harms that we must refrain from doing. For example, this line of argument is developed powerfully by Michael Walzer, in his defense of the principle of non-combatant immunity in wartime.[37]

Yet the general insight expressed by the Pauline principle

will be convincing only in those situations in which we judge that our responsibility to prevent some harm, or to bring about some benefit, is less exigent than our responsibility to refrain from some other sort of harm. There are situations in which such is not the case. We may be under a special obligation to prevent the occurrence of certain kinds of harms – as a physician is – or we may have a legitimate, even a compelling, reason to prefer the well-being of one person to that of another, or we may be faced with a circumstance in which the immediate, ineluctable result of our refusal to act will be worse, by any criterion, than the result of any action that we might take. In situations such as these, it is no longer so clear that the Pauline principle even applies, much less that it can resolve the dilemma that we face. Once again, we must recognize that there will be some situations in which we simply do not know how to apply our moral notions in such a way as to satisfy everyone.

There are other sorts of cases in which we simply do not know what to say, because we are faced with a combination of circumstances so horrendous, and at the same time (fortunately) so unusual, that we are hard pressed to know how to classify what is done in terms of the categories derived from our usual experiences.

For example, Alan Donagan describes a case that came before the courts in nineteenth-century England, *R. v. Dudley and Stephens*, in which two castaway sailors killed and ate one of their comrades in order to avoid starving to death themselves.[38] Fortunately, most of us will go through our lives without being forced to choose between killing somebody in order to eat her, and imminent death from starvation. For this very reason, however, it is difficult to find an appropriate general concept for this action, through which we can bring to bear socially accumulated wisdom as to whether this kind of thing might be justified or not. We are unclear whether to describe this action as murder, or not. It is significant, however, that, even in this case, we observe some of the same ambiguities as we found in debates over euthanasia and other dubious forms of killing: the circumstances are such that the agents were faced with extreme loss if they refrained from killing (that is, they would starve to death), and, at the same time, it is not clear that the reasons for prohibiting killing in most cases would obtain in this case (the boy who was killed was on the point of death from starvation himself).

So far, our analysis has proceeded as if our only options were to classify an action as murder, with the full onus that that description usually carries, or to describe it in such a way that it carries no moral onus at all. But our actual evaluative language is richer and more supple than that. To a large degree, the suppleness of moral language in this respect reflects the twofold function of moral language, namely, to indicate the boundaries of the community and to convey an evaluation of the agent. Ordinarily, these two functions readily fit together; someone who murders another, thereby egregiously transgressing the boundaries of the community, normally does indicate by that action that she is not to be trusted as a fellow-participant in the life of that community. But it is not always the case that these two judgements can be linked reliably, and both moral usage and legal practice reflect our sense of that fact. The case just cited represents a good example of the suppleness of moral language in use. The judge in the case, Lord Coleridge, ruled that the sailors' action did count as murder, thereby upholding the normative boundaries of the community. At the same time, however, he also acknowledged that, given the extraordinary circumstances, the sailors did not deserve the opprobrium that normally would have followed on a judgement that one has committed murder. Accordingly, he gave the prisoners the very light sentence of six months' imprisonment without hard labor.

MORAL DISAGREEMENTS, MORAL MISTAKES, AND GROSS MISUNDERSTANDINGS

In this chapter, I have attempted to trace some of the contours of moral thinking, in order both to expand upon, and to substantiate, the intuition that there is something distinctive about our basic moral concepts, something which is captured roughly in the claim that moral rules have a special quality of stringency. At the same time, I have attempted to show that moral thinking is rational, even though moral rationality cannot be understood in Kantian terms as a function of rules which determine a uniquely correct solution to every moral dilemma. Thus, I have tried to show how moral thinking functions in a rational way, even in those instances in which it encounters problems that cannot be resolved in a way that is compelling to all.

These two aims are, in fact, one. To say that moral thinking has a special stringency is to say, *inter alia*, that moral discernment is never a matter of individual choice *alone*, even though there is an ineradicable element of choice in any exercise of judgement of any sort. As Putnam observes, moral rules have the distinctive character that they do, in part, because they are meant to function in such a way as to safeguard consciences and to protect us from our own tendencies to selfishness and self-deception. If they are to fulfill this function, then it must be possible to offer an account of error in moral thinking. At the same time, one of the tests of rationality in any domain of thinking is precisely the possibility of offering an account of error, by which true and false, or valid and invalid, or serious and frivolous judgements can be identified.

How is this to be done, if we cannot fall back on an understanding of moral rules as comprising an infallible decision procedure for moral choice? Before attempting to answer this question, it is worth reminding ourselves again that this is not an issue that is generated by something distinctive in moral reasoning *per se*. Any set of empirical concepts, other than those of a perfected science, will give rise to some instances of ambiguity, which cannot be resolved apodictically. This does not mean that the set of concepts in question cannot be applied straightforwardly, and mistakes cannot be recognized and corrected, in most of the instances that arise in ordinary use. Furthermore, we can generally account for a mistake of this sort, to ourselves at any rate, if not to the person who is mistaken and confused. None of this need be theoretically or practically problematic.

With respect to moral judgements, however, the inevitable ambiguities that arise can be excruciatingly difficult, precisely because what is at stake in moral judgements is of such importance to us. This points to a second reason for attempting to offer an account of moral mistakes, beyond a general concern to validate the rationality of moral thinking. That is, we have a great practical need to be able to discriminate among the various ways in which it is possible to be mistaken or to misunderstand or to fail in moral judgement. There are some kinds of moral mistakes which really do reveal deficiencies or corruptions of the individual's capacities for judgement. Not every sort of mistake or disagreement does so, however, and, if we are to live together with a modicum of decency, it is important that we be able to tell which sort of mistake is which.

It may have been noticed that I have spoken throughout this section of mistakes and misunderstandings, rather than of moral wrongdoing more generally. By doing so, I do not mean to give the impression that every sort of moral wrongdoing can be understood in terms of a cognitive mistake. The general question of moral wrongdoing is difficult and complex, and it would take us too far afield to try to sort it out at this point. My concern here is more narrowly focused on the question of moral mistakes and misunderstandings, since that is the question that is immediately generated by a consideration of moral rationality. At the same time, some moral mistakes and misunderstandings do reflect moral deficiencies, and so our consideration cannot be altogether divorced from the wider issue of wrongdoing.

Let us turn, therefore, to the question of what counts as mistake or misunderstanding in moral judgement. To some degree, the answer to this question has been implied by what has already been said. In order to draw out this implication, I will begin by contrasting two situations that might both be experienced by the persons involved as dilemmas, in order to see what is at stake in the different judgements that might be made in each case.

Let us imagine, in the first case, a doctor who is treating a man in constant, extreme, and untreatable pain. The patient himself does not want to go on living, and yet for some reason (perhaps he is a paraplegic), he cannot commit suicide. He asks his doctor to kill him. What is the doctor to do?

For the second case, imagine a man who is desperately in love with a married woman. Her husband will not agree to a divorce, and she herself refuses to continue as her lover's mistress, even though she loves him and would gladly marry him if she could. Given the situation, she and her husband have decided to move away and to make a fresh start, somewhere where her lover cannot find them. In desperation, the man considers the option of killing his lover's husband, without her knowledge, so that she will be free to be with him. What should he do?

The first thing to be said about these two cases is that it is much easier to answer the question, "What should the person do?" in the second case. That is, anyone who is reasonably competent in moral judgement will recognize at once that one should not murder a rival in order to be with one's lover. In this case, at least as described here, there is no ambiguity about the application of the relevant moral notion; such an action would be murder, with all that that judgement implies. In the first case, however, there is a real doubt about whether it would be murder for the doctor to kill her patient, and, correlatively, there is room for genuine doubt about what she should do. Someone who advocated killing the patient in this case, or even someone who did it, would not thereby necessarily manifest fundamental confusion about the meaning of basic moral notions, as would be the case for someone who advises the man in the second case to kill his lover's husband.

Why is there a difference in the way in which we respond to doubt and disagreement in these two cases? The answer, surely, is to be found in considering the kinds of reasons that can be brought forward in defense of the act of killing in each case. In the former case, the advocate of euthanasia can argue in terms of the notion of murder itself, by offering reasons why that notion should not apply in this case.[39] We oppose murder because it takes away something of value to the person killed, she might argue, but, in this case, life is no longer of value to this suffering person; or, she might say, we oppose murder because it is a fundamental usurpation of human freedom, but, in this case, the putative victim wants to be killed, indeed, is pleading to be killed. Her interlocutor may well disagree, but he must none the less acknowledge that her considerations have some rational force, because they are derived from a consideration of the notion of murder, which they both share as a bench-mark for moral thinking. In contrast, there is no comparable justification for killing the husband in the second case. Someone could defend killing in this case only by refusing to acknowledge the validity and force of the concept of murder. In doing so, however, she would be, in effect, abandoning morality, or anything that we can recognize as morality. At that point, whatever we may or may not do in relation to such a person, we clearly cannot engage in rational moral dialogue with her, any more than we could engage in a scientific discussion with an astrologer.

Suppose that the unhappy lover in the second case goes ahead and murders the husband of his beloved. We would say that he has done something wrong, but what more are we to say in such a case? That is, what sort of failure do we encounter in such a case? Shall we say that the murderer has simply chosen not to act in accordance with one of the most serious of moral obligations, or must we also say that this sort of failure would not be possible unless the murderer had not also fallen into a defect of judgement?

The answer to this question is, surely, it depends. It depends on the particularities of the case, and it depends on the account that we give of what it is to understand a moral notion. This point is brought out powerfully by Raimond Gaita, in the course of an argument that someone who fully understood what it meant to murder someone could not make a clear, knowing choice to do it:

He must understand that if he murders his lover's husband then he becomes a murderer and that he must carry the significance of that into the future . . . He cannot possibly *want* what he gets – a love and a life polluted by murder. What he wants is her with her husband out of the way: he wants what he would have if her husband left her or if he died in an accident and *that is what the desire which tempts him pretends to be the achievable purpose of his deed.* Desire presents his deed to him as "getting her husband out of the way." But that is not the most significant thing he gets, and it can only appear to him to be so if he has only a partial understanding of the meaning of what he is tempted to do. He can live with her as though her husband were merely "out of the way" only if he plunges into a life of radical self-deception, but short of abandoning himself to the evil that will spread through his life, no degree of self-deception could hide his murderous self from him.[40]

It is all too possible to understand what it means to be a murderer, at least at some moments, and to go ahead and do the act anyway. Gaita's argument turns on this realization, because, as he observes, someone who really does understand what it is to be a murderer, and commits murder anyway, can only do so if he conceals that understanding from himself in some way, or else decides in despair to surrender himself to the evil that his act entails. What is more interesting from the perspective of this section, however, is what Gaita's remarks imply about the person who really does *not* understand what it would be to be a murderer, before or after the action.

Note, first of all, that the sort of inability that would be in question in such a case would not be an inability to understand the language of murder, in the sense that someone who did not speak English well might have some difficulty with the correct use of "murder," its distinction from "killing," and so on. Someone who is mentally handicapped may be unable to use the language of murder in the appropriate ways, but that is not the most significant sort of misunderstanding that is possible in this connection. It is possible to be capable of using the language of murder correctly, and yet to be incapable of understanding the concept of murder.

Gaita's remarks indicate, by a kind of negation, what such a person would be like. Her deficiencies would be located in her capacities for sensibility and perception, rather than in her cognitive capacities, narrowly construed. That is, she would not understand what it is to be a murderer, because she would not be able to respond in the appropriate ways to the prospect or the reality of murder. She would not feel horror at the prospect of being a murderer, and, if she did commit murder, she would feel no remorse. As a result of these deficiencies, moreover, her perceptions would be dulled or distorted in such a way that her construal of situations, and her appraisal of the options that she faces, would be systematically warped. Bernard Williams observes that one of the criteria for ethical understanding is that certain options simply do not occur to one, to be considered and dismissed: "One does not feel easy with the man who in the course of a discussion of how to deal with political or business rivals says, 'Of course, we could have them killed, but we should lay that aside right from the beginning.' It should never have come into his hands to be laid aside."[41] In other words, for someone who really understands what it is to murder someone, the option of murder would not even arise to be dismissed, unless the person is desperate.

What is the nature of the horror and remorse that we feel at murder, or at other lesser (but real) violations of morality? Gaita insists that the modalities of horror, guilt, and grief that we feel in these instances must be grounded in some sense of the value of the individual, whose life is destroyed or violated by an immoral action.[42] If we are really to understand what it is to destroy or violate a human life, we must be capable of some degree of empathy for the individual whose humanity is thus insulted. Even if we do not know the victim as an individual, we must be able to grasp what it would mean to know this person as an intelligible object of esteem, friendship, and love, someone who could both merit, and be expected to respond to, the graces of human relationships. In Gaita's terms, the person who is guilty of some assault on another is haunted by her victim, if she is at all capable of moral understanding and genuine remorse.

Gaita's account of remorse and related emotions is valuable because it reminds us powerfully of what is really involved in the stance of respect for the humanity of another that is central to morality. At the same time, it enables us to distinguish moral remorse from other forms of compunction. There are those who are devastated if they fail to use the correct fork at a dinner, or

fall into a grammatical error in a speech. More seriously, there
are those whose emotional energies are tied up with the observ-
ance of rules and obedience to authority *per se*, to the extent
that they lose sight of the value of the human lives that the rules
of a genuine morality are meant to safeguard. The psychologist
Alice Miller argues that this sort of attitude frequently results
from an upbringing that combines repeated abuse and humili-
ation with an insistence on respect for, and obedience to, one's
parents and other authority figures.[43]

It may seem that the failures of empathy and awareness of
others that Gaita and Miller describe are of limited importance, because they are speaking of extreme cases, which are
fortunately quite rare. It is not clear to me that instances of a
radical incapacity for empathy and moral understanding
really are that rare, but, in any case, we are all prone, in lesser
degrees and in more limited respects, to these sorts of incapaci-
ties. It is entirely possible to have enough sensitivity to the
value of another to refrain from the more obvious forms of
assault, and yet to be insensitive to the damage that is done by
sarcasm, by angry abuse, by gossip or rudeness or unkindness.
Someone who is aware enough of the value of another's sexuality to refrain from rape may yet be unable to appreciate the
kind of harm that is done by seduction. The same observations
could be made, in different areas of human life, over and over
again. Who among us can claim really to be aware of the value
of others, in every respect, and in every area of our lives?

On the other hand, the distinctive character of empathy for
the other that Gaita identifies with moral remorse can be found
in other situations, in which it is not so clear that it is appropriate to speak of guilt at all, or guilt of the sort that the
individual experiences. Consider Thomas Nagel's case of a
man whose careless driving brings about the death of another,
and who, therefore, is haunted throughout his life with remorse
and the stigma of having killed another, even though he never
intended to harm another through his carelessness.[44] If guilt is
to be understood in terms of what is intended, or even what is
knowingly permitted, then the unhappy driver in this situation
is guilty of nothing more than the same negligence that many

of us are guilty of, without having to bear the remorse of killing another by it. Yet a careless driver who kills another may well be haunted by his victim, and be remorseful and guilt-ridden, even though neither he nor anyone else would consider his act of carelessness to be morally equivalent to the action of someone who kills another deliberately.

In the case just described, the careless driver does appropriately acknowledge some guilt; what makes his case difficult is that the remorse that he bears seems disproportionate to the guilt that we normally feel as a result of everyday carelessness. In other cases, there may be no question of moral fault at all, at least in the terms that are generally accepted by one's community, and yet the individual may feel deep remorse for inflicting justified harm on another. The soldier, the police-officer, the executioner, even the person who kills another in self-defense may well be haunted by those whom she is forced to kill. A doctor may believe that abortion is morally justified, and yet be haunted by the nascent lives that she is forced to destroy. At a less serious, but still important, level, someone who is forced by unforeseen circumstances to break a promise will appropriately feel regret, and will attempt to "make it up" to the recipient of the promise, even though she may rightly feel that she was justified in acting as she did. Examples of this sort could be multiplied indefinitely. As was noted above, we cannot live human lives that are altogether free of the necessity of harming others in some ways, and for that reason, so long as we are morally aware persons, we cannot live lives that are altogether free of regret and remorse.

What are we to make of the phenomena of regret, remorse, and even guilt in the wake of actions that are not considered, by the agent herself or by her community, to be morally wrong? It would be a mistake, in my view, to conclude that the capacity to respond with guilty feelings to a wrongful action is not an essential component of moral understanding. To the contrary, a capacity to feel some modality of compunction at harm inflicted on another, whether justified or not, is a necessary precondition for feeling true moral guilt when that is appropriate. Moreover, feelings of guilt, remorse, and regret can play important roles in our interactions with one another, even when there is no question of a properly moral guilt. They can serve as an indication that, if we are to honor the individuality and humanity of another, whom we are forced to harm in some way, we must do what we can to make reparations, or, failing that, we must at least offer her some acknowledgment and some expression of regret. Moreover, feelings of guilt and remorse may well indicate that we have been too quick to excuse some form of harming another. Taken seriously, these feelings may even contribute eventually to a reformation, of ourselves and of our societies. These reformations happen too seldom, and almost never are they complete, yet they do happen.

So far, we have focused on drawing a distinction between someone who does not have the capacities for sensibility and empathy necessary for a genuine understanding of the basic moral notions, and someone who does understand them, and yet acts contrary to that understanding. There is a still more crucial distinction, at least for our immediate purposes, between the person whose failures of moral understanding reflect genuine deficiencies of character, and the person who makes a mistake in moral judgement, so to speak, competently and in good faith. This is the distinction that I hoped to suggest by the first example, that of the doctor who is inclined to accede to her patient's request for euthanasia. It may well be said that this would be a mistaken choice. None the less, it is important to realize that this sort of mistaken judgement, if it is indeed such, is very different in character both from the sort of failure experienced by someone who commits murder out of despair, and from the deficiency in judgement manifested by someone who cannot really understand the point of the concept of murder.

Sometimes, moral misjudgements reflect a corruption of mind, but that is by no means always the case. How are we to tell when a mistaken moral judgement (as we conceive it to be) reflects an honest error, as opposed to moral corruption? There is no infallible way to do so. Yet it is possible to make some distinctions. One of the marks of genuine mistake, or just honest moral disagreement, lies in the fact that the person making the judgement is capable of offering reasons that are publicly acceptable, because they are informed by some aspects of the moral notions that are shared by all parties to the debate. As the example given above suggests, one of the ways in which we distinguish between the advocate of euthanasia, and the murderous individual, is that the former, but not the latter, can give reasons for the course of action that she advocates in terms of the very notion that she and others are attempting to apply to the case at hand. Moreover, someone whose moral mistake reflects an honest error in judgement can be expected to display the sensibilities and the capacities for empathy that we expect of anyone who really understands what it means to be moral. That is, she will exhibit some awareness of the importance and value of other persons, some sense of their sufferings and some readiness to share their joys. The person who is manifestly callous is far more likely to reveal a corrupt mind through her mistaken judgements, than someone whose actions and demeanor reflect genuine concern for others.

It is hard to live a decent and humane life. We can fail in so many ways, not only through selfishness and a bad will, but also through callousness and carelessness and even misplaced compassion. Even in those instances in which we very much want to do the right thing, it can be hard, indeed, sometimes it will be impossible, to know what the right thing is to do. All this is so obvious as to be almost banal, and yet it is easy to forget it in the heat of academic disputation, or, even more, public debate. If we were more mindful of the very real difficulties of moral discernment and living, we would perhaps be less ready to accuse others of moral corruption and bad faith, when they simply disagree with us.

CHAPTER 3

Moral judgement in context: Thomas Aquinas on the moral act

In chapter 2, I defended an account of morality which was meant to show, among other things, that moral judgement is a rational process. Yet admittedly, on the basis of what has been said so far, moral judgement can be said to be rational only in a weak sense. While we can identify and account for gross failures of moral reasoning on these terms, it is not so clear that we can distinguish valid from mistaken judgements in those instances in which there is no question of a gross failure of judgement on anyone's part, but rather, we find ourselves in serious disagreement on difficult questions.

Is anything more needed? After all, if it is the case that moral reasoning cannot attain the certainty and completeness to which Kant and other modern moral theoreticians aspired, then perhaps we should simply be content with an account of rationality sufficient to distinguish between reasonable and grossly incompetent moral judgements. Within the very considerable community of those who are neither totally mad nor hopelessly bad, perhaps we will simply have to live with unresolved moral disagreements and an irreducible plurality of views. Given the conditions of contemporary life, perhaps this sort of pluralism is a positive good, a safeguard for democracy.

On one level, this is an accurate statement of the case. It is true that there will always be an irreducible element of disagreement and diversity within any moral community, because, logically, the kind of comprehensiveness and certainty that Kant and others sought in their moral theories simply cannot be attained. It is difficult to say that this is a *good* thing, as opposed to one of the sheer givens of our lives, but it is certainly good that the limitations of moral discourse be kept in mind, in democracies above all. Yet there are degrees of diversity. The fact that we cannot resolve *all* moral arguments, and should not try to do so, does not imply that we cannot resolve *some* of them.

Moreover, the undoubted value of pluralism does not obviate the importance of trying to resolve at least some moral arguments, both because consensus is also a social good, and, more fundamentally, because of what is at stake in these arguments. For the serious individual, who is contemplating a problematic moral choice, it will matter, very much indeed, that she does the right thing, because she does not want to harm others, or herself, to treat others unfairly, or to violate their claims to regard and care in some other way. That is, she will care about resolving her moral dilemmas in the best way she can, for precisely the same reasons that motivate her to attempt to live morally in the first place.

At the social level, the need to resolve some moral arguments is, if anything, more acute. A sustainable consensus must be secured, social roles must be agreed upon, rewards meted out, and sanctions imposed, children must be born and nurtured and educated, if a society is to function for any length of time. All of this presupposes a high degree of consensus; otherwise, common life could be sustained only at the cost of an unacceptable level of coercion.

It is important that we be able to mount a critique of the practices and institutions of our societies, in terms that will be intelligible and persuasive. While this sort of critique does not require a moral theory in the modern sense, it does seem to require an appeal to some kind of framework for evaluation and critique. That is why, in Joel Kupperman's words, most social reformers have incorporated "theory-like elements" into their arguments:

the moral pioneers who helped to change general thinking on such matters as slavery, the subjection of women, or the entitlements of the poor, had, at the least, theory-like elements in their thinking. They saw that all of the moral considerations that applied to whites also applied to blacks, that those which were applicable to men were

applicable to women, and that the general thrust toward the preven-
tion of misery which linked many elements of familiar morality had
special relevance to the plight of the very poor ... there is no
plausible way in which a group of people can begin to criticize an
established morality except by means of such theory-like elements. If
one's moral universe consists solely of an assortment of familiar rules,
with no attention given to connecting and underlying elements,
where is criticism to begin?[1]

It matters that we be able to discriminate between valid and
mistaken moral judgements, at least some of the time. We have
a stake in trying to make these discriminations for the same
reasons that we are committed to the moral life in the first
place, namely, out of our commitments to respect and promote
the well-being of other persons, and to help promote a social
order in which those commitments are institutionalized, as far
as may be possible. Correlatively, we have a stake in developing a stronger account of moral rationality than the previous
chapter provided. Yet how are we to go about doing so?

In this chapter, I will argue that the account of the moral act
developed by Thomas Aquinas in his *Summa theologiae* offers
invaluable resources for developing a stronger account of
moral rationality, which moreover does not fall into the opposite error of the strict rationalism of modern moral theories. In
order to appreciate the significance of Aquinas' contribution,
however, it is necessary to say something more about the
nature of moral argument and the strategies that are available
for resolving such arguments.

MORAL ARGUMENTS IN CONTEXT

Consider, once again, the example of the doctor who is asked
by her patient to kill him, in order to release him from his pain.
Suppose that she agrees to her patient's request for euthanasia,
and does kill him. Now suppose her to be in conversation with
someone who, like her, is morally serious and sensitive to all the
factors that make this such a difficult choice. Yet her interlocutor assesses these factors in a different way, and, as a result, he
comes to the conclusion that euthanasia would be wrong, at

least in this instance, perhaps in any case that he can imagine. How might he go about convincing her, or us, that her judgement is mistaken in this case?

As was noted in the previous chapter, he must first of all admit that her judgement is reasonable, in the sense that she can argue for it in terms of the basic moral notions that they share. Yet he can still argue cogently that she is mistaken, even granting that her claim is reasonable in the sense of being legitimately arguable. He might, for example, claim that she has overlooked, or failed to give due weight, to one aspect of the prohibition of murder that does apply to this case, or else he might claim that she has overlooked some aspect of her particular situation. He might say, "You have failed to take account of the central importance of respecting human life in all of its forms," or else, "It is crucially important that doctors, of all people, stay out of the business of killing people."

At this point, the physician might say, "You're right, I didn't think of that, and I see now that I need to reconsider the judgement that I made." Then again, she might not. It is more likely that she will answer that she has thought of everything that her interlocutor has mentioned, but she simply weighs the various factors in a different way than he does. At that point, is there anything further for him to say?

There is; he can still argue that, while the physician is correct to appeal to the considerations that she does, she has none the less misconstrued the proper relationships among them. So, for example, he might say, "Autonomy is important, but it is more important to respect the fundamental equality that is expressed by the injunction that individuals, acting on their own authority, should not kill other persons."

What the doctor's interlocutor must do, in short, if he is to make a cogent case that her judgement is mistaken, is to establish some perspective outside of the notion of murder itself, on the basis of which he can argue that her interpretation of that notion is inadequate or incorrect. He must be able to establish a vantage point outside this notion, because as we observed in the previous chapter, the prohibition against murder, like most of our other widely accepted moral rules, serves a variety of functions and expresses more than one commitment.

How are we to arrive at this wider vantage point? It might be thought that we could answer this question simply by appealing to the analogical unity proper to the concept of morality. Yet this response, taken by itself, would misrepresent the sort of unity that is in question when we consider morality (or any other similarly abstract and general concept in a natural language). The unity of the concept of morality, as it is instantiated in the basic moral notions, is manifested by the way in which these basic notions can be brought into intelligible relations to a focal meaning, which in this case is itself complex. Yet the basic moral notions are related to the focal meaning of morality in complex and diverse ways, as we have seen. An account of these diverse interrelationships, taken by itself, will not provide the wider perspective that is needed in order to distinguish correct and mistaken moral judgements. Otherwise, there would be no real distinction to be drawn between the analogical unity that is proper to the concept of morality, and a moral theory in the modern mode, which derives moral rules from a supposed first principle of morality.

In order to place the concept of morality within a wider context, it is therefore necessary to go beyond the considerations that inform our basic moral notions, in such a way as to introduce an order of priority into these diverse considerations. It is at this point that the long tradition of Christian ethics can offer a distinctive contribution to moral philosophy. The history of Christian ethics is precisely a history of reflections on a moral order which has been perceived, by and large, as existing prior to, and independently of, Christianity, and which, for that very reason, must be placed in a wider theological context if it is to be rightly understood and valued. Within that tradition, we find a rich variety of perspectives on the meaning of morality. However, I will not attempt a survey of these various perspectives. Rather, I intend to examine in some detail the implications of the thought of one Christian theologian on the nature of the moral act.

Specifically, I will argue that the account of morality developed by Thomas Aquinas in the *Summa theologiae* offers us a way to go beyond the weak account of moral rationality developed in the previous chapter. I do not intend to argue that Aquinas' understanding of morality is altogether congruent with contemporary views, or that we should accept it just as it stands. Yet Aquinas' understanding of morality, and, more specifically, his sense of what is problematic in moral judgement, are strikingly similar to our own. For that reason, his formulation of certain difficulties, and the solutions that he offers, are accessible and illuminating for us.

In particular, Aquinas' account of morality offers a way of introducing a wider perspective at what might be called the middle level of moral arguments. He recognizes (as we will see) that the generic notions of morality cannot be applied with absolute certainty to every individual act. However, he offers both models and substantive insights that are especially useful when what is in question is the proper relation between one kind of action and another, more general description, such as, "is euthanasia a form of murder, or a legitimate kind of killing?" Since this level of inquiry and controversy is especially important for socially sustained moral debate, Aquinas' account of morality has special relevance to those who are concerned to strengthen or critique the mores of their communities.

THE PRESUPPOSITIONS AND METHODOLOGY OF THE *SUMMA THEOLOGIAE*

In order to appreciate the significance of Aquinas' potential contribution, it is necessary first of all to address a common misunderstanding about the nature of his work. It is sometimes said that the work of Aquinas and his contemporaries anticipates the theoretical ambitions of the Enlightenment.[2] On this view, Aquinas' work comprises a theory on a grand scale, in which certain beliefs about God are foundational, and theological, philosophical, and moral claims are derived from those starting-points.

There is some truth in this perception. At the beginning of the *Summa theologiae*, Aquinas indicates that his purpose in writing is to "set forth those things that belong to the Christian religion in such a way as to be consistent with a beginners' level of proficiency ... we will try, with confidence in divine assistance, to lay out those things which pertain to sacred doctrine succinctly and clearly, in accordance with the logic of the subject matter" (*Summa theologiae*, Introduction).[3] Aquinas does intend to offer a unified, systematic presentation of the basic tenets of theology, seen as incorporating philosophical and moral, as well as more strictly doctrinal, matters, for the benefit of beginning students.[4]

Yet it is important to take careful note of the kind of unified account that Aquinas offers. The first principles of sacred doctrine are *sui generis*, since they consist in truths which are properly known only to God, and are revealed by God to us (1 1.2). There is no question of *understanding* these principles, since they reflect the mystery of God, which only God can comprehend (1 1.7 *ad* 1; 1 12.7). Correlatively, we cannot derive anything from these principles, and so we are not surprised to find Aquinas asserting that the purpose of argument in theology is to draw out the implications of revealed doctrine, to address seeming inconsistencies, and to respond to the arguments of critics of the faith (1 1.8). Whatever one thinks of this project, it is not the equivalent of modern philosophical foundationalism.[5]

Furthermore, Aquinas' method throughout the *Summa* is dialectical, rather than strictly deductive.[6] Nowhere in the *Summa* does Aquinas move deductively from premises to conclusions, in such a way as to establish his position definitively.[7] Rather, he moves back and forth among contrasting views, responding to them out of his own emerging position, while at the same time incorporating what he considers to be valid in them. In the process, he offers a progressive clarification and systematization of central concepts, seen through the prism of their various, seemingly inconsistent interpretations. In other words, he offers us an analogical exposition of the key concepts of his theology, in which focal meanings are arrived at through dialectical reflection on diverse views, and then used as the basis for reinterpreting and harmonizing seemingly incompatible positions, as far as may be done.

Thus, Aquinas' arguments in the *Summa* are meant to be seen as reflections of a discussion which is still ongoing and, therefore, incomplete. As Alasdair MacIntyre remarks:

Every article in the *Summa* poses a question whose answer depends upon the outcome of an essentially uncompleted debate. For the set of often disparate and heterogeneous arguments against whatever position Aquinas' inquiries so far have led him to accept is always open to addition by some as yet unforseen argument. And there is always the possibility that what has so far been accepted may yet have to be modified or even rejected. In this there is nothing peculiar to Aquinas' procedures. It is of the nature of all dialectic, understood as Aristotle understood it, to be essentially incomplete.[8]

The dialectical method of the *Summa*, with its emphasis on the balancing and weighing of arguments in an ongoing debate, enables Aquinas to invite his readers to enter as participants in a common inquiry. That is what I hope to do in what follows, in order to see what Aquinas can offer to us in the way of a more satisfactory account of moral rationality.

THE MORAL ACT IN THE *SUMMA THEOLOGIAE*: INITIAL CONSIDERATIONS

The general orientation of Aquinas' account of morality may be gathered from the introduction to the *prima secundae*:

Because, as Damascene says, the human person is said to be made in the image of God, in so far as through "the image" is signified "the intellectual [capacity], freedom of judgment, and the power of self-movement," consequently, having spoken of the exemplar, that is, God, and of those things which proceed from the divine power in accordance with his will, it remains to consider this image, that is, the human person, in so far as he also is the originating principle of his works, as if he had free judgment and the power to originate his works.

For Aquinas, as for us, the starting-point for an account of morality is the concept of action. At the same time, to the reader who has arrived at this point through a reading of the *prima pars*, it is apparent that the concept of action is itself an analogical concept, which takes its focal meaning from human action, and is applied analogously both to sub-rational creatures and (in a very different way, of course) to God.[9] His development of the concept of action, in turn, is intimately bound up with the concepts of goodness and being. It is perhaps easier to see these connections if we begin with his remarks on goodness.[10]

According to Aquinas, the concept of goodness, like the concept of being, can be applied to anything at all that has real existence, in so far as, and in the mode in which, it exists (I 5. 1–3). This assertion is immediately qualified, however, with the proviso that the focal meaning for the concept of goodness is *perfected* being, which is equivalent to being that has fully actualized its potentialities: "For every being, in so far as it is a being, is in act, and is in a certain way perfect, because every act is a certain perfection" (I 5.3). Thus, the concept of goodness is convertible with the concepts of being and action.

This qualification helps us to understand what would otherwise be a puzzling remark, taken from Aristotle, that "the good is that which all desire" (I 5.1). How is it possible to desire what one already is? As Aquinas explains, all things seek the good, in so far as they desire their own perfection in accordance with the potentialities of their specific kinds (I 5.4, 5; I 6.1; I 60.3, 4; I 62.1). Moreover, since all created existence and goodness can be said to be a similitude of God's perfect existence and goodness, all creatures can be said to desire God in so far as they desire their own specific forms of perfection (I 6.1 *ad* 2; I–II 109.3).

So much is true of all creatures, from the angels to the most indeterminate forms of matter. What is distinctive about the human person is that she, unlike lower kinds of creatures, can only seek her perfection knowingly, through actions which are directed towards the attainment of that end (I 83.1; I 103.5 *ad* 2; I–II 1.2, 8). In what does that perfection consist? Like all other creatures, the human person is first of all oriented towards her own proper specific good, which, in our case, is to live in accordance with reason (I–II 5.5, 57.5, 58.2; II–II 47.6; cf.

1 62.1).[11] Again, it is true for us, as for all other creatures, that this orientation ultimately directs us towards God, who would be naturally known and loved above all else, even apart from any supernatural destiny (1 60.5, 1 62.1; 1–11 109.3). At the same time, we are also called to a more perfect union with God, culminating ultimately in the beatific vision, that is, the direct vision of God as Triune (1 12.1; 11–11 23.1, 6).

At every level in this complex account of human perfection, moreover, the concept of action plays a central role. At the natural level, happiness can be said to consist in action in accordance with virtue (1–11 5.5). The supernatural happiness of the beatific vision is itself a form of activity (1–11 3.2), and cannot be attained except through human actions, informed by the grace of God (1–11 5.7).

Thus, it comes as no surprise that Aquinas organizes the second volume of the *Summa theologiae* (comprising both the *prima secundae* and the *secunda secundae*) around the concept of human action, considered both as an expression of the potentialities and perfection of the agent, and as an object for evaluation by some standard. After the preliminary discussion of human perfection, or happiness, which comprises the first five questions of the *prima secundae*, we read:

Since, therefore, it is necessary to arrive at happiness by certain acts, consequently, it is proper to consider human acts, in order that we may know by which acts happiness is attained, or [else], the way to happiness is impeded. But since operations and acts are concerned with singulars, therefore every operative knowledge is perfected in a particular consideration. Moral consideration, since it concerns human acts, should therefore deal with the universal first, and secondly, the particular.

With respect to the universal consideration of human acts, however, the first topic that arises for consideration concerns human acts themselves, and the second, concerns their principles. (1–11 6, introduction)

Following through on this schema, Aquinas goes on to outline the plan of the remainder of the second part of the *Summa*. The consideration of "human acts themselves" leads him to consider the immediate originating principles of action,

including the will and the passions. He then turns to the
principles which give meaning to human action, including the
virtues, the different forms of law, and divine grace (I–II 49,
introduction). The *secunda secundae* is taken up with a consideration of the specific norms of human action, organized around
the schema of the three theological and the four cardinal
virtues.

After an extended discussion of the nature of voluntary
action and the will (I–II 6–17), Aquinas takes up the question
which, in different forms, has preoccupied us, namely, what
are the criteria by which a particular action is judged to be
either good or bad (I–II 18)? It is here that he begins to lay out,
in a preliminary way, what he sees as the criteria for the moral
evaluation of actions.

Aquinas begins this discussion with a question that would
seem odd from our perspective, asking at I–II 18.1 whether it is
the case that every human action is good, or is it possible that
some action should be bad. Once we recall his general account
of goodness, however, it quickly becomes apparent that this is a
more serious question for him than may at first appear. The
difficulty is not only that anything that exists in any way
whatever, including actions, must be said to be good in some
sense. The very meaning of goodness, for Aquinas, is active
perfection, and, for this reason, any action must be understood
as a manifestation of the agent's existence and goodness. At the
same time, it is necessarily the case, for Aquinas, that an action
be directed towards some good, at least a partial or seeming
good. On Aquinas' terms, it would be difficult to know how to
describe an event as an action, if it were not in some way both
expressive of goodness, and directed towards the good.

The solution that Aquinas offers is not surprising, given his
general understanding of goodness. He applies the same
general formula that he invoked for creatures generally: "So,
therefore, we should say that every action, in so far as it has
something of being, to that extent, it has something of goodness; in so far, however, as it lacks something of the fullness of
being which a human action ought to have, to that extent it is
deficient in goodness, and so is said to be bad" (I–II 18.1).

This is a very considerable standard for goodness. Taken without further qualification, it might seem to imply that no human action is ever good *simpliciter*. After all, every human action lacks *some* goodness, if only because it involves choosing some goods and refraining from the pursuit of others. Aquinas does not consider this possibility directly, but it is sufficiently clear, from what follows, that this is not his view. Rather, what he means is that a human action which falls short of one of the general criteria for moral goodness (which, therefore, "lacks something of the fullness of being which a human action *ought to have*"; my emphasis) is therefore a bad action.

But what are these criteria, and what is their interrelationship? In the first place, Aquinas says, the object of the action must be appropriate (I–II 18.2). Secondly, the action must be done in the proper circumstances (I–II 18.3). Finally, the aim or purpose of the agent must be good (I–II 18.4).

Significantly, Aquinas insists that these criteria must be kept distinct in the description and evaluation of specific actions. And so we read, in I–II 18.7, that the end for which the agent acts is distinct from the object of the action, unless there is some internal relation between the two (as fighting well is internally ordered to attaining victory). A difficulty arises at this point, because Aquinas also says that the end for which the agent acts determines the moral species of an action, just as the object does. How, then, are we to understand the situation in which the object and the end have no natural relationship to one another, as for example, in a case taken from Aristotle, when someone steals in order to have the means to commit adultery? In such a case, Aquinas explains, we must say that the agent "commits two transgressions [*malitias*] in one act" (I–II 18.7).

Similarly, the circumstances of an action do not ordinarily change its moral species, even though they do increase or diminish its goodness or evil (I–II 18.10, 11). Yet, if a particular circumstance is relevant to the determinations of moral reason in some way, it can lead to a redescription of the act. The circumstance of place would not ordinarily change the moral description of an act of theft, but, if I steal the silver-plate from my local parish church, in that case, the circumstance of place *would* add a new qualification to the proper moral description of the act.

At this point, Aquinas introduces an important qualification for the understanding of his overall analysis of the moral act. He considers the objection that something can only be in one species. He grants that this is true of natural objects. It is not true, however, of something, such as a human action, the correct description of which is determined by human reason:

> the process of reason is not determined to any one thing, but when anything is given, it can proceed further. And therefore, that which is considered in one act as a circumstance added onto the object, which determines the species of the act, can be considered a second time by ordaining reason as a principle condition of the object that determines the species of the act. And so, to take what is another's has its species from the formal notion of "another" [*ratione alieni*], and by this fact [the act] is constituted in the species of theft; and if the notion of place or time should be considered beyond this, [such a notion] would fall under the formal description of a circumstance. But since reason can ordain also with respect to place or time, and other things of this sort, it happens that the condition of place is considered with respect to the object, as contrary to the order of reason; as, for example, that reason ordains that no damage should be done in a sacred place. (I–II 18.10)

Aquinas' criteria for the moral evaluation of actions cannot be separated from his criteria for the correct descriptions of individual actions. These, in turn, are not ineluctably given in the act itself, but must be discerned from a consideration of the norms for action generated by reason. One implication of this argument is that it is possible for an action to have more than one object, in accordance with the different descriptions that can correctly be applied to it (cf. II–II 154.1 *ad* 2). It is not incorrect to describe an act of stealing silver from the church as an act of theft, even though it is also an act of sacrilege.

This point must be kept in mind if we are to understand one of the most puzzling aspects of Aquinas' analysis of the moral act, namely, his discussion of the object of an act. Certainly, this notion plays a central role in that discussion. Yet it is not immediately clear what he means by this component, which is neither a part of the circumstances nor determined by the agent's aim in acting. At some points, Aquinas almost seems to equate the object of an action with the physical entity that is at the receiving end, so to speak, of what the agent does (at I–II 18.2 *ad* 1, for example). However, this can hardly be his view, since it would suggest that there is no difference, with respect to the objects of the respective acts, between my act of deliberately smashing my sugar bowl, and my act of deliberately smashing your sugar bowl. Nor is it consonant with Aquinas' own favored examples of the object of an action in this question, namely, to make use of what is one's own, and to take what is another's (I–II 18.2 and following).

The key to understanding Aquinas at this point is given at I–II 18.10, in the passage quoted above. As his remarks indicate, the object of an action is nothing other than the generic concept under which an action is correctly described, when considered from the standpoint of moral reason. His examples suggest, further, that he thinks of the object of the act primarily (although not exclusively) with reference to the norms of non-maleficence which are included, for him, under the rubric of justice. The object is, therefore, roughly equivalent, in our terms, to the basic moral notion under which an action falls. We are further encouraged to draw this parallel by the fact that Aquinas says that the object of the act gives the moral species to the action, *not* the other way around (I–II 18.5). That is, once we have determined the object of the action, then we are in a position to determine its correct description from a moral point of view, although the object alone does not determine that description.

It is sometimes assumed that, for Aquinas, the object of an action is always unambiguously given by a straightforward description of the act. The text just cited should caution us against accepting such a view. We cannot move from a description of an action to a judgement about its object, since the correct description of the action from the moral point of view is determined precisely in and through a determination of the object of the act. (It should be noted, again, that there may be more than one such correct description, since an act may have more than one object, considered from different vantage points.)

Moreover, for Aquinas, as for us, the correct description of an action will be clear in most cases, but not in all cases. For him, the premises of a true science, which deal with universals, cannot be applied with certainty to contingent particulars. There can be no true science of morality, nor can there be an art of morality, since Aquinas associates art with practical deliberation carried out in a specified, determinate way.[12] Consider his explanation of why there can be no such thing as a speculative prudence:

> every application of right reason to something that is to be done pertains to art. But nothing pertains to prudence except the application of right reason to those things about which there is counsel. And with respect to these sorts of things [that is, matters about which one takes counsel], there are no determinate ways of arriving at an end; as is said in *Ethic.* III. Because therefore speculative reason does certain things, for example, the syllogism, the proposition, and other things of this sort, in which one proceeds in certain and definite ways, so it may be that the character of art can be preserved with respect to these things [i.e., matters of speculative reason], but not the character of prudence. Therefore, one finds a certain speculative art, but not a speculative prudence. (II–II 47.2 *ad* 3)

In order fully to appreciate the significance of this passage, it is necessary to realize that prudence, for Aquinas, is an intellectual virtue, grounded in the practical intellect, by which the agent is enabled to choose and to act in accordance with the rational principles of human action (I–II 57.5, II–II 47.2). The upshot of this passage is that there is no determinate way to move from the rational principles of human action to a specific choice of a concrete action.

We find a similar sense of the limitations of practical reason in Aquinas' discussion of the precepts of the natural law.[13] According to Aquinas, the precepts of the natural law are grounded in the deliverances of the practical reason as these are applied to actions, specifically to those external actions which are the province of the virtue of justice (I–II 90.1 *ad* 2, I–II 100.2). These determinations take place at what we have identified as the level of the basic moral notions; that is, they serve to specify and extend the fundamental concept of morality, and, as such, they stand as an intermediate stage between the abstract concept of morality and judgements regarding specific actions. In Aquinas' terms, the precepts of the natural law, which are more or less equivalent to the precepts of the Decalogue, follow with only a minimum of reflection from the fundamental precepts to love God and neighbor, which, with respect to human persons at least, is equivalent to the basic injunction of non-maleficence (I–II 100.1, 3 *ad* 1, 5).

At this level, there is little or no room for error. However, the further we move from general principles to specific determinations, the more difficult it is to say with any certainty whether, and how, a determinate precept should be qualified and extended:

as was said above, those things pertain to the law of nature, to which the human person is naturally inclined; among which, it is proper to the human person that he is inclined to act according to reason. However, it pertains to reason to proceed from what is general to what is specific ... The speculative reason is constituted in one way with respect to this [procedure], however, and the practical reason, in another way. Since the speculative reason deals chiefly with necessary things, concerning which it is impossible that it should proceed otherwise [than it does], the truth is found without any defect in specific conclusions, as also [it is found] in general principles. But practical reason deals with contingent things, among which are human operations, and, therefore, even though there is some necessity in [its] general principles, the more one descends to specifics, the more defect is found ... with respect to things that are done, there is not the same truth or practical rectitude for all people with respect to specifics, but only with respect to general principles; and with respect to those things about which there is the same rectitude in specifics for all, it is not equally known to all. (I–II 94.4)

Moreover, it is clear from an examination of Aquinas' more extended discussion of the norms of justice that he is aware of the need to qualify and extend the basic norms of the natural law at the level of socially sustained reflection, as well as at the level of individual decision. Let two examples suffice.

Aquinas recognizes that, in some sense, it is always bad to kill a human being. He also acknowledges that there are some situations in which homicide is allowed by the norms of justice, specifically, in prosecution of a justifiable military action, or in capital punishment (II–II 64.2). It is not the case that these latter kinds of actions are justified murders; rather, they are not murders at all. Aquinas justifies this distinction by appealing to the rationale of political authority, which has responsibility to care for the good of all, and which may sometimes sacrifice dangerous individuals to the good of the whole. For the same reason, however, he goes on to say that a private individual, who is not responsible for the good of all, is not justified in killing a convicted criminal (II–II 64.3). By the same token, political authorities may not kill the innocent on any pretext whatever, because the life and well-being of the innocent members of a community are the very rationale of human society (II–II 64. 6).

Similarly, Aquinas asserts that it is wrong to take another's possessions, against the will of the other (II–II 66.3, 5). Yet political authorities may punish wrong-doers by confiscating their goods, or allowing them to be taken as spoils of war, again, because they have authority to act on behalf of the good of all (II–II 66.8). Moreover, anyone at all may take from another what is necessary to sustain her life, in an emergency situation, because the very point of the institution of property is precisely to guarantee that each individual is provided with the necessities of life. Such an action is not to be considered to be justified theft or robbery, Aquinas adds, because it does not have the character of theft or robbery at all (II–II 66.7).

Thus, it would be a mistake to examine Aquinas' analysis of the components of the morality of an action, in the hope of finding a decision procedure for determining the correct moral description of every single action (or every kind of action) with apodictic certainty. His account does offer, however, an initial formulation of the ways in which the various components of an action enter into our description and evaluation of it. For Aquinas, as for us, the most basic terms of moral evaluation are provided by generic moral notions, which identify kinds of actions that exemplify wrongness, or, more rarely, praise-worthiness, and which may be understood and applied in terms of the rationales of the correlative moral rules. These rationales, in turn, reflect our shared consensus on what we owe to one another and may expect of one another, on the point of our basic institutions, and on the overall aims of our lives together.

There is one other aspect of Aquinas' analysis of actions that calls for special attention. We have already noted that Aquinas usually defines the appropriateness or inappropriateness of the objects of actions in reference to the aims and the institutional structures of human life. More generally, Aquinas makes a distinction between the natural and the moral species of an act, as, for example, between killing and murder, or between sexual intercourse and adultery (1–11 1.3 *ad* 3, 1–11 18.5). The language of natural kinds of actions is perhaps unfortunate, but Aquinas' point is well taken. There are certain kinds of actions which are integral to human existence as such, which would feature in any account of the natural history of the human animal, as, for example, sexual intercourse or killing.

The basic moral prohibitions are generally associated with these natural sorts of actions. The notion of murder includes, as it were, the notion of killing; the concept of theft includes the idea of taking or appropriation; and both adultery and rape presuppose that an act of sexual intercourse has taken place. At the same time, however, it is possible to kill without committing murder; to appropriate what is another's, without stealing; to engage in sexual activity that is not adultery or rape. The relation between killing and murder, between appropriation and theft, and so on, can be expressed, roughly, in terms of a distinction between necessary and sufficient conditions; that is, it is normally a necessary, but not a sufficient, condition, for an act to be counted as murder, that it be an act of killing someone, and so for the rest.

It is true that the non-moral correlates of the basic moral action-kinds do not, in themselves, carry with them a moral judgement. They do not determine the object of the action, morally speaking, nor do they necessarily determine the intention of the agent. It is also the case, however, that these sorts of actions do carry a kind of moral significance, precisely because they are correlated with generic moral concepts, and serve to raise the question, as it were, whether one of these concepts might apply to the specific act in question.[14]

Aquinas, therefore, offers an account of morality that is consistent with our contemporary understanding of the functioning and the limits of moral rules. This is a point of contact between Aquinas' understanding of morality and our own. In order to see the distinctive contribution that Aquinas offers to contemporary thought, it is necessary to go beyond this shared starting point. How does Aquinas adjudicate among the diverse considerations that inform basic moral notions, so as to arrive at one judgement rather than another in problematic cases? That, after all, is the question that has emerged as central for our own understanding of moral judgement.

The general answer to this question, to which Aquinas repeatedly returns, is that moral norms are determined by reason, just as are the specific actions of the virtues (for example, at I–II 1.1 *ad* 3, 18.8, 64.1, 90.1, 91.2; II–II 47.6). But, taken by itself, this response is unhelpful. What does it mean to act in accordance with reason?

The answer, once again, is that the meaning of acting in accordance with reason is analogical. The focal meaning, in every instance, is that the human person, unlike lower animals, directs her actions in accordance with a reasoned understanding of the good (I–II 91.2, especially *ad* 3). But what that means, concretely, is determined by the specific context of the choice in question. With respect to the virtues which are concerned with the passions, the judgement of reason is generally determined with reference to the situation of the agent herself, and what is appropriate to her own constitution and situation (I–II 60.2, 64.2). With respect to justice, on the other hand, the judgement of reason is directed to the attainment of an objectively just state of affairs (again, see I–II 64.2; cf.II–II 57.1). What this means in individual cases must, again, be determined with reference to the specifics of the situation at hand.

However, Aquinas does not limit himself to gesturing towards the deliverances of individual judgement. As we have already seen, he is prepared to articulate distinctions at the level of the basic moral notions as well.

On what basis does he make these distinctions? If we examine the treatise on justice in the *secunda secundae*, it becomes apparent that he appeals to more than one such basis. But the most important criterion, which he takes to be definitive of the virtue of justice itself, is the norm of equality, which must be understood in tandem with the fundamental injunction to avoid doing harm (II–II 58.1; cf. I–II 100.5). Someone who violates one of the basic norms of non-maleficence, for Aquinas, "dishonors" the victim, "by depriving him of some excellence on account of which he has honor" (II–II 72.1). In other words, the malefactor injures her victim by refusing to acknowledge his status as fundamentally equal with respect to their shared humanity, and paying him the regard that is, as such, his due. It does not follow that this is the only way in which the malefactor harms her victim, or that the more tangible kinds of harms, killing, seizing property, and so on, somehow do not count morally. To the contrary, Aquinas holds that the fundamental norm for behavior to other people, from which all others are derived, is the dual injunction not to harm anyone, and to respect one's special obligations (I–II 100.5; cf. I–II 100.3 *ad* 1). In fact, these amount to the same thing, since, as we read further on, it is a kind of harm to fail to respect one's special obligations to parents, kin, and the like (II–II 44.8 *ad* 1). At the same time, for Aquinas as for us, the commitment to equality conditions the way in which this fundamental norm is formulated and qualified.

How does this commitment to equality serve to bring an ordering of priority to the various components of basic moral concepts? We have already seen one example of Aquinas' use of this concept in his discussion of murder and legitimate homicide (II–II 64). The fundamental distinction that is operative in this discussion (except in reference to self-defense) is a distinction between what private individuals may do and what the state, acting through its sanctioned authorities, may do (II–II

64.2). The point is that we as individuals are on the same plane with one another, at least with respect to something as fundamental as life itself. The state, as such, is not; political authorities have a responsibility for the common good, in a way that no private individual can have, and, moreover, the representatives of the state act for the collective community, and so do not stand on the same plane, as it were, with the individual. The same reasoning runs through Aquinas' discussions of whether, and under what conditions, and by whom, other sorts of harms may be inflicted on persons (II–II 65.1,3; II–II 66.8; II–II 67.1).

It also informs, although less clearly, his discussion of property, and his distinction between robbery or theft and a legitimate form of appropriation of property held by another. In this discussion, Aquinas reflects the patristic conviction that all property is a form of institutionalized inequality, which is permissible, under the circumstances of everyday life, but is not fully consistent with God's original plan that the goods of the earth should be held in common by all (again, see II–II 66.7). That is why, if the institution of property fails to fulfill its purpose in a particular case, the claims that it generates are superseded by the more exigent claim that material goods must be placed in the service of the needs of all.

It would take us too far afield to go through all the other examples of Aquinas' appeal to equality. There is one other that calls for special mention, however. This is his discussion of the obligations of obedience, which, for him, include the obligations of servants to masters, as well as the obligations of those under religious vows to their superiors, and, in general, every sort of obligation of a subordinate to a superior (II–II 104.5). As we would expect, Aquinas is quite prepared to defend the general institutions of subordination and superiority that structure his society. What may be surprising is that he places strict limits on the extent of this obedience. For him, there is no such thing as an obligation of *unlimited* obedience between one person and another. The requirements of obedience are limited by the point of the relationship, for one thing (II–II 104.5 *ad* 2). More importantly, there are limits on the sorts of obedience that can be exacted of anybody, under any circumstances.

These limits are set by the fundamental inclinations of human life, which all persons share, and with respect to which all are equal: "However, one person is held to obey another with respect to those things which are to be done externally through the body. Nevertheless, in things which pertain to the nature of the body, one person is not held to obey another, but only God, since all persons are equal in nature" (II–II 104.5; cf. I 96.4). He goes on to explain, no one can command another either to marry or not to marry, for example, because this concerns a fundamental aspect of human existence which is common to all persons.

Aquinas' discussion of obedience is particularly significant because it illustrates his dialectical approach to the various components of his moral tradition, and, correlatively, it serves to clarify the senses in which he is, and is not, committed to a general norm of equality. It is certainly true that Aquinas, like nearly all his contemporaries, is no advocate of political, social, or gender equality, as we would understand these norms. At the same time, however, he is committed to an understanding of justice as equality, which he articulates in terms derived from Aristotle, but which owes even more to the Stoic and patristic tradition of the natural law. So understood, a commitment to equality involves the recognition that all human persons are (at least potentially) equal as moral agents, and should be treated accordingly.

What, concretely, does this mean? It does not mean that all institutions of subordination and dominance must be eliminated, first of all; not only does Aquinas believe that these are necessary to social existence, but he also holds that they do not transgress upon the fundamental equality of persons as moral agents. Certainly, Aquinas' substantive interpretation of equality is not adequate, and it would be regressive to attempt to return to his specific vision of social relations. Yet before we accuse him of hypocrisy on this score, it is worth asking how many advocates of equality have been prepared to eliminate *all* social distinctions among persons. We certainly are not; the institutions of property and wage labor, to name only two forms of structured domination, are defended among us more zealously than they would have been defended by anyone in the thirteenth century.

At the same time, it would be a mistake to assume that Aquinas simply collapses equality into a vague sort of equality of dignity. For him, the normative content of equality is given by what he takes to be the central inclinations of human life, including self-preservation and the desire to have and raise children. Understood in this way, equality does do real normative work, setting constraints on the sorts of obligations that individuals can place on one another. One of the most interesting things about Aquinas' discussion of obedience is that it illustrates so well his dialectical approach to moral reasoning. The general norm of equality serves to modify the norm of obedience, even as that norm is qualified in its turn by the incorporation of a limited form of legitimate subordination.

So far, it would seem that Aquinas still has nothing of substance to add to our understanding of the formulation of moral norms. I have just said, after all, that his twofold commitment to equality and non-maleficence is essentially similar to our own concept of morality. Granting that he can offer insight and clarity on specific questions, is there anything of substance that we can learn from Aquinas, beyond what is common to the moral tradition that we share?

In order to answer this question, it should be noted that Aquinas' understanding of equality is importantly different from anything that would be defended by most of our contemporaries. He identifies certain "commonalities of human nature" as providing the focal meaning for equality. While the resultant normative claims would correspond, more or less, with our own intuitions (we also are against forced marriages, for example), it is worth noting that almost no contemporary would spell out the meaning of equality in quite this way. Usually, equality is understood solely in terms of some mental capacity or quality of consciousness, as, for example, the ability to exercise choice, or the capacity to feel.[15] The question that arises, therefore, is, how does Aquinas arrive at this particular explication of the idea of equality? Does it amount to nothing more than a set of assumptions, or does it reflect a well-thought-out position?

The latter is the case, although it may not be obvious from this passage, taken in isolation from the rest of the *Summa*. Once this text is taken in its wider context, however, it becomes apparent that it reflects the metaphysical framework within which Aquinas works out his accounts of the basic moral notions. What governs Aquinas' thinking on moral matters, from beginning to end, is a certain understanding of what it is to be a human creature, and, more generally, what it is to be a creature *tout court*. He does not *derive* moral norms directly from this account, but he does make use of it to bring order to the diverse sorts of considerations that inform the basic moral notions. It is at this point that he offers a distinctive contribution to our own moral reflections.

The clearest indication of Aquinas' approach in this regard lies in a passage that may well be one of the most discussed and most misunderstood passages in the whole *Summa*. This occurs in the course of his account of the natural law, specifically at I–II 94.2. The question that he considers in this article is, "whether the natural law contains many precepts, or only one?" Certainly, there are diverse precepts to be found in the natural law, but is that all there is to say about them? Or is there a principle of unity underlying them and bringing coherence to the moral life? At stake here is the unity and coherence of the natural law, and, therefore, its reasonableness.[16]

We would expect a thoroughgoing rationalist such as Aquinas to assert that there is a principle of coherence underneath the various precepts of the natural law, and so he does. In order to justify this claim, he begins by observing that, just as there are first principles of reasoning, which must be respected if one is to reason at all, so there is a first principle of action which necessarily informs every action, namely, "good is to be done and pursued, and the bad is to be avoided." As Germain Grisez observes, this is not the first principle of morality *per se*; it is rather an expression of the fundamental principle that must be embodied in any putative action, if it is actually to be intelligible as such.[17] Aquinas goes on to say that this orientation towards the good, which we share with every other creature, assumes the form of certain fundamental inclinations in us, some of which we share with all other creatures (to remain in existence), some of which are proper to us as living creatures (to reproduce), and some of which are distinctively human (to live in society, to worship God). These inclinations serve to provide a principle of ordering for the precepts of the natural law: "Therefore, the order of the precepts of the law of nature is in accordance with the order of the natural inclinations" (I–II 94.2).

The last point should be underscored. Commentators on this passage sometimes assume that Aquinas is saying that the norms of the natural law are *derived* from the inclinations. That is not what he says, however. We have already observed that, on his view, the norms of the natural law are derived from the twin injunctions to love God and neighbor, or, equivalently, with respect to human relationships at least, the injunction to avoid harm (I–II 100. 1, 3, 5). What he says here is that the inclinations bring *order* to the precepts of the natural law. Just as our own basic orientation towards the good is articulated by the inclinations, so the moral norms through which we fulfill our goodness as creatures are similarly ordered in accordance with these inclinations.

The inclinations themselves, in turn, are identified, and placed in correct order, by an observation of basic human impulses as these are interpreted in the context of Aquinas' metaphysics of being. Our fundamental inclinations are interpreted by analogy with the inclinations of lower creatures: "The natural inclination in those things devoid of reason makes manifest the natural inclination belonging to the will of an intellectual nature" (I 60.5). This sort of analogical interpretation, in turn, presupposes that created existence manifests a gradient of degrees of causal scope and power, and, therefore, of perfection, which begins with creatures that merely exist, proceeds through plants and animals to rational animals (that is, us), and beyond us to the angels (I 47.2). The human inclinations that Aquinas mentions at I–II 94.2 represent our own participation at each (materially instantiated) level of this gradient of being.

John Finnis argues that Aquinas cannot really mean what he plainly says in this passage, because, if he did, it would follow that we are morally justified in violating a moral norm associated with one of the lower inclinations, in order to pursue a good associated with a higher inclination.[18] This does not follow. It is true that, for Aquinas, a human life that is lived only at the level of the more basic inclinations would be deficient, culpably so if the agent chose it. However, when the inclinations are applied to the norms of non-maleficence which comprise justice, the more basic inclinations are generally associated with the more exigent claims. For example, the preservation of life generates more exigent duties than does respect for property, which is a rational human convention.

This appeal to the ordering force of the inclinations is further qualified by Aquinas' views on the exercise of causal efficacy. He takes it for granted that the range of activities for any creature, ourselves included, will proceed outward, from the individual himself, to those who are most nearly connected to her (II–II 26.4, 6; II–II 31.3). Similarly, he argues that, since the impulse for self-preservation is the most basic human inclination, and since no one has a greater obligation to care for the life of another than for her own, then the (necessary) use of lethal force to defend oneself from a lethal attack does not count as an instance of murder, but, rather, as a justified act of self-preservation (II–II 64.7).

In general, the metaphysical context of the account of morality as developed in the *Summa* allows Aquinas to determine the scope and the limits of moral responsibility, and, therefore, to distinguish between actions which fall within the scope of one of the basic moral norms, and those similar actions which are legitimate none the less. In general, any action which can be described as a *rational* fulfillment of one of the basic inclinations is justified; fornication, for example, is not morally justified, because those who procreate outside the framework of marriage do not reflect due care for the well-being of their future offspring (II–II 154.2). Similarly, those constrictions of care and concern which reflect the limitations of a creature's causal scope are likewise justified, simply by that fact. Aquinas has no

difficulties with special relationships (again, see II–II 26.4, 6).[19]
He even allows that it is legitimate for us, from our limited
perspective, to will something that is substantively different
from what God wills from the universal perspective of divinity
(I–II 19.10).

This provides one point at which Aquinas' account of morality does offer a substantive contribution to the moral debates
of our time. That is, Aquinas weighs in on one side of a
recurrent debate over the scope of moral responsibility. Over
against utilitarians and other sorts of perfectionists, he offers us
the resources to defend a more circumscribed account of moral
obligation. Ultimately, the responsibilities of persons spring
from, and are congruent with, their status as individual
creatures, whose existence and identity are enmeshed in a web
of local causalities, particular concerns. Those who are in
public office have a wider scope for action, and, therefore, a
wider responsibility than most. But in Aquinas' universe, no
one has responsibility for the good of the whole world, except
the Governor of the world. This is one of the most attractive
implications of Aquinas' account of the moral life; it allows
God to be God, and frees us to be our limited individual selves.

A CASE IN POINT: THOMISTIC PERSPECTIVES ON MURDER AND KILLING

The debate with utilitarianism is not our central concern,
however. Let us return to the question that was raised at the
beginning of this chapter. When we are in doubt as to the
application of one of the basic moral notions, because more
than one such application can be defended in terms of considerations which inform the notion in question, how do we
choose among competing interpretations? That is, how do we
distinguish among primary and secondary considerations in
our application of the basic moral notions?

Aquinas offers us at least the beginnings of an answer to this
question, in the form of a normative account of human nature,
in terms of which it is possible to make distinctions of priority,
and even validity, among the different considerations which

inform our basic moral notions. This much was implicit in the preceding section.

It is worth emphasizing that the normative account that Aquinas offers is quite minimal, as far as its actual content goes. He begins with a set of very general, even banal, observations about tendencies that are ubiquitous in human life, together with a metaphysical argument that these are constitutive inclinations of human nature. This minimal account is consistent with a great many more specific versions of what human nature consists in, what is normative in it, and what is not, without necessarily implying a commitment to any of them. Aquinas' own more specific arguments along this line are not always convincing. Yet a revision of Aquinas' thicker account of human nature does not affect the core of his normative account, because, at this point, what is central to his argument is his overall metaphysics, and not his specific judgements about what is proper to the human creature. The price of this flexibility is of course a high level of generality. Even so, this minimal account does a surprising amount of normative work. It can do the same in the context of our own moral reflection.

In this section, I will defend the cogency and the contemporary relevance of Aquinas' views in the most direct way that I know, by applying them to some actual problems. I will focus on questions which have recurred as examples throughout the discussion so far, and which are not discussed by Aquinas himself in any detail. I do not claim that my application of Aquinas' views would have represented his own opinions, or, much less, that every other Thomist would agree with my particular judgements. Still, there would be little point in studying Aquinas as a source for contemporary moral reflection, unless it were possible to argue that his approach makes a real difference in practice.

This exercise in casuistry will serve another function as well. An account of morality which allowed for no growth and revision would be impoverished indeed. There can be no doubt that both our understanding of human life and our social situation are very different from what they were in Aquinas' day, so much so that we cannot view the world precisely as he and his contemporaries did. Yet Aquinas' account of morality is flexible enough to allow for development and revision in the light of changed perspectives and needs, without undermining what is central to that account.

I begin with a summary of what I believe to be central to Aquinas' account of morality. Aquinas, as I understand him, takes the focal meaning of morality to consist in a commitment to non-maleficence, understood in the context of the essential equality of all persons. So much is common ground between him and us. He further interprets this commitment in the light of his minimal account of what is normatively human. This account enables him to give a substantive meaning to equality, which, in turn, allows him to place the various considerations underlying the basic moral rules into some order, thus fulfilling the program set forth in I–II 94.2.

In the preceding section, I examined the way in which Aquinas' commitment to equality informs the distinctions that he draws between murder and various forms of legitimate homicide (II–II 64). We saw that a commitment to equality was central to these distinctions, since, for Aquinas, the only person who can deliberately and directly take the life of another is a representative of political authority, who does not stand on the same plane, so to speak, with a private individual. It seems to me that these distinctions are generally persuasive, although I will offer some qualifications below.

My chief concern in this section, however, will be with issues which Aquinas did not address in detail, namely, euthanasia and abortion. It could be said that Aquinas *did* address these forms of killing, and condemned them, in his blanket condemnation of the killing of the innocent. In my view, however, that response would be too quick. With respect to euthanasia, the new circumstances generated by the increased efficacy of medical treatment have made a real difference, at least in that they have increased the urgency of the issue of euthanasia. It would be foolish to ignore that fact. As for the question of abortion, we will see that it is not clear that Aquinas himself would have understood his strictures on killing the innocent to apply to abortion in every instance.

Let us turn to the question of euthanasia. What makes this question so difficult is that many of the considerations which inform our prohibition against murder would not seem to apply to euthanasia. On the assumption that what we are talking about is really a *mercy* killing, under circumstances in which death is a "blessed release," as we say, it does not seem to be the case that the putative victim is actually harmed, even though we may well say, with Ronald Dworkin, that the end of a human life in any circumstances whatever involves a loss which should be regretted and mourned.[20] As for the violation of her freedom, if she has been permanently deprived of consciousness, she has no freedom left to violate; or it may be the case that she actively wants to be killed. (In a case in which someone who is ill does *not* want to be killed, one of the most powerful considerations underlying the prohibition against murder does come into play, and, in such a situation, it seems to me, there can be no doubt that killing the individual would be murder.)

Yet there is another consideration informing the prohibition against murder, which does remain in play in such situations. That is, the patient and her physician, or whoever else is caring for him, are both private individuals. Thus, even granting that the physician who kills her patient does not harm him in any obvious way or usurp his freedom, she none the less violates the fundamental relationship of equality that should obtain between one human person and another. Yet equality is not just one consideration among others which go to make up our moral concepts; it is a fundamental component of the concept of morality, and, once it is undermined, the attitudes of mutuality and respect for one another, which are basic to moral judgement, are likewise called into question. For this reason, the violation of equality involved in euthanasia would seem to me to be decisive, and I would argue that euthanasia cannot be justified, however compelling the motivations for it in a particular case.

It might be objected that the act of the physician in the case described above, who carries out euthanasia at her patient's request, does not involve a violation of equality. She is carrying out the patient's wishes, and, therefore, she is actually honoring the relationship of equality that subsists between them, precisely as free, rational creatures.

It is at this point that Aquinas' account of the inclinations does normative work. One of the implications of that account is that it provides substantive content to the idea of equality; that is to say, it gives us some concrete indication of the respects in which persons are equal. More to the point, it provides a way out of the desperate expedient of assuming that autonomy is the only thing that is normative in human nature, or that the norm of equality can be understood solely in terms of respect for the wishes of another. In this case, the physician and her patient are equal, not only as free creatures, but simply as human creatures, each with a life of his or her own. And the equality that subsists between them at this level is more fundamental, and more exigent, than the equality that exists between them as free creatures.

This raises a difficult question, which cannot be resolved, but which should at least be raised. That is to say, what does this position imply about the general norm of respect for freedom or autonomy?

Anyone who is familiar with Aquinas' overall account of morality will realize that respect for freedom *per se* does not play a large role in his moral universe. This is odd, given his insistence that the capacity for self-direction through free action is what is distinctive to human existence (I–II introduction). It is not itself the object of one of the basic inclinations, but it is the mode in which all the inclinations must be sought, if they are to be pursued and lived out in a truly human way. Thus, it would seem that on his own terms, Aquinas should give respect for autonomy more of a central place than in fact he does.

Even so, it does seem to me that a Thomist would have to acknowledge more constraints on respect for autonomy than a strict libertarian would allow. Specifically, I believe that the Thomist is committed to the view that there are certain kinds of actions that cannot be directed to other persons, *even with their consent*. The taking of human life seems to me to be a very clear example of an act that should not be done even with the consent of the person whose life it is. There are other examples which are, admittedly, less clear, but which seem to me to be persuasive; for example, it would be wrong to prostitute someone, as a pimp or as a client, even with the consent of the person involved, because of the deeply dehumanizing effects of this sort of transaction. (Most prostitutes are subject to some degree of coercion, which means that the actions of pimps and clients are even worse than this example suggests.) It also seems to me that the Thomist can allow for, or even consider to be obligatory, some forms of coercion directed towards persons who are not capable of rational self-direction, for example, the insane, or even children.

Having said all that, it should also be said that there is nothing in a Thomistic account of morality that would justify us in the paternalistic coercion of rational adults "for their own good," or in withholding from people the conditions for full rational choice, such as knowledge and sufficient education to acquire independence of thought. I believe that the principles of such a morality would require us to *provide* these pre-requisites for rational self-direction, but I cannot argue the point here.

Let us return to the question of euthanasia. Suppose that the argument for a general prohibition of euthanasia is granted. Does it follow that the physician must do everything in her power to keep her suffering patient alive? Not at all. This is one case in which the distinction between acting directly to bring about an end, and merely allowing something to happen, makes perfect sense. The physician who allows a suffering patient to die, or who withdraws treatment when there is no hope of a recovery of even the most limited well-being, does not take on the active role of her patient's deliverer and killer; she simply withdraws from her role as physician, and allows the processes of human dying, which, after all, are also a part of human life, to run their course. This is no violation of equality, but an acknowledgement of shared finitude.[21]

In my discussion of euthanasia, there is one question that is noteworthy by its absence. That is, what are we to say about a situation in which the patient herself contemplates suicide, either with or without her doctor's assistance?

Aquinas' own view on this subject is very clear. Suicide clearly falls within the scope of the prohibition of murder. It involves an irrational act against the instinct of self-preservation and the obligation of self-love entailed by charity; it usurps the authority of the human society, to which the individual is responsible; finally, it usurps the authority of God, to whom alone belongs the right to decide when our lives will end (II–II 64.5). How far are these arguments persuasive?

The first argument, that suicide violates the inclination to self-preservation and the obligation to love oneself in charity, is elaborated at II–II 64.5 *ad* 3, in which Aquinas considers the various reasons that persons might have for committing suicide. It is clear, from this extensive discussion, that suicide is condemned because it is an *irrational* act, and, therefore, contrary to charity, as well as to the natural law. As Aquinas says, it is not legitimate to kill oneself "to avoid any miseries, of whatever kind, of the present life. Since death is the last of the evils of this life, and the most terrible ... so to put oneself to death in order to avoid other miseries of this life is to take on a greater evil in order to avoid a lesser evil" (II–II 64.5 *ad* 3). With respect to most of the considerations that Aquinas mentions, this argument is indeed persuasive. It is not so clear that it is persuasive with respect to the person who is dying, and who chooses suicide in order to avoid pain or degradation in the dying process. Might we not describe this as a choice to die in one way and not another, rather than as a choice to die instead of living?

Of the three arguments that Aquinas offers, his appeal to the interest that the state has in the life of the individual seems to me to be much the weakest in this context. It is difficult to see what practical interest the state could have in the continuance of the life of someone who is already in the process of dying and is racked with pain. Aquinas does not seem to be thinking of the sorts of cases that arise at the end of life, and that admittedly lends some plausibility to his argument. It *is* plausible that the state has an interest in the preservation of the life

of a healthy, potentially productive, but despondent, individual. That, however, is not what is in question in this
instance.

Aquinas' appeal to the authority of God is more difficult to
address. No one who is committed to the Christian tradition
can afford to dismiss the argument that certain aspects of our
lives are God's domain, within which we do not have the
authority to simply do as we wish. Apart from the fact that
there are considerable (but, I think, inconclusive) scriptural
warrants for such a view, this way of thinking is deeply intertwined with a sense of the sacredness of human life. This sense,
in turn, expresses something very deep in the Christian sensibility, and not only the Christian sensibility. As such, it ought to
be cherished, and not lightly dismissed.

And yet ... If the only good argument against suicide
consists in the claim that it usurps the authority of God, it
follows that someone who is terminally ill and subject to
extreme and untreatable suffering must be told to continue to
endure her suffering for an indefinite future, *only* because it
would usurp the authority of God for her to end her life.
Suffering is a part of life, and we should be prepared to endure
what we must; we need no gospel to tell us that. Yet there is
something deeply disturbing about the argument that people
ought to be prepared to accept suffering, pain, or radical
diminishment of life, which could be alleviated or prevented,
for *no other reason* than that God has not given us the authority
to act in the appropriate ways. Is the God of love so easily
offended, or is God's authority so precarious? After all, the
mainstream of the Christian tradition has allowed for a considerable scope for human action, without feeling that the
authority of God is threatened by our own efforts to shape our
lives.

It is also the case that appeals to God's authority are perhaps
the most easily abused of all the repertoire of arguments in the
Christian tradition. It is all too easy for a defense of God's
authority to be elided into a defense of the authority of the
human individuals and institutions which claim a share of that
authority for themselves. Therefore, a certain skepticism about

these appeals would be in order. I do not mean to say that such a claim would never be legitimate, but there would need to be overwhelmingly clear warrant for it. And, in the case of suicide, it does not seem that such warrants exist.

It does not seem that Aquinas' arguments against suicide are finally convincing. More generally, it does not seem that there is any compelling argument against suicide that would rule it out, at least for someone who is certainly dying.[22]

This raises a further question, because very often there is no sharp line between the act of euthanasia and assistance in suicide. Certainly, if suicide is a morally legitimate option, then there can be no moral objection to providing someone with assistance in committing suicide, so long as that assistance does not consist in actually killing the patient at her request. The latter would count as an act of euthanasia, rather than assistance in someone else's act of suicide, and, as such, it would be ruled out for the reasons given above.

I have argued that euthanasia is ruled out because it violates the essential relationship of equality that exists among private individuals. This suggests the possibility that euthanasia might be justified, if it were carried out by the state, through its designated representatives. The visions that this conjures up are so dreadful as to call into question the whole argument as it has developed so far.

Yet it does not follow, from what has been said so far, that, because euthanasia violates a primary relationship of equality between individuals, it would therefore be legitimate if it were carried out by the state. Certainly, there is nothing in Aquinas himself to support such a conclusion. Even though Aquinas argues that the state may take the life of malefactors, he is adamantly opposed to the suggestion that the state could also take the life of those who are not malefactors (ii–ii 64.6).

It is easy to see why state-sponsored euthanasia would be morally objectionable. The modern nation-state is very different from the political regimes with which Aquinas would have been familiar. The emergence of the nation-state was, in many ways, a force for liberation. It opened up possibilities for institutional reform that Aquinas and his contemporaries could not have imagined. Yet it also generated what quickly became a defining problem for modern political and moral thought. How can the individual be protected from the overwhelming power and the expansionist tendencies of the nation-state?

This is not the place to rehearse all the answers that have been given to this question. The relevant point is this: precisely because the modern nation-state is so drastically *unequal* to individuals, the power of the state over human life and death should be kept within the strictest limits possible. The use of violent, even lethal, force by armies and police forces will be a responsibility of any political community that can be imagined, unless the conditions of human life were to be radically altered. But there can be no justification for the state to take life when there is no question of protecting the security of its people (or sometimes third parties) against aggression. This would certainly rule out state-sponsored euthanasia. It would also, incidentally, rule out capital punishment, unless this were the only means to protect society from violent crime (and there is overwhelming evidence that such is not the case).

Much more could be said on the question of euthanasia, and all the troubling questions which it raises. Yet every discussion must come to closure at some point, and so I now turn to the other life and death question that has been much debated, namely, the question of abortion.

The reasons for the explosive nature of the abortion debate are complex. To some extent this debate is so intense because it has become a focal point for complex and ambiguous attitudes towards women and children, towards sexuality, and towards the rapid changes in gender roles. Yet this is not the whole explanation. The debate over abortion is difficult because the question itself is a difficult one, and both sides on this debate can claim to be defending cherished values.[23]

One common argument against abortion appeals, again, to the fundamental principle of equality. The fetus is, after all, a living human being like ourselves. Of course, there are considerable differences between a fetus and an adult human being, or even between a fetus and a child; although actually there is not a great deal of difference between a late-stage fetus and a newborn child. Yet however great the differences between ourselves and nascent human life, they are bracketed off from our deliberations by the stringency of the commitment to equality. So the argument would go.

On the other side, it may be asked how plausible it is to claim that the differences between the fetus and ourselves are not morally relevant at all. In the earliest stages of its development, a fetus has none of the characteristics that we generally associate with personal identity, beyond sheer existence. In its earliest stages, it has no capacity for consciousness, much less for independent life. Furthermore, it has no social identity as an individual and no personal history. Not only can it not relate to us in even the most rudimentary ways, we cannot relate to it as to a distinct human being. Moreover, in its earliest stages, without doubt, and probably throughout gestation, it has no desire to go on living and no fear of death. Whatever else may be said about the act of killing it, there can be no question here of doing something against the victim's will, because the fetus has no will.

These considerations, which seem to pull in contrary directions, are further complicated by the fact that the relationship between a woman and her unborn child is *sui generis*. That, too, makes it difficult to know how to respond morally to the act of abortion. As we have already had occasion to note, our moral concepts are formed against a background of judgements about the limits of human capacities and responsibilities. It may be said that an unwanted pregnancy can place a uniquely insupportable burden on a woman, at least in some circumstances, so that she should not be required to carry the pregnancy to term, for reasons analogous to our reasons for allowing someone to kill another in self-defense. (Note that this does not imply that abortion *is* an act of self-defense in some cases; this argument is sometimes made, but, as it stands, I think it is unconvincing.) On the other hand, the contrary argument is sometimes offered, that women stand in such an intimate relationship to their unborn children that they have a *greater* responsibility to them than we normally have to one another, perhaps even to our own (born) children.

The strongest argument against abortion rests on the appeal to equality. The considerations brought forward in this chapter indicate why this argument should have the force that it does. A commitment to equality is not just one consideration among others underlying our basic moral notions; rather, it informs all our moral judgements. If it were the case that the fetus has exactly the same moral status as the rest of us, it is very difficult to see how abortion could be justified, except perhaps in extremely rare cases.

Yet it is far from clear that this is the case. That is why abortion is so difficult, and it is why we cannot finally offer any sort of judgement on the morality of abortion without first coming to some conclusions about the status of the fetus. Understandably, people on all sides of the abortion controversy have attempted to do just that. Arguments justifying abortion are sometimes put forward to the effect that, even if the fetus is a person, its mother's rights override its right to life. On the other hand, it is sometimes said that, even if we think the fetus *might* be a person, we should give it the benefit of a doubt and refrain from ending its life. Neither argument is convincing, in my view. Admittedly, it might well be the case that, even if the fetus is a person, its rights can be overridden in the way suggested, but it seems obvious that, once we attempt to apply this argument to cases, we must sooner or later come to some conclusions about the status of the being whose supposed rights are being overridden. We need far stronger reasons to justify killing a person, than to justify ending a human, but non-personal, existence. On the other hand, the quietist argument against abortion simply refuses to take account of the enormous cost in human suffering that such an absolute prohibition would involve. The possibility that the fetus is a fully personal human life raises a grave moral question, but so does the suffering of the countless women and their families who find themselves faced with pregnancy in difficult circumstances. It is frivolous not to confront the question of abortion directly.

Aquinas himself held that the developing fetus did not receive a rational soul until it reached a sufficient degree of physical organization to be potentially capable of rational life (1 118.2 *ad* 2). It is sometimes said that this view has since been invalidated by developments in embryology which Aquinas could not have foreseen, but I would agree with Joseph Donceel that this is not the case.[24] Aquinas' reason for denying that the fetus can receive a rational soul before it has reached a certain stage of development follows from the claim that the rational soul is the form of the human person. As such, it cannot subsist in a developing human being until that being develops the bodily capacity for rational functioning. In other words, on Aquinas' view, the early-stage fetus does not have the metaphysical or moral status of a person, because it does not yet have any capacity, nor even the physical substratum of a capacity, for the distinctively human mode of functioning. And, as far as his biological presuppositions go, Aquinas was essentially right on this point.

In my own view, Aquinas' view is philosophically cogent and theologically compelling, but I will not here undertake the complex arguments that would be necessary to defend it.[25] I will content myself with drawing out what seem to me to be the implications of this view. (It is worth remarking again that this is my own interpretation of the implications of Aquinas' thought; I do not claim that it would have been his own conclusion.) If Aquinas is correct, it follows, first of all, that the early-stage fetus is not a person, and does not fall within the ambit of the principle of equality. It is a developing human life, and, as such, it deserves reverence and protection. But this claim can be overridden, more readily than can the claim of immunity from killing that each of us has against all others. The moral legitimacy of abortion in the early stages of pregnancy, before the development of the fetal brain must, therefore, be granted, at least in some cases. It is worth noting that a Thomistic position on abortion, which rests on metaphysical claims which are admittedly not in wide currency, would be in accordance with what I believe to be a widespread intuition, that early abortions are sometimes justifiable, even though later abortions are (even) more problematic morally.

This conclusion leaves important issues to be addressed. As

was the case with respect to euthanasia, I cannot undertake to address them all. Two in particular, however, are obvious loose ends.

First of all, what are we to say about the status of the fetus in its later stages? Secondly, does it follow, from what has just been said, that we would be justified in killing someone who is gravely retarded, or who has suffered brain damage that renders her permanently non-sentient? These questions should be addressed together, because they both force us to go further in our reflections on what it means to be a human person.

Even though the capacity for rational functioning is the defining characteristic of the human person, on a Thomistic view at least, this capacity is not the only consideration that is relevant to the question of abortion. The identity of a human person does not just reside in her rational capacities. It is also grounded and manifested in her affective life, her bodily existence, and even in her social identity and her participation in a shared communal history. All of these are aspects of personal existence, and they all exercise a claim.

In its early stages of development, a fetus has none of these qualities except for its bodily existence; neither rational capacity, nor capacity for any sort of sentience, nor a social identity as a distinct individual, nor a place in the community. However, the same cannot be said about a fetus in its later stages. Once the brain has developed, the fetus has the physical capacity for thought and feeling, and it may be that, in the later stages of its development, it has rudimentary consciousness. Similarly, even the most damaged human being, once born, has a separate, visible human existence, and, as such, it has at least the capacity for sustaining a social identity. Persons who are not so gravely damaged, but who are none the less seriously impaired, are not only capable of rudimentary rationality, but (more importantly) they share in the world of human perceptions, interactions, and feelings.

All this complicates the issue of abortion in its later stages. My own view is that, after the fetus has reached that stage in its development at which its brain has developed, it is a person, and, therefore, it enjoys the same immunities against being killed as the rest of us do. Or nearly so; for, even after this point, the fetus is still a developing life, with organic links to its mother and perhaps to other siblings, and this does still make a moral difference. The claims of a developing life that will foreseeably be cut short are not so stringent as the claims of a person, even a dying person, who is already among us, and, for this reason, I would argue, we can abort a fetus that is doomed to death anyway for a serious reason, for example, to save the mother's reproductive capacities, or to save another sibling (if, as does happen occasionally, a woman is carrying too many children to bring them all to term), or to save the fetus itself a life of extreme suffering followed by early death. Alan Donagan has argued that, because a child owes its very existence to its parents, but not the other way around, a woman is not obliged to die in childbirth to bring her child into the world; I agree, and, therefore, I also hold that abortion can be justified to save the life of the mother.[26] It does not seem to me that abortion can otherwise be justified, once the brain of the fetus has developed.

As for the situation of those who are gravely impaired, either congenitally, or as a result of disease or accident later in life, these individuals stand in precisely the same relation, and exercise the same claims of equal regard, as all the rest of us do with respect to one another. A capacity for human functioning that is defective in some way, or which cannot be exercised fully for some reason, is none the less a capacity for human functioning, which is grounded, in my view, in the deeper core of a personal being. Even if this is not granted, it is still the case that even the most impaired individual has an identity and the possibility of relating to others, if she is capable of consciousness at all. Even if someone has no capacity for consciousness, she none the less has an identity and a place in the human community, simply in virtue of having a separate human existence.

Much more could be said on all these issues, but every discussion must come to an end at some point. If the preceding section has served to indicate the relevance of Aquinas to contemporary moral problems, and to further the conversation on the issues themselves, it will have fulfilled its purpose.

CHAPTER 4

Moral acts and acts of virtue

In his *Quandaries and Virtues*, Edmund Pincoffs protests against what he refers to, "for convenience and disparagement, as 'quandary ethics.'"[1] That is, he protests against the widespread view that moral philosophy properly focuses on moral problems. On this view,

> the ultimate beneficiary of ethical analysis is the person who, in one of these situations, seeks rational ground for the decision he must make ... ethics is therefore primarily concerned to find such grounds, often conceived of as moral rules and the principles from which they can be derived ... meta-ethics consists in the analysis of the terms, claims, and arguments that come into play in moral disputation, deliberation, and justification in problematic contexts.[2]

Pincoffs urges us to turn to a more careful consideration of topics that have been neglected in moral philosophy, particularly the issues of integrity of character and the virtues. His recommendations have been widely heeded, so that, at this point, it is hardly the case that questions of virtue and character have been neglected by moral philosophers or theologians. A rejection of moral theory in the Kantian mode is often accompanied by a turn to the language of the virtues as a way of understanding moral judgement.[3]

It may seem by now that I have thoroughly implicated myself in the project of "quandary ethics." Even if the analysis of the basic moral notions and their correlative rules offered in chapter 1 were not sufficiently compromising, the extended discussion of hard cases and the moral law in the previous two chapters would be decisive for many readers. Those who are charitably inclined may conclude that I have been led by my eagerness to do justice to the concerns expressed by Putnam and others to take up a style of moral philosophizing that was already becoming outdated even as Pincoffs' work appeared. Others will suspect that I have read more Aquinas than is good for me. Perhaps there is some truth in both perceptions, but matters are more complex than that.

An account of moral judgement that is limited to an analysis of the functioning of basic moral notions will be, at best, incomplete. That would be the milder version of Pincoffs' challenge, and that, at least, is certainly true. Any adequate account of moral judgement must say something about the nature of the human agent who judges, as well as the concepts by which she judges.

At the same time, the dichotomy that Pincoffs and others have drawn between "quandary ethics" and a morality of virtuous character and prudent judgement is wrong-headed in the assumptions that it reflects. That is, the distinction between following a rule and acting out of a virtue presupposes a mistaken idea of both the traditional moral rules and the virtues, and of the nature of the distinction between them.

It is at this point that Aquinas can make a further contribution to contemporary attempts to understand moral judgement. His account of the virtues is noteworthy precisely because he is one of the very few to synthesize a fully developed account of the virtues with an equally extensive account of the moral law, without collapsing either kind of consideration into the other. In the process, he raises, and partially addresses, deeper questions about the capacities of the agent which inform moral judgement. He offers, finally, a substantive and cogent account of prudence which does the work that contemporary appeals to prudence are meant to do, without emptying prudence of any substantive content.

In order to see how Aquinas can speak to contemporary discussions on the virtues and their relationship to moral judgement, we need a better sense of that discussion. Accordingly, I begin with an examination of Pincoffs' own account of the virtues, which remains one of the best and most thorough treatments. Through reflecting on the limits of Pincoffs' analysis, we will be led to consider the logic of the language of the virtues and the differences, and the similarities, between ideals of specific virtues and the rules associated with the basic moral notions.

In *Quandaries and Virtues*, Pincoffs offers an account of the virtues which, in his view, provides an alternative to "quandary ethics." In order to understand what he finds attractive about an appeal to the virtues, it is, therefore, necessary to see why he rejects quandary ethics. One difficulty has already been noted; he recognizes that it is not possible to arrive at determinate solutions to every moral difficulty by means of apodictic rules. He also sees at least two other difficulties with the project of quandary ethics.[4] In the first place, this mode of moral thought does not allow any place for reflection on character, and the ways in which it matters to us that our actions both express and shape individual character. Moreover, this approach imposes a false unity on the moral life, because it does not leave room for the recognition of the diversity of considerations which inform our judgements of ourselves and one another.

In Pincoffs' view, an account of the virtues offers an attractive alternative to the modern theoretical approach, because it offers an alternative which respects the heterogeneity, inconclusiveness, and contextual sensitivity of actual moral discourse. Seen from this perspective, one of the most appealing aspects of the language of the virtues, for Pincoffs, is precisely its diversity.

To illustrate the point, he offers a list, compiled with Robert Audi, of qualities that might serve as an answer to a question about the sort of person that somebody is. We need not examine the whole list. Here is a representative sample: able, affectionate, brainy, charitable, conscientious, cosmopolitan, decent, devout, dignified, equable, fair-minded, frank, generous, gentle, humorous, independent, just, kindly, learned, lively, methodical, open-minded, persistent, polite, prudent, reasonable, self-confident, sensitive, serious, sober, tender, tolerant, virile, witty, youthful, and zany.[5]

The first point that strikes us about this list is its heterogeneity. Many of the traits on this list would appear in almost any standard list of the virtues, but many others would not, either because they seem to reflect natural endowments or matters of temperament, rather than moral accomplishment ("brainy," "witty"), or because they are not always praiseworthy or desirable qualities ("polite," "obedient"), or, finally, because they are desirable only from the perspective of a set of values that is not generally shared ("cosmopolitan," "virile").

It is true, as Pincoffs goes on to observe, that these qualities have certain things in common, over and above the basic fact that they can all be attributed to human beings. For one thing, they are indeterminate. That is, there is no one clearly identifiable kind of action which can be linked to the possession of a virtue; we cannot teach a child to be kind or gentle or brave by training it to perform some one definite kind of action, on command, as it were. In addition, Pincoffs mentions two other features that these qualities share:

> They are not static [properties], such as specifying weight or place or birth; they are dynamic, having to do with tendencies, or dispositions ... They also seem, at least potentially, to be grounds for preference or avoidance. But the preference or avoidance is of a different sort from that in which we would, for example, prefer a person who weighs over 150 pounds for an experiment in nutrition.[6]

It is important to take note of these similarities, because they help to identify the field of discourse in which we speak of someone's virtues and vices. At the same time, they do not add up to anything like a systematic theory of the virtues. In Pincoffs' view, it would be a mistake to try to develop this sort of systematic theory. The language of virtues and vices offers a valuable resource for moral reflection precisely because it is a repository of the heterogeneous values that inform moral discourse. Evaluations in terms of virtues allow us to do justice to the rich variety of qualities and excellences that we prize, without requiring us to impose the false unity of a moral theory on them.

In his introductory remarks, Pincoffs speaks of moral rationality in terms that clearly reflect his allegiance to Quine:

I will hold that there are mutually irreducible types of moral consideration, that there is no hierarchy – with the king consideration at ease on the apex – no one-principle system that incorporates all of the moral rules ...

In thinking of the way that we reason about moral issues, think of nets. Nets are suspended by cords that run to points on the periphery. The strength of the net is the joint strength of the woven cords of which it is made and the points to which they lead. Think, then, of the leading types of moral consideration as points to which the cords run ... To reason morally is to weave a net (or if fallacies crop up, to mend a net). To decide rationally is to compare the joint strength of one set of considerations to the joint strength of alternative sets.[7]

For Pincoffs, there is finally no way to get beyond the surface of moral language, to an underlying rationale or purpose in terms of which to systematize that language. We value a variety of different characteristics in persons, and the language of the virtues reflects this. But, for Pincoffs, there is no possibility, as there is no need, to systematize the language of the virtues by means of some theoretical superstructure.

Or so it seems, when Pincoffs is most at pains to draw a distinction between moral theory, and the richer forms of moral discourse that are available to us. Yet, as he moves on to address other concerns, there are indications that some of these other concerns are not so readily reconciled with his emphasis on the diverse and non-systematizable nature of moral language.

Early on, he discusses the possibility that integrity of character might not be compatible with the emphasis earlier in this century on the universalizability of moral norms.[8] His point is that it is perfectly reasonable for someone to acknowledge that, while a particular course of action might be legitimate for someone else, it is not legitimate for the individual herself, not consonant with her character or the standards that she has set for herself. Pincoffs' criticism of universalizability is well taken.

Yet it sits oddly with his insistence that the language of the virtues is irreducibly diverse. If there are no intrinsic connections among different qualities of character and action, how could a particular course of action be inconsistent with a settled character? It might be that the proposed course of action is so horrendous or shameful that nobody with any character to speak of would do it. But, as Pincoffs imagines it, what is in question is a kind of action that it is possible to imagine someone else performing, with justification at least, if not with honor. If that is the case, then how could I rule out the possibility that *I* might perform it? That is, how could there be a criterion of consistency or integrity, even one which is internally generated, if the language of the virtues does not admit of any sort of ordering in terms of more fundamental principles or commitments?

When we arrive at the last section of the book, it becomes still more clear that Pincoffs needs a more discriminating account of the virtues than, on his own terms, it appears possible to have.[9] In this section, he takes up the question of moral education, with an aim to determining whether there is any real difference between training children in the virtues and indoctrinating them, as the Catholics and communists do. He argues that there is a distinction, because, while the former teach their children to accept a particular and questionable way of life as if it were beyond criticism, the moral educator forms children in those virtues which everyone must recognize as desirable.

One smiles at Pincoffs' parade examples of moral indoctrination, even while admitting that he has a point. Indoctrination is a bad thing, whoever is practicing it. And there is something intuitively right about the distinction between indoctrinating a child, and teaching her to be honest or kind. Yet it is not so clear that Pincoffs can make sense of this distinction, on the terms of his own account of the virtues. It is significant, however, that, for Pincoffs, this distinction depends on a prior distinction between questionable ways of life, such as Catholicism, and qualities whose desirability or otherwise cannot be questioned: "Dishonesty, if it were a subject for debate, which I deny, is at least not so in the way that Catholicism or communism or trial marriages are."[10]

It is true that no one can seriously deny that dishonesty, selfishness, cruelty, and the like, are bad qualities, or, correlatively, that truthfulness, thoughtfulness, and kindness are good qualities. Someone who consistently and seriously denied the viciousness of dishonesty and the desirability of truthfulness (for example) would be, in effect, withdrawing from anything that we could recognize as a discussion of the human good. These sorts of qualities exemplify our more general concept of personal goodness, directly or indirectly as the case may be. Yet no one who wants to participate in moral discourse can deny that murder, theft, and lying are bad kinds of actions, either, and for the same reason; that is, these are notions of kinds of actions which exemplify and give content to the more general concept of morality.

Even so, there is another sort of question that can be asked with respect to qualities such as cruelty or thoughtfulness. That is, what counts as cruelty or thoughtfulness? These sorts of questions are parallel to such questions as, "what counts as murder?" and they arise for the same reason; our notions of virtues and vices cannot be applied with apodictic certainty to every situation.[11]

Pincoffs himself remarks on the indeterminacy of concepts of the virtues and vices, but he does not recognize that this indeterminacy makes his distinction between moral training and indoctrination very difficult to sustain.[12] After all, this distinction depends on the claim that the teacher who shapes her young pupils to be kind, for example, is only training them in a quality that is unquestionably good. But no one trains children to be kind in the abstract; children are taught to be kind in specific ways, and, in the process, they are taught to endorse one *substantive* version of kindness, while being discouraged from others. And, while the general desirability of kindness may be beyond debate, specific construals of that ideal are, to the contrary, quite debatable. Thus, the further the teacher moves from abstract advocacy to actually forming children in the virtues in concrete situations, the more this process will come to resemble indoctrination as Pincoffs understands it.

This becomes still clearer when Pincoffs raises the question of what it means to be a virtuous person, or, on his terms, to be one of "the right sort":

To become the right sort of person is to become the sort of person that the community needs, must have, if it is to continue as a desirable association. "Desirability" must be defined largely by considering what the community would be like in the presence of dishonesty, injustice, cruelty – the vices.[13]

This suggests that the ultimate standard for applying the language of the virtues is given by one's community. I say "suggests" advisedly, because these remarks might also be taken to imply that there is some intrinsic, communally embodied standard, perhaps generated by the exigencies of community life itself, which gives content to the language of the virtues.[14] Yet Pincoffs does not make any such claim, and for this reason, it is very difficult to see how he *can* appeal to any standard other than the practices of his own community to give content to the ideals of the virtues and vices.

If this is so, then it is very difficult to see how he can sustain any distinction, except a polemical one, between indoctrination and the language of the virtues. After all, Catholics and communists and other disreputable groups can and do lay claim to the language of the virtues and vices, interpreted in accordance with their own community standards and practices. Like Pincoffs, they can claim that they are only training their children in virtues which everyone must approve, and which are essential to the maintenance of their community life. To be sure, they interpret the virtues in terms of their own communal practices, but so does Pincoffs. They can as readily accuse him of indoctrination as he does them.[15]

None of this implies that Pincoffs' account of the virtues is without merit. To the contrary, he offers one of the best and most detailed accounts of the way in which the language of the virtues functions. Yet, for that very reason, the limitations of his account serve to remind us that an appeal to the virtues cannot serve as an *unproblematic* alternative to appeals to moral rules. At any rate, it is clear that further examination of the logic of the virtues is in order.

IDEALS OF VIRTUE AND THE BASIC MORAL NOTIONS

We noted above that Pincoffs recognizes that the language of the virtues is indeterminate. That is, we cannot tie virtues conceptually to specific behaviors, nor can we readily identify specific kinds of actions that are clearly inconsistent with particular virtues. Yet Pincoffs apparently assumes, as many moral thinkers do, that the indeterminacy of concepts of the virtues constitutes a critical difference between a form of moral judgement that is grounded in the language of virtues, and moral reasoning that is governed by moral rules. To the contrary, this quality of indeterminacy is one point of *similarity* between the basic moral notions and concepts of the virtues. Our examination of the basic moral notions and their correlative rules has made this clear. The language of particular virtues (and vices) is indeterminate with respect to its concrete applications, for the same logical reason that the basic moral notions, together with nearly all other empirical concepts, are indeterminate.

At the same time, the indeterminacy of virtue concepts should not be taken to imply that these concepts have no content at all. Just as our basic moral notions are understood in terms of paradigmatic instances of actions, which would generally be accepted as examples of (for example) murder, so our notions of the virtues are also understood in terms of paradigmatic examples of actions which would generally be accepted as instances of the virtue in question. Otherwise, the language of the virtues would be, not indeterminate, but vacuous.

Once we let go of the modern understanding of rules as algorithms, there is no reason to deny that our notions of particular virtues, too, *are* rules. Like the traditional moral rules, they provide criteria by which to evaluate our actions, either prospectively or in retrospect. In order to make use of these criteria, we must use judgement to apply general notions of kinds of actions, which are held to be desirable or blameworthy, to specific instances of choice and action. Yet exactly the same can be said of the rules associated with the basic moral notions. However, in deference to common usage, I will continue to limit the expression, "moral rules," to the rules correlated with basic moral notions such as murder.

At the same time, it is true that there are differences between the functioning of the basic moral notions and their correlative rules, and the functioning of our notions of the virtues. First of all, the traditional moral rules generally do have some conceptual link with fairly specific kinds of actions, described in non-moral terms. The notion of murder is linked to the notion of killing, that of theft is linked to the notion of appropriation of property, and so on. For these sorts of moral notions, the non-moral action descriptions serve as (more or less) necessary, but not sufficient, conditions for the application of the rule in question, as we noted in the previous chapter. There does not seem to be a similar link between ascriptions of non-moral action descriptions and the ascription of particular virtues or vices; that is, there does not seem to be any specific kind of behavior that must be displayed, in order for us to be in a position, logically, to describe the act in question as an act of a specific virtue or vice.

The basis for this difference lies in the different functions that are played by the concepts associated with the moral rules and those which are associated with the virtues. (A recognition of this point does not commit us to the view that the virtues are to be understood and valued *only* in terms of their social function, as Gaita points out.[16]) The moral rules serve to set boundaries within a community, by identifying kinds of harms which are not consistent with the basic attitudes that we should take towards one another. For this reason, they tend to be tied, conceptually, to fairly definite non-moral action descriptions.

Our concepts of virtues and vices, on the other hand, play a rather different role. As Pincoffs observes, they serve to point to personal qualities which offer "grounds for preference or avoidance," as persons *tout court* and not as cooks, Southerners, or fathers.[17] As such, they cannot be tied so neatly to particular non-moral kinds of actions, because the relationships among specific actions and the character traits of their agents are quite complex. Again, it does not follow that there are no links at all. We could not even begin to characterize traits of character, without some idea of the kinds of actions which are *typically* associated with given character traits. With respect to some virtues and vices, indeed, the link between the concept of the virtue or vice, and some non-moral kind of action, can be very strong; for example, we typically associate courage with an act such as charging the enemy line, just as we associate cowardice with running away. Yet, even where this sort of link is strongest, it remains only a presumptive link between qualities and their typical manifestations. There are many ways to be courageous besides the heroism of the soldier, and many ways to be cowardly besides running away; we can imagine circumstances in which running away would be an act of courage. There seems to be neither a necessary, nor much less a sufficient, link between particular non-moral action descriptions, and concepts of virtues or vices.

Moreover, our concepts of the specific virtues are not only indeterminate, they are downright ambiguous. That is, it is possible to make out a credible case that two contrary courses of action are *both* exemplifications of a particular virtue, or at least are both consistent with it.

This sort of ambiguity is not commonly found among the basic moral notions. It may be difficult to say whether an act of killing is murder or not, but it is hard to imagine making out a credible case that a given act is the *opposite* of murder; partly because it is hard to say what would count as the opposite of murder. Robin Hood's distinctive approach to the redistribution of wealth might just count as an act of giving, rather than an act of taking, but, even in this case, I think our ordinary linguistic intuitions would not allow us to describe his act of taking from the rich as *itself* an act of giving to the poor, even though we recognize that he is taking something *in order to* give it to the poor.

With respect to the language of virtues and vices, on the other hand, it is very often the case that a specific act can be construed as either virtuous or vicious, depending on the point of view that is taken towards the action. It is even possible sometimes plausibly to describe one and the same act as an act of a specific virtue and of its contrary vice. We would not describe one and the same action in contrary ways from the same vantage point, but it is significant that we can often see the plausibility of such contrary descriptions from different standpoints. For example: ordinarily, we think of a glutton as a big eater. The person who eats sparingly would seem clearly to offer an example of moderation. Yet C. S. Lewis suggests, credibly, that daintiness of appetite can actually reflect a kind of gluttony, if gluttony is understood as an inappropriate focus on food.[18]

Why is the language of the virtues ambiguous in this way, whereas the language of the moral rules generally is not? The reason is that our concepts of specific virtues and vices tend to be understood in reference to one another, in a way that the concepts associated with the moral rules (normally) are not. Typically, our concepts of virtues and vices are paired together, as for example, courage and cowardice, chastity and lust, kindness and cruelty, and so on. Moreover, many of our concepts of specific virtues are linked with vices considered to be false versions, or similitudes, of the virtue in question; for example, courage and rashness, chastity and frigidity, kindness and squeamishness, or tough-mindedness and cruelty.

Because our concepts of specific virtues are not only open-textured, but interlinked with one another, we normally cannot apply this language to concrete actions without making some reference, whether implicit or explicit, to a wider context of evaluations. We have already observed that the same may be said of the basic moral notions. Even so, in the majority of cases, where the application of a basic moral rule is straight-forward, we can make use of the relevant language in an intelligible fashion without necessarily needing to place it in any wider context. It is only when we cannot be sure how to apply a given moral rule that we feel the need of appealing to a wider context of interpretation. With reference to the virtues, on the other hand, we normally stand in need of such a wider context in order to apply the relevant language intelligibly and cogently. It is possible to apply concepts of specific virtues and vices without making any such reference, moving simply at the level of the typical instantiations of the relevant qualities. But, as Pincoffs' treatment of indoctrination and moral education illustrates, this sort of application breaks down very quickly.

It will not do, therefore, to turn from the language of moral rules to the language of the virtues, as if these were two alternative approaches to moral judgement, one of them problematic, the other not so problematic. For one thing, these two sorts of normative concepts perform different functions, neither of which can be reduced to the other, or eliminated from our repertoire of normative discourse. More to the point, the language of the virtues is, if anything, *more* problematic than the language of the traditional moral rules.

It does not follow that the virtues should, therefore, be relegated once again to the marginal status that they had until recently in moral philosophy. Pincoffs and his colleagues who insist on the importance and centrality of the virtues are surely right to point out that this language reflects insights and concerns which are present only obliquely, or not at all, in the basic moral notions and their correlative rules. Nor do we stand in need of a modern theory of the virtues, if we are to recover these insights. Yet a miminalistic account of the virtues such as Pincoffs offers does not have enough substantive force to enable us to use the language of the virtues in a cogent way. Once again, we find ourselves in need of a third alternative, which will enable us to bring some coherence and critical perspective to an area of normative discourse, without forcing it into the Procrustean bed of a moral theory in the modern mode.

In the previous chapter, I argued that Aquinas orders the basic moral notions, and thus expands their normative power, by placing them in a wider metaphysical context. It will not be surprising to find that he gives order and normative force to his account of the virtues in the same way.

Before turning to an examination of Aquinas' account of the virtues, one caveat is in order. My emphasis on the *language* of the virtues might suggest that our first concern as moral agents should be to develop a facility in that language. That is not at all the case. To the contrary, the same thing must be said in this connection as was said with reference to the basic moral notions and their correlative rules: what is essential for the person as a moral agent is not the capacity for using the language of morality, but, rather, the capacity to *understand* the concept of morality, which capacity is centrally manifested in the capacity to *act intelligently* in the application of this concept. Yet, if we are to give a philosophical account of that capacity, there is no way to do so except by reflection on the relevant concepts, as those are mediated through language.

VIRTUE AND THE PERFECTION OF ACTION

In the previous chapter, we noted that Aquinas organizes the second part of the *Summa theologiae* around an analysis of human actions, including the criteria for their evaluation. Given this, we would expect to find that he places his account of the virtues in the context of his overall account of what it is for the human person to act, and to act well in pursuit of her natural and supernatural happiness. As he indicates in the introduction to I–II 6, quoted in the previous chapter, that is indeed his plan. Thus, we would expect that Aquinas brings order and coherence to his treatment of the virtues by placing this account within the wider context of the human good, just as he did with reference to the basic moral notions. In order to understand his treatment, it will, therefore, be helpful to review the main points of his general account of goodness, before turning to his account of the virtues as such.[19]

Recall that the concept of goodness, for Aquinas, is intimately connected with the concepts of being, causality, and order. To be good without qualification is to fulfill the ideal of some specific kind of creature, that is to say, to be perfect in accordance with that ideal. Correlatively, whatever exists is good to some degree, since it is *ipso facto* perfected to some extent or it would not exist at all (I 5.3). The creature's exercise of causality is thus to be interpreted normatively, in terms of its orderly progression from a less to a more complete instantiation of its own specific ideal (1 5.4). At the same time, in and through this progression, the creature fits into a wider causal matrix which also has its proper order, and, therefore, enjoys a kind of goodness and existence in its own right.

Aquinas holds that the rational creature is to be distinguished from all lower kinds of creatures by the fact that, whereas the latter are directed towards their final end by the natural unfolding of their causal powers, the rational creature can only attain her specific perfection through actions which are knowingly directed by her towards the attainment of that end, understood under the rubric of happiness (1 22.2 *ad* 4; 1 103.1 *ad* 5; I–II 1.3, 8; I–II 12.5). Correlatively, those of her active powers which presuppose consciousness for their operation are all dependent in some way on the functioning of her intellect. Not only is her will, which is the form of appetite proper to a rational creature, dependent for its activation in a particular act of choice on an intellectual judgement that a given object is good (1 82.4; I–II 8.1), but her passions, which exist in some form in all animals, always presuppose some cognitive judgement, grounded in reason, that a particular object is desirable or noxious (as the passions of sub-rational animals do not; 1 81.3). That is to say, the active powers of the human creature are not directed to particular objects, as the powers of sub-rational creatures are (1 105.4; I–II 10.1, 2). These powers must be qualified by dispositions over and above their natural dynamisms, if the human person is to be able to move towards her individual perfection and the attainment of wider forms of goodness through actions knowingly directed towards that goal (I–II 49.4; I–II 55.1).

These abiding dispositions, which direct the active powers of the human creature towards particular sorts of actions, are nothing other than the virtues (I–II 55.1). At this point, we should note that the term, "virtue," is wider than our discussion so far has suggested, since it includes intellectual qualities such as knowledge and wisdom, as well as practical capacities such as proficiencies in the arts (I–II 56.3; I–II 57; I–II 58.3). And of course, virtues of these sorts are morally neutral. However, those virtues which shape the passions and the will, and the intellect, in so far as it is directed towards human action *per se*, are necessarily moral, since the desiderative faculties are the immediate springs of action, and Aquinas holds that particular actions are never morally neutral (I–II 18.9). To the extent that an individual's moral virtues are perfected, that is to say, moral virtues in the most proper sense, they will perfect her active powers in such a way as to lead to actions which are good without qualification, in that they fully promote or instantiate the attainment of her specifically human good (I–II 55.3,4; I–II 65.1). In other words, perfected virtues will always give rise to morally good actions, in contrast to the imperfect virtues, which also qualify the desiderative faculties, but in such a way as typically to result in actions which are good only in some limited respect (I–II 65.1). And so, Aquinas accepts Augustine's definition of a moral virtue, not as any habit, but as a habit which is productive of good actions: "Virtue is a good quality of the mind, by which we live righteously, of which no one can make bad use, which God brings about in us, without us" (I–II 55.4; the last clause, Aquinas adds, applies only to the infused virtues).

At this point, we must ask what it means, more specifically, to say that the virtues perfect the active powers of the human person in such a way as to give rise to actions that are good without qualification. We must recall that the human person, unlike sub-rational creatures, can only move towards her specific perfection through her own actions, knowingly directed towards the attainment of that end, understood under the rubric of happiness. In other words, precisely because she is a rational creature, capable of determining her own actions on the basis of rational knowledge, the human person's capacity to act well will be a component, and not merely a disposable means, of her attainment of perfection as a human being. Thus, virtue, which enables the human person to act well, that is to say, in accordance with her specific nature as a rational animal, can be understood as a disposition by which the human soul is informed by reason (II–II 47.6; compare I–II 57.5; I–II 58.2). At the same time, in Aquinas' view, human goodness cannot be understood in terms of a purely formal adherence to the canons of reason. In order to act in accordance with reason, it is necessary that the person act and sustain action in accordance with a correct understanding of what it means to be a good human being (I–II 1.2,7; I–II 3.2).

Perfected moral virtue, for Aquinas, is thus a disposition by which the individual translates her general knowledge of that in which her good consists into specific actions. But just how does this translation take place? Is it sufficient for the individual to know what her true good is, in order to do it? Understood in this way, the virtues would consist in nothing other than a settled tendency to act in accordance with one's correct conception of the human good.

But Aquinas rejects this conception of true virtue. After setting forth this view, which he attributes to Socrates, he goes on to say:

> This, however, proceeds from a false supposition. For the appetitive part does not obey reason entirely at command, but with some contradiction; hence, the Philosopher says, in I *Politics*, that reason commands the appetitive parts by a political rule, by means of which, that is to say, one [rules over] free people, who have the right, in some instance, of contradicting [one's directives] ...
>
> So, therefore, in order for the human person to act well, it is necessary not only that the reason be well disposed through a habit of intellectual virtue, but also that the appetitive power be well disposed through the habit of moral virtue. And so, just as the appetite is distinguished from the reason, so moral virtue is distinguished from intellectual virtue. Hence, as the appetite is the principle of the human act in so far as it participates to some degree in reason, so moral habit has the character of human virtue, to the extent that it is conformed to reason. (I–II 58.2)

It is not enough to attain an intellectual grasp of the human good in order to be good without qualification; a right conception of the human good is essential, on Aquinas' view, but it must inform the agent's passions and will, as well as her intellect, if she is to attain human goodness.

Moreover, it must be remembered that, for Aquinas, human goodness does not just consist in the attainment of an external standard of rationality or perfection; it also, and intrinsically, consists in the perfection of the human capacities which are exercised in act. It is not enough for the individual to do the right sorts of things, in order to be truly virtuous; she must do them well, that is to say, out of well-formed passions, a good will, and intelligent judgement. Done in this way, a particular act is good, not only by the external standards of the basic moral notions, but also as a manifestation of the perfection of the individual's powers of action:

A virtue implies the perfection of a power . . . Now it is necessary that the end of which any power is capable is good, because every evil implies a certain defect, and hence Dionysius says . . . that every evil is a weakness. For this reason, it is necessary that the virtue of anything be said to be ordained to good. Hence, human virtue, which is an operative habit, is a good habit, and is productive of the good. (1–11 55·3)

The overall concept of virtue must be understood in terms of the dual meaning of goodness, as that is applied to the human agent. A good act is an act which corresponds to the general standard of human action, that is, conformity to reason. At the same time, it is also good in the sense of actualizing, and therefore perfecting, the powers of the agent, including passions, will, and intellect. This dual reference for goodness and virtue provides Aquinas with the framework that he needs in order to bring coherence to the language of the virtues.

It provides him with a framework, not a theory in the modern sense; this point should be underscored. Aquinas does not *derive* an account of the virtues from his general account of goodness in action. Rather, he begins, as we do, with a diverse and heterogeneous tradition of the virtues, which is mediated to him through the diverse sources which inform the *Summa*, in addition to the scholarly and practical conversations which animated his own society. He brings coherence to this tradition by means of his overall framework for understanding the virtues, but the resultant account is dialectically argued, and the different virtues are related to one another analogically. Aquinas' treatment of the virtues is, in this respect, similar to his treatment of the basic moral notions. That is, he brings order to a received account by means of an overall, meta-physically informed framework, but he does not attempt to impose a strict deductive order on that account; his analogical reasoning is looser, if you will, but also more flexible than Kant's derivations.

How does the framework of Aquinas' overall account of virtue enable him to bring some order to his account of the virtues? We now turn to that question.

THE DIALECTICS OF VIRTUE

At the beginning of his discussion of the virtue of justice, Aquinas offers an important key for understanding his account of the virtues. He remarks, "For since every virtue is a habit which is a principle of a good act, it is necessary that a virtue be defined through the good act concerning the proper matter of the virtue" (II–II 58.1). The matter of the virtue, properly speaking, is the recurring situation of human life which provides the immediate context for the virtue in question; for example, justice is concerned with actions which involve others, and not just the agent herself. However, since these recurring contexts are themselves mediated, in part, through traditions of reflection on the virtues, Aquinas' appeal to the matter of a virtue requires him to begin with the virtues as they are actually understood in these multiple traditions. At the same time, the qualification, "the *good* act" introduces an element of normative judgement into Aquinas' appropriation of these traditions.

In this way, Aquinas sets up a dialectic for understanding a particular virtue which enables him to move between the paradigmatic instances of the virtue, as mediated by the traditions on which he draws, and the area of concern which gives these paradigms their point, as he attempts to arrive at a more adequate concept of specific virtues. This dialectic is controlled, in turn, by the notion of goodness, which is understood both in terms of external normative criteria and in terms of the perfection of the agent's powers.[20]

At the same time, this dialectical method enables Aquinas to redescribe virtues, and their correlative vices, without cutting the threads that bind him to a particular traditional discourse.

By using this dialectic, Aquinas is able, first of all, to draw illuminating distinctions between virtues and their similitudes. For example, he distinguishes between true prudence and prudence of the flesh on the grounds that the former directs the intellect towards what is truly good, whereas the latter involves cleverness in attaining partial and limited goods (II–II 55). That much is obvious and uninteresting. However, Aquinas is able, in addition, to take account of the fact that shrewdness resembles prudence in so many ways, in such a way as to acknowledge and illuminate the ambiguity of the traditional language about prudence (note his comment at II–II 55.1 *ad* 1). He does so, first of all, by acknowledging that prudence and prudence of the flesh both concern the same exigencies of human life, and are conceptualized in terms of paradigmatic actions which are very similar, at least over a wide range of examples of truly and seemingly prudent acts. As he says in the introduction to II–II 53, the similitudes of prudence (which include prudence of the flesh) have "a certain false similitude to prudence, which comes about, that is, through the abuse of those things which are required for prudence." In this way, he does justice to the lived context which renders both prudence and prudence of the flesh intelligible. At the same time, by reminding us of the distinction, obvious enough in itself, between the truly good and the seeming or partial good, he introduces a further qualification into our understanding of the matter of the virtue of prudence, in terms of which we can understand prudence of the flesh as a distorted form of prudence. Finally, because a distortion preserves, and is intelligible in terms of, the good that it distorts, Aquinas is also able to do justice to the traditional insight that there *is* after all something admirable about prudence of the flesh, as well as prudence.

Aquinas proceeds in a similar way when he turns to the more interesting problem of virtues which are in some way incomplete or limited in scope, but which are none the less truly good qualities in a restricted sense. The key to his method of proceeding here is provided by a distinction that he draws between perfect and imperfect virtues:

Moral virtue may be taken either as perfect, or as imperfect virtue. Imperfect moral virtue, indeed ... is nothing other than a certain inclination in us to do some work of a kind that is good, whether that inclination is from nature or custom. And taking the moral virtues in this way, they are not connected. For we see one who, from nature or from some habit, is prepared to do works of liberality, who none the less is not prepared for works of chastity. However, a perfect moral virtue is a habit directed to a good work done well. And taking the moral virtues in this way, we ought to say that they are connected, as nearly everyone agrees. (I–II 65.1)

We will return to the claim that the virtues are connected at the end of this chapter. What is of importance at this point is the distinction that Aquinas draws between "a certain inclination in us to do some work of a kind that is good" and "a perfect moral virtue," which "is a habit directed to a good work done well." This distinction clearly reflects his overall understanding of goodness, with its dual reference to external norms of action and the perfection of the agent's powers of action. At the same time, it enables him to acknowledge the common usage, according to which any capacity to do good works can be called a virtue in some limited sense, however it is acquired and whatever the details of its functioning may be. From the perspective of his more adequate understanding of a virtue, Aquinas is able to turn to the traditions that he draws on, and to interpret the good qualities that they celebrate as being virtues in a secondary and derivative sense, derivative, that is, from the perspective of what he has established to be the primary sense of virtue. Yet this is not a sheer imposition of an arbitrary criterion onto a traditional framework; to the contrary, Aquinas' proposal for the focal meaning of the concept of virtue is validated in part by its explanatory power, seen in terms of his ability to make sense of the diversity of traditional ideas of virtue. Thus, Aquinas' reformulation of the traditional idea of a virtue in the light of his overall account of goodness provides him with a perspective for evaluating received traditions, but it does not cut him adrift from those traditions or prevent him from acknowledging what is valid in them.

The distinction between perfect and imperfect virtue, or

some analogue of that distinction, is pressed into service in a variety of contexts. We have just seen that Aquinas employs it to distinguish between the good qualities, derivatively understood as virtues, which are possessed by persons who are not good overall, and the virtues, properly so called, of the truly virtuous person. In another context, he distinguishes between the self-restraint of the continent individual, who desires what is not in accordance with her overall good but acts appropriately none the less, with the temperance of the virtuous person, who desires what is truly good for her (II–II 155.1). Self-restraint is good, says Aquinas, but it lacks the quality of true virtue. Similarly, modest shame is a good quality, but it lacks certain essential qualifications of true virtue; it is a simple passion, and its presence presupposes a defect, namely, the real danger that the individual might fall into vice (II–II 144.1). Finally, we should note that even those qualities which *are* virtues in an unqualified sense, that is, the acquired virtues of someone who has attained complete human virtue, fall short of the standard of perfection that is set by the theological virtues (I–II 62.2 *ad* 2).

Finally, Aquinas' dialectical approach to the language of the virtues provides him with a framework within which to bring an analogical unity to traditional ways of naming and classifying the virtues. What concerns Aquinas at this point is not the problem of distinguishing virtues from their similitudes, or virtues *tout court* from virtues, derivatively speaking. Rather, the issue here is the correct interrelationship of the true virtues. Moreover, since the language of the diverse virtues is interlinked, as we saw in the first section, an account which brings an order into this language will also necessarily provide a framework within which to redescribe the virtues in terms of higher virtues.

This framework is structured around Aquinas' interpretation of the traditional schemas of the cardinal and theological virtues, which he inherited from a variety of sources in his tradition. At I–II 61.3, he explains the rationale for the traditional schema of the four cardinal virtues, that is, prudence, justice, fortitude, and temperance, as follows:

So therefore, we can consider the aforesaid four virtues in two ways. In one way, they can be considered as general formal reasons. And according to this way [of understanding them], they are said to be principle [virtues], as if general to all the virtues: as, for example, that every virtue which brings about the good respecting the consideration of reason, is said to be prudence; and every virtue which brings about the good of what is due and upright in operations is said to be justice; and every virtue which restrains and presses down the passions is said to be temperance; and every virtue which brings about firmness of soul against any of the passions is said to be fortitude . . .

They can be considered in another way, however, in accordance with the way in which these virtues are named from that which is principle in each respective matter. And so [understood], these are special virtues, divided over against others. For they are said to be principle [virtues] with respect to other [virtues] because of the greater significance of the matter [of each]: as for example, that prudence is said of [the virtue] which is directive; and justice, [of the virtue] which is concerned with due actions among equals; temperance, [of the virtue] which restrains desires for the pleasures of touch; and fortitude, [of the virtue] which strengthens against dangers of death. (I–II 61.3)

The four cardinal virtues are interpreted analogically, with the latter interpretation providing the focal meaning (as Aquinas indicates at I–II 61.4). What is striking about this passage is the way in which Aquinas draws on the focal idea of goodness in action to bring coherence to a complex and diverse tradition. Taken in the first sense, the cardinal virtues are understood in terms of general characteristics of virtuous action. Taken in the second, and primary, sense, they are understood as specific virtues, grounded in those faculties of the soul that are the springs of human action, which represent the most paradigmatic or essential form of the perfection of the respective faculties. Understood in this latter sense, each of the cardinal virtues provides the focal meaning in terms of which the diverse virtues of the faculties of the human soul can be organized and understood.

The cardinal virtues, taken as qualities which can be acquired by human effort, are directed to, and in some degree constitutive of, human happiness, understood as the perfection of the human agent in accordance with the ideal of her specific kind of being (I–II 5.5; I–II 62.1). Aquinas also believes that the human person is directed towards the supernatural end of direct personal union with God, who will be known and loved in the beatific vision as a personal reality, and not merely as the First and Final Cause of the created order (I 12.1; I–II 109.3 *ad* 1). Because this aim exceeds the natural capacities of the human creature (or any other creature, for that matter), it can only be attained through the exercise of operative capacities which are bestowed by God "entirely from without" (I–II 63.1). Chief among these are the theological virtues of faith, hope and charity (I–II 62.1, 3). Moreover, since charity can only work in and through the various faculties of the person, it is always infused with analogues to the acquired cardinal virtues (I–II 65.3). The infused cardinal virtues are specifically different from their acquired counterparts because they are directed towards a different end, and, moreover, they are experienced and lived out in a somewhat different way, even though they are grounded in the same faculties of the soul and concern the same matter as do their acquired analogues (I–II 63.4 *ad* 2; cf. II–II 26.6). Thus, the wider framework of the theological virtues bestows a further context in terms of which the virtues can be redescribed.

The framework of the cardinal and theological virtues provides Aquinas with the organizing schema of much of the *secunda secundae*, in which he offers a critical and constructive account of the normative traditions that he has received. In order to extend this framework to take in the details of that tradition, he introduces a further set of distinctions by means of which to extend his analogical account of the virtues. That is, he introduces the notion of the parts of the virtues, in terms of which he can relate diverse specific virtues to the central cardinal or theological virtues. Lee Yearly offers a lucid summary of Aquinas' methodology:

Aquinas argues that a virtue can have three parts. First are the qualities, the component parts, that help shape a single virtue's action; for example, memory and foresight in prudence. Second are those distinctive virtues, allied virtues, that share the essential characteristic of the primary virtue but fail to express it fully, even if they may express other qualities of the primary virtue more fully than it does; for example, the wit to judge when exceptions to rules are needed (*gnome*). Third are those separable and substantially different activities of a virtue, the types of a virtue, that appear when the virtue operates in distinct spheres of life; for example, military and political prudence.[21]

He goes on to explain how this set of distinctions provides Aquinas with a way of organizing a heterogeneous tradition of ideals of the virtues:

Aquinas uses these ideas to organize into one systematically organized whole the panoply of virtues and ideas about specific virtues that he inherits. Augustinian ideas about patience, for example, can be seen as component or allied parts of courage, even though courage largely is defined in Aristotelian terms; Cicero and Aristotle's different accounts of magnanimity can be "synthesized" and fitted into courage's hierarchical structure.[22]

At the same time, this framework allows, and requires, Aquinas to redescribe virtues in terms of one another, and to allow for multiple redescriptions from the perspective of different virtues within his overall framework. No one can exercise moral virtue in the full sense apart from prudence, nor can prudence function without the moral virtues (I–II 57.5, I–II 58.4,5); thus, every act of moral virtue, in the unqualified sense of virtue, will also be describable as a prudent act, and every act of prudence will also involve the exercise of some other moral virtue. Similarly, because the common good, which is the object of justice, supersedes the good of the individual (in some respects), any temperate or brave action can also be described as an act of justice (II–II 58.5), and some kinds of actions which are most readily understood as violations of the norms of temperance are also correctly described as acts of injustice (II–II 154.1 *ad* 2).

Thus, Aquinas offers a way of addressing the difficulties inherent in the language of the virtues that were identified in the first section of this chapter. He offers a framework within which he can distinguish virtues from their similitudes and virtues *simpliciter* from virtues derivatively so called. Moreover, he offers a way of understanding how the virtues are mutually interpreting, in a framework structured around the notion of goodness in action.

This framework, however, is only one part of Aquinas' account of the virtues. It provides us with the grammar of the language of the virtues, as it were, but it offers little insight into the substantive content of the concept of virtue and notions of the virtues.

This brings us to a further aspect of Aquinas' reformulation of traditional language in the light of his understanding of human goodness and the goodness of action. Aquinas inherited from Aristotle the doctrine that virtuous action is activity in accordance with a mean, which he takes to be equivalent with activity that is in accordance with reason. Yet this language is far from clear as it stands, so much so that Daniel Nelson concludes that it is empty of any content, over and above the *ad hoc* deliverances of prudence in specific instances of choice.[23] This conclusion is too quick; Aquinas does give a substantive meaning to action in accordance with reason, thus, to the mean of a virtue, although, as we noted in the previous chapter, these expressions, too, must be understood analogically.

At the same time, it is impossible to understand Aquinas' interpretation of the mean of the virtues without a closer examination of his account of prudence and its relationship to the moral virtues properly so called. (Prudence, which is strictly speaking an intellectual virtue, is counted as a moral virtue in a derivative sense because it is the virtue of the practical intellect; I–II 58.3 *ad* I.) We now turn to that account.

PRUDENCE AND THE MORAL VIRTUES

At the beginning of Aquinas' account of prudence in the *secunda secundae*, we read that prudence is an intellectual virtue (II–II 47.1), and, more specifically, a virtue of the practical intellect (II–II 47.2), which has as its distinctive matter the application of general principles to particular actions (II–II 47.5), with an aim to the overall perfection of the agent's life (in contrast to the arts; I–II 57.4). As such, prudence is necessarily concerned with contingent singulars, and, even at its most perfect, the deliberations of prudence lack the certainty of science, which deals with universals (II–II 47.3). Its central actions are to inquire with respect to what is to be done in a given situation, to form a judgement based on that inquiry, and to command the action or actions so determined (II–II 47.8). The component parts of prudence are memory, reason, intellect, teachableness, cleverness, foresight, circumspection, and caution (II–II 48.1). As we would expect, such a complex capacity is not easily acquired, for it requires experience attained over time (II–II 47.14 *ad* 3), as well as a facility in judgement that is unevenly distributed (II–II 47.15). Nor is prudence invariably retained, because it can be corrupted through distortions of the passions, or obscured (although not corrupted) through the disintegration of the intellect (II–II 47.16).

Just as prudence perfects the practical intellect, so the moral virtues properly so called perfect the appetites; fortitude and temperance perfect the passions, and justice perfects the rational appetite of the will. The former two virtues inform the passions in such a way that the agent desires and feels aversion to what is truly good or bad, seen from the perspective of her overall true good as a human being. The will, which is already directed towards the individual's overall good by its very nature, is perfected by justice in such a way as to orient the individual towards the common good (I–II 56.6).

We have already observed that, on Aquinas' view, the cardinal virtues are connected, in such a way that whoever fully possesses one of them necessarily has them all (I–II 65.1). More specifically, he asserts that the moral virtues properly so called cannot exist without prudence (I–II 58.4), nor can prudence in its turn exist without the moral virtues (I–II 58.5).

There are at least two ways of reading these texts which would be natural, but wrong. On the first of these readings, Aquinas is saying that prudence enables the agent to discern the sorts of actions that she should be doing, and the virtues of the passions and the will simply bring the appetites into line with aims that have been discerned, in advance, by prudence itself. As Giuseppe Abbà shows, in his excellent study of the development of Aquinas' thought on this subject, that was indeed Aquinas' view in his earlier writings, particularly in the *Scriptum super sententiis*.[24] In those works, moral virtue is understood in terms of participated rectitude, through which the passions are conformed to aims that are presented to them, as it were pre-formed, by reason. Yet by the time of the writing of the *Summa theologiae*, the language of participated rectitude no longer plays a central role in Aquinas' account of the virtues. This would suggest that by this point, he does not interpret the relation between prudence and the moral virtues in this way.

We can be sure that he does not, because he explicitly says that prudence does not set the aims of the moral virtues. In II–II 47.6, after asking whether prudence determines the end of the moral virtues, Aquinas denies that it does:

The end of moral virtues is the human good. Now the good of the human soul is to be in accordance with reason ... Hence, it is necessary that the ends of the moral virtues preexist in the reason ... certain things are in the practical reason as conclusions, and among these are those things which are directed toward an end, at which we arrive from a consideration of the ends themselves. And these [that is, those things that are directed towards an end, and therefore are in practical reason as conclusions] belong to prudence, which applies universal principles to the particular conclusions of operations. (II–II 47.6)

More specifically, he adds, natural reason, functioning as synderesis, determines the ends of the moral virtues (II–II 47.6 *ad* 1). At the same time, it is important to remember that intellectual knowledge of the appropriate ends of action does not suffice, by itself, to generate actions in accordance with those ends. It is also necessary that the agent be disposed in such a way as to want to act in accordance with reason, whatever specifically that may mean in a given situation. These dispositions are provided by the moral virtues: "an inclination towards a due end ... is [given] through the habit of moral virtue" (I–II 65.1; cf. I–II 58.2, I–II 65.3).

Taken by itself, II–II 47.6 might suggest that prudence is simply a capacity to discern effective and appropriate means by which to attain the predetermined ends of the moral virtues. But an examination of the next article corrects that impression. For there we read that it does belong to prudence to determine the mean of the moral virtues. The mean, Aquinas goes on to explain, is nothing other than conformity with reason, with respect to that area of life that is the matter of the virtue in question (II–II 47.7). At the same time, conformity with reason has different, although analogous, meanings for the different virtues. For temperance and fortitude, it is specified by a direct reference to the individual's own good, whereas, for justice, it is specified with reference to the good of another (I–II 64.2). Thus fortitude and temperance aim at a rational mean, whereas the mean of justice is a real mean; it reflects impersonal standards of equity, and not simply the exigencies of the individual's good, narrowly conceived. In either case, however, what concretely counts as the good of oneself or another in a given respect must be determined by prudence (II–II 47.7, especially *ad* 3; cf. I–II 66.3 *ad* 3).

The critical point is this. Any interpretation of the inseparable connection between prudence and the moral virtues properly so called must take account of the intimate dialectical interrelationship that obtains between them in practice. The mistaken interpretations that we have been considering go wrong precisely because they oversimplify that interaction, taking either prudence or the moral virtues to set criteria for virtuous action independently, thereby placing the other in a secondary, essentially ancillary role. But Aquinas insists on the interconnectedness of the cardinal virtues in practice, because he has come to realize that both the moral virtues and prudence play an irreducible part in determining the norms of virtuous action.[25]

On the one hand, the virtues of the appetites are not just desires to do good deeds, which are independently prescribed by prudence. Rather, they find expression in the individual's desires for the good, both in general terms, and in terms of her admiration and desire for the fitting, the noble, the decent, the praiseworthy, as these ideals have been inculcated in her by her upbringing. These desires, in turn, set the orientation of the whole person, her mind as well as her passions and her will. Precisely because she desires the good, in general and in a variety of specific ways, the virtuous person notices certain features of a situation, and does not see, or discounts, other features. Some aspects of a state of affairs have a saliency for her that they would not have for someone who is not generally concerned about goodness.[26] Thus, the desires of the virtuous person inform her judgements in such a way as partially to determine the descriptions under which she views situations and thinks about her prospective actions.

At the same time, prudence consists in something more than the capacity to figure out how to attain the ends set by virtue. A little consideration makes it clear that this is not a realistic way to speak of virtuous activity anyway. While there may be circumstances in which the virtuous individual knows clearly what she needs to do in a given situation, and is puzzled about the means by which to carry out her good aim, normally the uncertainties of the well-meaning, virtuous person will not be like that. Compare, for example, the uncertainties of the individual who feels moved to give something to a charity, but cannot decide which charity is most effective, to the uncertainties of the father who wants to be generous to his son, but is worried that a large present of money would really be ungenerous, because it would encourage dependency and passivity on the boy's part. In the latter case, unlike the former, it is uncertain precisely what would count as a generous act. Prudence provides in the latter sort of case, in other words, a determination of what would count as a virtuous action in a specific situation; that is what it means to say that prudence determines the concrete content of the mean of the virtue, in specific instances of choice.

What this implies will vary from virtue to virtue and from case to case, however. With respect to fortitude and temperance and their associated virtues, the deliverances of prudence will have an ineluctable relation to the agent herself, because the mean of these virtues is determined with reference to the agent's own individual good (i–ii 60.2; i–ii 64.2; ii–ii 57.1; ii–ii 141.6). While the prudent person will be guided in her deliberations by the paradigms for sobriety or patience or whatever, her determinations of what counts as sober behavior (for example) for her will necessarily involve some reference to the balance of indulgence and abstinence that is most in accordance with her overall good.

On the other hand, the mean of the virtue of justice is determined with respect to objective criteria of fairness and equity between persons (i–ii 60.2; ii–ii 57.1). As such, the objective requirements of justice can be discerned and carried out, at least in some cases, by those who are not particularly virtuous or prudent; so much would seem to be implied, at any rate, by Aquinas' remarks at i–ii 100.1, to the effect that the norms of the Decalogue are readily apparent to most persons (and Aquinas does not have high expectations for the majority of persons; see i 49.3 *ad* 5; i 63.9; cf. i–ii 109.2). At the same time, it would be a mistake to conclude that the demands of justice are secondary or external to the life of virtue.[27] Justice, after all, is itself a virtue, one of the two principle virtues of the will (the other being charity), and, therefore, like temperance and fortitude, it is a perfection of the capacities for action of the individual who possesses it (i–ii 56.6; i–ii 60.3). Specifically, it directs the individual to the common good, which for Aquinas is necessary for the full perfection of the individual herself (i–ii 56.6; ii–ii 47.10; ii–ii 58.12); at the same time, it qualifies both temperance and fortitude, providing norms by which true temperance and fortitude can be distinguished from incomplete or counterfeit forms of these virtues (ii–ii 58.5,6).

This brings us to the question of the relation of prudence to the traditional moral rules. Many of those who would reject moral theorizing in the modern mode argue that we would do better to follow the example of the person of practical wisdom or prudence. On this view, what characterizes the prudent individual is precisely that she does not act in accordance with rules; at most, she might refer to maxims or summaries of the wise decisions of the past in discerning the proper course of action in a given circumstance. This view is well summarized by Martha Nussbaum, who remarks that rules can be helpful so long as we realize that they are "summaries or rules of thumb, highly useful for a variety of purposes, but valid only to the extent to which they correctly describe good concrete judgements, and to be assessed, ultimately, against these."[28] Similarly:

Rules and general procedures can be aids in moral development, since people who do not yet have practical wisdom and insight need to follow rules that summarize the wise judgements of others. Then too, if there is not time to formulate a fully concrete decision in the case at hand, it is better to follow a good summary rule or a standardized decision procedure than to make a hasty and inadequate contextual choice. Again, if we are not confident of our judgement in a particular case, if there is reason to believe that bias or interest might distort our particular judgement, rules give us a particular constancy and stability ...

But Aristotle's point in all these cases [and Nussbaum's, too] is that the rule or algorithm represents a falling off from full practical rationality, not its flourishing or completion.[29]

According to Nelson, this general position is also Aquinas' view.[30] However, this interpretation presupposes a dichotomy between practical wisdom or prudence, and rule-governed behavior, that Aquinas did not draw and that is wrong-headed in any case. As we saw in chapter 1, the understanding of rules as algorithms is not just inadequate or limited, but impossible as a way of following rules which are correlated with most of the generic concepts of a natural language. The prudent person applies moral rules through a process of judgement rather than employing a decision procedure similar to that of a mathematician, because *there is no other way to apply rules* of this kind. The imprudent or immature or wicked person would apply the same rule in the same *logical* way, although she would most likely do so badly in some way or another. Moreover, there is no fundamental difference between following a moral rule and acting out of a virtue. In each case, the intellect is guided by a set of paradigmatic examples of kinds of actions, which must be applied to a specific choice through an act of judgement. There are differences between the logic of moral rules as these are traditionally understood, and the logic of the virtues (apart from justice, as Aquinas understands it), but these are differences which can be traced to the substantive content and the point of each class of concepts, as we saw earlier in this chapter.

Is there any advantage, then, to being virtuous and prudent? What can the practically wise individual do, that the rest of us cannot? In order to answer this question, let us look again at the claim that, for the wise person, moral rules function as maxims.

There is some truth in the claim that moral rules function as maxims. Certainly, it is true that moral rules cannot be understood apart from some knowledge of the cases that exemplify them. However, the language of summarizing, the insistence on seeing rules as maxims or rules of thumb, suggests that rules are nothing more than condensed accounts of cases, which provide a shorthand reminder of past decisions, but add no new element to what we could (and ideally would) learn from a seriatim study of the cases themselves.

Yet this is hardly a realistic picture even of an ordinary summary, much less of the traditional moral rules. No summary is simply a collection of items. Every summary is guided by a rationale, and, unless that rationale is understood, neither can the summary itself be understood *as* a summary. The same can be said about any sort of classification whatever. In order to understand the biologist's system for the classification of animals, it is not enough to be able to say what sorts of creatures have been fitted into what categories. One must be able to explain the *point* of the classifications that have been made, and to make use of those classifications by applying them intelligently to new sorts of creatures.

Have I contradicted myself at this point, since I argued in chapter 1 that someone who grasps a concept, even in the context of a wider conceptual framework, will *not* be able to apply it with apodictic certainty in every case? No, because the capacity for intelligent application cannot, and need not, be equated with an ability to resolve any and all dilemmas of application with apodictic certainty. This capacity *does* involve, however, first of all, the ability to apply the concept in question in most cases, readily and with assurance, in such a way as to be generally persuasive to those who share the same conceptual scheme. If someone cannot *ever* apply a concept in such a way as to secure general agreement that she has done so correctly, then something is wrong, either with the individual's understanding, or with the concept itself. And, secondly, someone who can apply a concept intelligently will be able to interpret cases of ambiguous application in terms of the different considerations which inform the concept in question. That is, she will be able to explain what criteria for applying the concept are lacking in this case, or underdetermine its application, or perhaps, why the relevant criteria are in conflict in this instance.

Consider, again, what is involved in understanding the concept of murder, or, correlatively, the rule prohibiting certain kinds of killings, namely, murders. It is certainly true that we cannot understand the concept of murder unless we are familiar with cases of murders, cases, that is, in which it has been judged to be wrong to kill a human being. Yet it is not enough, in order to understand the concept of murder, simply to go through a list of cases in one's mind. Someone might be able to list a series of cases that counted as murder, and yet not realize that the salient similarities among the cases include the fact that, in each of them, someone is killed. Other sorts of misunderstandings are also possible. Consider the following reactions to a new sort of case: "That wouldn't be murder, because the person being killed is not from our country." Or, "That wouldn't be murder, because it involves killing people with bombs, and not with a knife, poison, or a gun." These sorts of responses would indicate that the individual making them had not grasped the point of the notion of murder.

The prudent person, then, will be characterized by her intelligent grasp of the point of the basic moral notions, and of the virtues, which will enable her to apply them intelligently in the various choices of her life. It should be emphasized again that her capacity is fundamentally a capacity for intelligent *action*, and not a capacity to describe good actions or to explain what she does, although normally she will have these capacities as well.

For the person who is not so prudent, however, the moral rules will function in the way that Nussbaum suggests they do, that is, as reminders of seriatim lists of cases. Because she has little or no intelligent grasp of the point of the rule, she will be reduced to the desperate expedient of attempting to imitate the moral paragons of the past without understanding. This deficiency may result in moral flightiness, or else in rigidity and a veneration for rules for their own sake.

THE CONNECTION OF THE VIRTUES

So far, I have skirted the issues raised by Aquinas' assertion of the connection of the virtues (which is a more accurate and less misleading way of speaking than the more traditional expression, "the unity of the virtues").[31] Yet this issue cannot be avoided indefinitely, because it is central both to Aquinas' account of the virtues, and to the alternative account of rationality that he offers to contemporary moral thought.

What does Aquinas mean when he asserts that, for the individual of perfected virtue, all the virtues are connected? Consider what he says in defense of this claim:

For this [the connection of the virtues], a twofold reason is assigned, in accordance with the diverse ways in which the cardinal virtues are distinguished. For as has been said, some distinguish them according to certain general conditions of the virtues, in so far as discretion pertains to prudence, rectitude to justice, moderation to temperance, firmness of the soul to fortitude, in whatever matter these things may be considered. And, according to this, the rationale for the connection [of the virtues] is clearly seen, for firmness does not have the praise of virtue if it be without moderation, or rectitude, or discretion, and the same rationale applies to the others ...

Others, however, distinguish the aforesaid virtues in accordance with their matter. And, according to this, the rationale for their connection is given by Aristotle in the 6th book of the *Ethics*. For, as has been said above, no moral virtue can be had without prudence, in that it is proper to moral virtue to make a right choice, since it is an elective habit. However, for a right choice [to be made], an inclination towards a due end, which is directly [given] through the habit of moral virtue, does not alone suffice, but one must also directly choose those things which are directed towards the end, which is done through prudence ... Likewise also, prudence cannot be possessed unless the moral virtues are also possessed, since prudence is right reason concerning things that can be done, towards which one is rightly related through the moral virtues. Hence, just as speculative science cannot be had without the understanding of principles, so prudence cannot be had without the moral virtues. From which it manifestly follows that the moral virtues are connected. (I–II 65.1; compare I–II 61.4 *ad* 1)

When Aquinas claims that the virtues are connected, he is actually making two claims. On the one hand, he claims that the general conditions for any virtuous act, which are traditionally associated with the cardinal virtues, must all be present in any specific action for it to count as virtuous in an unqualified sense. He also makes a second, more interesting claim, that the cardinal virtues, considered as specific and discrete virtues, are all necessarily present in the character of the truly virtuous person. Let us consider each of these claims in turn.

What are we to make of the first claim that the cardinal virtues, considered as general conditions for any virtuous action, are connected? On the face of it, this version of the connection of the virtues would appear less problematic. After all, if we are prepared to agree with Aquinas that an action which is in any way defective cannot be said to be a good act *simpliciter*, then it is not difficult to admit that an action which is deficient in one of the general characteristics of virtue is not fully virtuous. And this conclusion is congruent with our general perceptions. We may well admire the courage of the bank robber, or the cleverness of the extortionist, or the audacity of the high-stakes embezzler. But it is one thing to admire some aspect of an individual's action, and another to admire an action or an individual without qualification. We are unlikely to emulate the embezzler, or to hold Jesse James up as a model for the young.

The claim that the cardinal virtues are all connected in the character of the virtuous individual, in such a way that anyone who truly possesses one of these virtues, necessarily possesses them all, is more interesting. It is also a great deal less plausible, at least on first examination. After all, very few of us can claim to be perfect, or to know many saints, whether secular or ecclesiastical. Does it follow that the virtues possessed and exhibited by our imperfect selves are not true virtues? Aquinas apparently is forced by the logic of his analysis to say precisely that. It would seem that this claim can only be defended, if we take it as a kind of stipulation, to the effect that nothing counts as a virtue unless it is governed in its exercise by prudence, and informed by a grasp of the true human good. But this sort of stipulation, it will be said, is not terribly interesting, the more so as it sets up a condition for true virtue that is not likely to be met.[32]

It would be easy, faced with these objections, to dismiss out of hand Aquinas' assertion of the connection of the virtues. Yet to do so would involve giving up what is most attractive in his overall account of the virtues. His claim that the virtues are all connected in the character of the virtuous person is not simply an empty stipulation, but a necessary corollary of his overall account of virtue. As his explanation of this claim quoted above indicates, the thesis of the connection of the virtues follows from the logic of his analysis of the relationship between the moral virtues, properly so called, and prudence. The moral virtues cannot operate without the guidance of practical reason, which determines what counts as an appropriate action in each instance of choice. Correlatively, the intellect could not even begin to operate in a humanly good way, without the impetus of settled desires for goodness in its various forms, which both move the agent to act and direct her attention and her perceptions in the appropriate ways. If we are to understand virtue in this substantive way, then it follows ineluctably that the judgements and actions of someone who is deficient in one of the virtues will be systematically impaired and distorted, not only with respect to the typical actions of that virtue, but with respect to much or all that she does.

If Aquinas' thesis of the connection of the virtues is to be rejected, therefore, we should consider just what it is that we would want to drop from his overall analysis. Would we be willing to agree that fully virtuous action can take place without some process of reflection on what is truly good and what it means to do what is good, which is what prudence essentially involves? Or would we be prepared to admit that someone can be truly virtuous in the absence of settled desires for the good, and the sensibilities generated by those desires, that are central to the moral virtues? In the former case, we would find ourselves commending unthinking conformity, to someone's directions or to social conventions, as a fully good and admirable human life; in the latter case, we would be left with a cold fish as a paradigm for human goodness. My suspicion is that very few would be willing to admit that someone who is really virtuous, praiseworthy, and admirable without qualification, could be deficient in either intellectual judgement or feeling in these ways. If this is so, then the difficulty generated by the gap between Aquinas' claim of the connection of the virtues, and the reality of our experience, is a problem not only for him, but for us as well.

Moreover, the thesis of the connection of the virtues enables Aquinas to distinguish between virtues and their similitudes, because it implies that an action which is truly expressive of one cardinal virtue can be redescribed as an act of other cardinal virtues as well. We have already noted that every act of moral virtue, on Aquinas' terms, will necessarily also be a prudent act, and it will be an act of justice as well, at least in an extended sense. In this way, the thesis of the connection of the virtues gives content and force to Aquinas' definition of virtue as a *habitus* which produces good works, done well, and, correlatively, it provides him with the dialectical methodology through which he brings coherence to received traditions of the virtues.

There are at least two responses that might be made at this point. On the one hand, it might be said that while the logic of Aquinas' analysis has some merit, it is too rigid. He characterizes the virtues as absolutes, which one either has or lacks, whereas they are better understood as intensive qualities; one can be *somewhat* prudent, *minimally* chaste, and so on. Or it might be said that the ideal that Aquinas holds out is unrealistic because it does not take account of the complexities of psychological development. Someone who possesses both prudence and the moral virtues, generally speaking, may be limited in some area of life by psychological debility or the effects of conditioning.

However, Aquinas' account of the connection of the virtues can allow for both of these possibilities. He acknowledges that the ideal of perfected virtue cannot be attained in this fallen world, so long as what is in question are the acquired cardinal virtues (i–ii 109.2). Those who have received charity possess all the theological and cardinal virtues by infusion, since as we noted above, all the cardinal virtues are infused together with charity (i–ii 65.3). This does not mean that all those who are justified by God's grace are paragons of goodness, however. The infused cardinal virtues may be potentially present in an individual, who none the less has difficulty exercising them because of the effects of past habits, or some other similar cause (i–ii 65.3 *ad* 2). Indeed, one of the most important differences between the acquired and the infused cardinal virtues is precisely that the latter, unlike the former, can truly be possessed even by those who consistently experience some difficulty in exercising them. Thus, Aquinas does speak of at least some of the virtues in intensive terms (see, for example, ii–ii 47.12 *ad* 2, 3), and, while he naturally does not mention the negative effects of psychological conditioning and mild mental illness, his overall account could incorporate both under the rubric of impediments to the full exercise of the virtues.

It may be objected that Aquinas' account of the infused cardinal virtues will only be convincing to someone who accepts his doctrine of grace. That is true, of course, but my aim here is not to defend Aquinas' account of the acquisition of the virtues. My point is rather that Aquinas himself recognizes that the person of perfected acquired virtue represents an ideal, rather than an attainable possibility, given the actual conditions of human life. Yet this ideal is not meaningless. It provides a standard of integral goodness which can be sought after, and even approximated, although it can never be fully attained.[33]

Another objection would be that, if this interpretation is

correct, Aquinas' thesis of the connection of the virtues is vacuous after all. If this thesis holds out an ideal which we all fail to reach, then surely, it will be said, the ideal itself has no *practical* significance, and, therefore, no real meaning. Yet not all failures are of the same sort. Aquinas can allow that the individual of true infused virtue may have only a minimal degree of either insight or good feeling, and, moreover, he can admit that such an individual might have difficulty in exercising the virtues because of some impediment to action. He cannot admit that a truly virtuous individual, understood in terms of either the infused or the acquired virtues, might have a bad conception of the human good, or might consistently act without any reference at all to such a conception. That is, on Aquinas' view, the truly virtuous individual will possess both practical wisdom and moral virtue, even though her practice of both may be limited or impeded in various ways, and, furthermore, these virtues will be interconnected. Thus, even though the ideal of the connection of the virtues can only be approximated, none the less, the distinction between the individual who falls short of this ideal, and the individual who fails more seriously to attain virtue, does reflect real differences among individuals.

Correlatively, Aquinas' interpretation of the connection of the virtues illuminates certain kinds of moral failures, specifically those which can be traced either to some form of thoughtlessness or to insensibility.[34] Moreover, it suggests options for self-examination and self-improvement for those (and who among us is not included here) who do find themselves prone to moral failures that are persistently traceable to some failure of understanding or sensibility.

The central point of Aquinas' claim that the virtues are connected is not that the virtuous person is altogether perfect; rather, he insists on the integral practical connection between prudence and the moral virtues, if any of the virtues is to operate without distortion. What Michael Stocker says of Aristotle would apply to Aquinas as well:

Aristotle suggests that the virtues are inseparable, and in this sense unified, because of the relations between *phronesis*, practical wisdom, and the virtues ... The mutual determination just spoken of gives us another way to understand their inseparability and unity: wherever two or more virtues come into play, the mean of each is determined by all.

Because of the complexity of such mutual determination, we might well expect there to be no algorithm giving us the mean of each and of all – at least none that is available to us ... Thus, we see the need for practical wisdom and why practical wisdom ineliminably involves judgement.[35]

Above all, the ideal of the connection of the virtues is centrally important because it gives substance to the claim that the moral life, broadly construed to include the life of virtue, is coherent and can be lived in a rational fashion. Just as an appeal to the fundamental inclinations towards goodness provided Aquinas with a set of criteria for bringing order to the norms of justice, so the connection of the virtues, seen in the context of their dialectical interconnection and ordering, provides him with a criterion for bringing coherence and order into the life of virtue *tout court*. It may well be that this criterion sets up a standard for behavior that no one will ever meet. Without some such criterion, however, we would not be able even to conceive of what it would be to pursue a truly good and admirable life in a self-reflective and deliberate way. We would be at the mercy both of our own prejudices, and of whatever fragmentary ideals our society presented to us.

So understood, Aquinas' claim that the virtues are connected is not so much a philosophical/theological thesis, nor much less a rule for discriminating truly virtuous people from the not so virtuous, as it is a program for action for all those who want to grow in personal goodness. It offers a criterion for truly virtuous action, and it suggests a way of reflecting on our acts in the light of the context set by the ordered ideals of the cardinal virtues. This process, in turn, sets up its own dialectic of action and reflection, which is self-corrective and expansive. Here, again, we are given some substantive insight into what it means to be a prudent person; that is, the person of prudence is someone whose life displays this pattern of self-corrective reflection.

It is true that Aquinas' account of the virtues is cast in terms of a psychology that is dated in some respects, and, moreover, it incorporates some values that are problematic. Yet the fundamental ideal of moral rationality that is contained in that account is sound and potentially quite fruitful. In the next chapter, I will explore how this ideal might be reformulated in the light of a contemporary understanding of the human individual and the relation between the individual and society.

CHAPTER 5

The virtues reformulated

There is one further question that must be considered, if Aquinas is to serve as a genuine interlocutor in contemporary discussions of the virtues. That is, how far is it possible to defend Aquinas' account of the virtues, given the considerable distance between his understanding of the human agent, and our own?

It is no part of my purpose to defend Aquinas' philosophical psychology in its entirety. His analysis of the capacities of the human person in terms of distinct faculties of the soul is notoriously difficult to understand.[1] At any rate, we have simply moved too far beyond Aquinas to be in a position to appropriate his psychology as it stands. Aquinas has no sense of the dynamic development of the psyche, and, perhaps more importantly, he also has very little sense of the significance of social forces in shaping individual identity.

None the less, I do hold that Aquinas' account of the virtues is fundamentally sound, and it still retains its normative power. This claim depends on a certain interpretation of what *is* essential to Aquinas' account, as opposed to what can be left behind without sacrificing his central insights. On my reading of him, Aquinas' account of the virtues depends centrally on the prior account of goodness in action, according to which fully good human actions are both perfective of the powers and capacities of the agent, and good in their correspondence to the norms of reason, analogically understood in the context of the kind of act that is in question. This central insight, in turn, enables him to offer a cogent explanation of the traditional doctrines of the cardinal virtues and the connection of the virtues, and to make use of both doctrines to bring order and critical perspective to the diverse traditions that he incorporates into his *Summa*.

Aquinas' account of the virtues depends, in the final analysis, on his philosophical and (ultimately) theological account of goodness, in general and especially as applied to human persons and their acts. Yet, as we saw in the previous chapter, Aquinas does not simply impose a metaphysical schema onto traditional accounts of the virtues; rather, he allows these traditions to function as independent witnesses to the nature of goodness in action, extending and correcting his overall account through dialectical reflection on them. Approached in this way, the traditions and the practice of the virtues offer possibilities for understanding good action, and, therefore, the human good, which cannot be attained in any other way.

In this chapter I will offer a reformulation of Aquinas' account of the virtues in terms of a contemporary understanding of the human agent. If this reformulation is persuasive, it will indicate that Aquinas' overall account of goodness is at least plausible and worthy of further consideration, although that will be a task for another day. Moreover, this reformulation will bring to light a further implication of Aquinas' account of the virtues, which is more immediately relevant to the concerns that have emerged in our consideration of the moral act. Once his account of the virtues is reformulated in the light of a contemporary understanding of the human person, the self-critical and constructive power of that account becomes more evident than it was in Aquinas' own formulation.

That is, once this reformulation is completed, it will be easier to see how the prudent and virtuous person, as Aquinas would understand her, is capable of rational self-criticism and transformation of her individual and cultural ideals for virtue, precisely in and through her continued reflective practice of the virtues. This reformulation will further extend our understanding of what it is to be an individual of prudence. Even more, it will indicate that Aquinas' account of moral judgement, comprehensively construed to include the practice of the virtues, includes an account of rationality which is strong enough to generate principled social criticism, as well as individual self-reflectiveness.[2]

A full defense of the philosophical psychology that I find persuasive would call for yet another book. In what follows, I draw on an understanding of the human agent which, for me, ultimately is grounded in the thought of George Herbert Mead, but which also reflects many other streams of thought in the twentieth century, and which I believe would be widely shared, at least in its broad outlines.[3] Admittedly, for those who do not share my views on psychology, this reformulation may not appear to be much of an improvement on Aquinas' own views. Yet, even if that were the case, this exercise in reformulation would still serve to indicate that the central insights, and the normative power, of Aquinas' account of the virtues do not depend on the details of the psychological framework in which he casts them.

In my reconstruction, I depend upon the widely held view that the mental processes of the human agent presuppose, and are deeply conditioned by, the complex interactions between the individual and the wider community, as it is mediated to her by caretakers, peers, and the institutions of her society. It does not necessarily follow that the human person is wholly and irreducibly a product of her society, or much less that she does not have legitimate moral claims over against her community.[4] This view does imply, however, that the formation of a sense of individual identity, and the awareness of oneself as one human being among others, are both dependent on a capacity for empathetic identification with others. This capacity for identification begins to emerge as the child is taught to observe the norms of her society, to participate in its rituals, and, not least, to talk, and it continues as she tries on the roles and the recurrent narratives of her community through play-acting. As she is socialized in all these ways, she learns how persons in particular roles or recurrent situations can be expected to think and to feel, and this fund of information enables her both to orient herself in terms of her actual and potential place in her community, and to align herself correctly in relation to others with whom she enters into a network of mutual claims and expectations. If all goes well, the person who moves in this way through childhood and adolescence to adulthood will gradually arrive, through a complicated process of choice and discovery, at a sense of herself as a unified center of activity, who occupies a variety of roles and situations within her community, but cannot be reduced to any one of them or to their heterogeneous sum.

Let this suffice as a sketch of the psychology that I am supposing; further specifics will emerge as my reformulation of Aquinas' account of the virtues develops.

TEMPERANCE, FORTITUDE, AND THE EXIGENCIES OF ACTION

In the previous chapter, we saw that Aquinas defends the traditional identification of certain virtues as cardinal or principle on the grounds that these virtues are both necessary to, and especially expressive of, full human perfection in action. Certainly, it is the case that Aquinas' cardinal virtues of the passions, temperance and fortitude, name qualities of character which must be present, in some degree, if the agent is to act at all. Admittedly, the integral connection between these virtues and the capacity to act is obscured by the associations that have grown up around the traditional language of temperance and fortitude. For this reason, it may be helpful to begin by reminding ourselves of near-synonyms of these virtues, bracketing the question of whether, and in what sense, these really are names for exactly the same virtues.

The significance of temperance is more readily apparent if it is redescribed as self-control, or, perhaps, as self-restraint, or identified with one of its specific parts, such as chastity, sobriety, or moderation. In contemporary parlance, it might be described as a capacity for acting appropriately with respect to the fundamental organic processes of human life: appropriate consumption of food, appropriate use of stimulants and intoxicants, appropriate sexual behavior. Similarly, the virtue traditionally known as fortitude would be more recognizable to us if it were given its still more traditional name, courage, or identified in terms of one of its parts, for example, perseverance or patience.

However these virtues may be redescribed, they have in common some reference to what might be described as ubiquitous standing temptations of human life, which are built into the organism, so to speak. That is, they all find their context in recurring forms of desire or aversion that easily could, and often do, deflect individuals from pursuing wider aims through ongoing activity, and which often lead them, moreover, to act at variance with their standing commitments. In other words, these virtues are cultivated in response to a series of worries, so standard as to be almost banal. I want to live a healthy, reasonably successful life, but I am afraid of my tendencies to overeat and to lie in bed all morning, so I try to cultivate moderation at table, early rising, and a taste for exercise. I want to maintain a modicum of self-respect, the respect of others, and emotional security, but I am afraid of my tendencies to indulge in sexual pleasure and the delights of ersatz intimacy, so I cultivate sexual chastity and restraint in potentially erotic situations. I want to be a smashing success in my chosen profession, but I worry about my tendencies to be too easily discouraged, my fear of ridicule, my diffidence about putting myself forward, so I cultivate persistence and a certain fearlessness about speaking out and putting my work forward.

These examples have been deliberately chosen to set forth aims for action which are not especially praiseworthy, although they are not bad either. By so doing, I intend to underscore the point that some degree of temperance and fortitude, however understood, is necessary in order to pursue any sustained course of action whatever. Without some capacities for self-restraint, persistence, and courage, it would be difficult or impossible to sustain even the most ordinary aims and courses of activity. An agent who did not possess these qualities at all would be able to perform discrete actions, but she would not be able to do most of the things that involve sustaining a course of activity; the fulfillment of role responsibilities, the pursuit of aims that can only be attained by a series of actions, participation in most social actions, promising, contracting, all these would be prohibitively difficult for her. She would, therefore, scarcely be able to function even as a member of her society, much less as a self-determining agent.

So far, we have been speaking as if temperance and fortitude and their analogues were essentially capacities for self-control, exercised through a persistent pursuit of one's aims in the face of countervailing desires and aversions. Aquinas himself is ambivalent on this point. Sometimes, he speaks as if this were his view as well (see, for example, II–II 123.3; II–II 141.3 *ad* 2). However, his explicit account of these virtues is somewhat different. On this alternative view, what distinguishes the individual who possesses true temperance and fortitude from the individual who is merely capable of self-control is that, whereas the self-controlled person feels desires and aversions that are contrary to her aims and convictions, but manages to act appropriately anyway, the truly virtuous person does not even experience such contrary desires and aversions (II–II 155.1; cf. II–II 123.1 *ad* 2). She always responds emotionally in a way that is in accordance with her overall aims and commitments.

How plausible is this latter view? Does it seem likely that even the most saintly individual could attain a state in which she simply does not feel tempted to act contrary to her overall aims and commitments? And, if it does, would we consider this degree of self-consistency to be humanly desirable, something that is good for both the individual and the community?

The answer to these questions will vary with the virtue in question. Aquinas' view is most persuasive with respect to the virtues that have to do with desires, particularly desires for the simpler physical pleasures. We are more likely to approve of, and to try to emulate, the person whose desires for food, drink, and sexual pleasure are appropriate to the situation and to her overall aims. It is difficult to admire the man at the cocktail party who clearly longs to stuff himself with the sausage rolls, and to put away five or six martinis, even if he manages to hold himself in. It is better for him and for us that he does so, but we would be more likely to admire him, and he would probably be more comfortable with himself, if food and drink mattered less to him.

Some of the virtues associated with fortitude can also plausibly be understood along these lines. For example, the individual who needs to make an effort to be patient at every red light is preferable to the one who curses them all, but we would probably feel that it would be still better if she were sufficiently calm not to feel annoyed at petty difficulties. However, matters are somewhat different with respect to courage construed as persistence in the face of real danger. As Aristotle points out, there are some dangers so great that they would generate some fear in anyone.[5] If this is so, then it would appear that even the truly courageous individual might sometimes have to act contrary to real fear, yet we are not so likely to judge that her fears diminish her praiseworthy character, as we would be likely to deprecate the person whose desires are immoderate. This difference in judgement reflects a sense of what we can normally expect from one another. It is not all that difficult for most of us to cultivate appropriate attitudes towards physical pleasure, but almost no one, to the contrary, can avoid some fear at the prospect of death and at least some other dangers.

None the less, even granting these difficulties, and acknowledging Aquinas' own ambivalence on the question, there is a valid insight in his claim that, ideally, the temperate and brave individual does not have to struggle against passions which are contrary to her overall reasoned judgements about the good. This account of temperance and fortitude is positive rather than negative in its estimation of the passions and their place in a well-integrated character. The truly virtuous person is one who has succeeded in integrating the multitude of desires and aversions into a unified character, who is able, therefore, to perceive the world clearly from the standpoint of her central commitments, and to act accordingly. Granting the necessary qualifications with respect to serious fears, the person whose reactions are consistently at variance with her settled convictions indicates, by that very fact, that she has not yet attained that unity of character that is the bedrock of a fully virtuous life. Not only will she have to struggle in order to be good, but her perceptions of reality, the ways in which she construes her situation and her choices, will invariably be distorted on some occasions.

We now come to a critically important question, about which Aquinas does not say as much as we would like. That is, how are the virtues acquired? Aquinas' definition of a virtue as a *habitus* has led some to conclude that the virtues are acquired through the repeated imitation of the paradigms for virtuous behavior that the individual receives from her community (with some textual support; see I–II 55.2, I–II 63.2).[6] But clearly, this cannot be the whole story. True virtue, as Aquinas understands it, presupposes capacities for reasoned judgement that cannot be learned simply by imitating the example of someone else's goodness. Yet, as we have already noted, specific virtues cannot be conceptualized apart from some such paradigms either. Without some fund of agreed-upon paradigmatic cases, persons within a society would not have a shared conception of a virtue at all. Correlatively, there would be no basis on which to teach children and other beginners what is expected of them within society. There is a role for imitation in the acquisition of virtue, and yet, if an individual is to become proficient in virtue, she must at some point make the transition from imitation to a reasoned grasp of the point of the paradigms of virtuous action that she has learned. How does this come about?

It is here that a reformulation of Aquinas' account of the virtues in terms of a more socially grounded conception of the human person can begin to be illuminating. Let us consider how the acquisition of the virtues might be understood from such a perspective.

Seen from this perspective, it would appear that the process of learning a virtue begins as a process of internalizing the paradigms of that virtue, incorporating these into one's sense of oneself. For the child, this process will get underway through the coercion, more or less benevolent, of the child's caretakers and peers, through which she is forced to act in accordance with these paradigms. ("Don't be greedy! Don't gobble your food like that! And leave some for your little sister . . ." "What are you, chicken? Come on, I dare you!") Little by little, as the child acts on these paradigms, the ideals that inform them are internalized, until they become a part of her expectations for herself. At the same time, she develops in her understanding of them, she begins to get the "feel" for appropriate behavior, as she begins to grasp the point of self-restraint, persistence, and courage.

What is involved in coming to see the point of these virtues? It should be noted that the child who is forced, and then induced, to act in accordance with certain ideals of conduct is thereby subjected to a process of formation that extends to both intellect and emotions. By being forced to act in certain ways, and experiencing the responses of others to her actions, the child comes to think and to feel in ways that correspond to those actions. In this way, the raw materials of organic desire and aversion, which are the basic stuff of the psyche, are shaped in one direction rather than another, in such a way, that is, that the child gradually comes to want to practice self-restraint, persistence, and courage, and to see the world and the situations that face her accordingly. In the process, she becomes self-conscious about her own desires and aversions, comes to construe her inner world in a certain way and to attempt to act on herself, just as she attempts to act on others. Without this capacity, she would not be able to become an individual who functions within her society, without being absorbed by it.

At some point in this process, if all goes well, the child who internalizes the ideals of these virtues will reach a point at which she is able to see for herself what would be involved in acting in accordance with them. At first, this capacity will be limited to situations in which she simply prompts herself to act in a familiar situation, in the same way as her parents taught her to act in the past. At this level, she needs little more than the capacity to call to mind the internalized other and to act on that self-applied stimulus. But gradually, as her mind and feelings develop along the lines set by her early training, she will find herself able to act in accordance with these ideals in unfamiliar situations. Because she wants to live up to an ideal of herself as a certain kind of little girl, and construes the situations that face her accordingly, she will be increasingly able to discern the sorts of actions that correspond to those ideals, and to act in accordance with her perceptions, even in unprecedented circumstances. This capacity will develop more or less consciously as the child matures; it will be guided by explicit reasoning at some points, and, at other points, by a simple sense that some courses of action feel right, and others do not. This capacity will never enable the child, or the mature adult, to dispense with the correctives provided by the reactions of others to her actions. Yet the attainment of this capacity marks a critical point in the moral maturity of the child, for it is now that she begins to be capable of analogical reasoning.

As the child continues to mature into an adolescent and a young adult, she increasingly comes to see herself as someone with purposes, commitments, and responsibilities that she must pursue or fulfill over time. To a large degree, especially for the adolescent, these long-term aims will be bestowed on her by the expectations of her society and the specific roles that she assumes. But to some extent, at least, these aims will be her own, in the sense that she herself cares about them and is committed to attaining them. Even if most of the aims in which she has invested herself were originally bestowed on her by her culture (and that is surely one of the things that a culture is for), they become her own through her willing adoption of them as such, and they are further personalized by being integrated into the unrepeatable history and the wider ensemble of commitments and aims that give her her distinctive personal identity.[7]

In the course of investing herself in, and continually pursuing, these aims, the young person will quickly come to realize that, if she is to succeed in them, she must draw on the qualities of self-restraint, persistence, and courage that were formed in her as a child. That is, she comes to realize, in and through her intelligent action, that these virtues are desirable and necessary for her precisely as a human agent, whatever particular aims and ideals she may care about. This is so, no matter what wider aims were inculcated in the course of her earliest formation in those virtues. For this reason, once the maturing youth begins to draw on these virtues in pursuit of her own aims, she thereby progressively acquires the capacity to bring her own conception of what is good and worthwhile to bear on the particular ideals, the specific paradigms of self-restraint and the rest that provided the starting-points for her formation in these virtues.[8]

An example may help to clarify this point. A young man who has been raised in the tradition of the martial virtues, and who therefore grows up valuing courage in the face of physical danger, may find himself, on maturity, a deeply committed pacifist. As a result of his principled pacifism, he may find himself committed to refusing to fight when his country is at war, to oppose the war in public, and to undergo the penalties that he incurs as a result of his opposition. At first, this stance may feel like a painful break with his past, and, in many respects, it is. Yet, as he stays on the difficult path that he has chosen, the youth may come consciously to realize, what is surely the case, that the qualities of courage and persistence in the face of danger which he learned in the context of incorporating the martial virtues are still in play in his life. But now, instead of serving the aim of glory on the battlefield by nerving him to face death in battle, these qualities are employed in the service of his commitment to pacifism, by nerving him to face disgrace, imprisonment, possibly even death. In the process, the ideal of courage that he learned as a child is reconfigured. The ideal of courage appropriate to the soldier is not the same, is not lived in the same way, experienced in the same way, as the ideal of courage appropriate to the martyr for a cause. Yet they are not dissimilar, either. And, because they are not, the young man can come to recognize that there is a sense in which his activities as a pacifist exhibit courage, even though he learned the ideal of courage in a very different context. Once that conclusion has been reached, moreover, he will be in a position to critique his old conception of courage, and the wider ideal that informs it, from the standpoint of his newer conception of courage, with its own configuration in a new set of ideals.

It is important to realize that this sort of critical reflection upon, and revision of, one's ideals of the virtues, would not be possible without some practical commitment to the ideal of the unity of human goodness, and, therefore, to the connection of the virtues. (I say *practical*, because this sort of critical reflection does not presuppose a self-conscious and articulate commitment to these as philosophical or theological claims.) Lacking such a commitment, someone who found herself confronted with a serious incongruity between the ideals of virtue presented to her as a child, and her own deepest convictions, would have no way to understand this incongruity except in terms of a sheer heterogeneity between what she was once taught, and what she has come to believe. She would have no resources by which to recover the elements of goodness in her earlier training, because she would not know how to allow the ideals of one virtue to be corrected and reformulated by another. And that would be an unfortunate situation, to say the least, since it would leave the individual in a position of being unable to claim her own past, by integrating it into her present.

There is another kind of consideration that also enters into the maturing individual's reassessment of the particular ideals of temperance and fortitude in which she was formed as a child. These ideals, whatever forms they take, offer some determination to fundamental human desires and aversions. Yet, while these basic impulses are malleable, they are not infinitely malleable. Being grounded in the organic life of the person, and the exigencies of that life, they cannot be altogether suppressed or too drastically reconfigured without threatening the psychic balance that is critical to the well-being of the individual. A paradigmatic ideal for self-control that is so rigid that it requires perpetual malnourishment, or an ideal for courage and patience that expects persons to live in constant fear, will inevitably come under scrutiny and criticism, at least by some within a society, as individuals experience the costs of living out such ideals.

Because this corrective dynamism is built into our basic

desires and aversions, there is a grain of truth in the classical idea that human nature sets parameters around the appropriate expressions of our desires and aversions. There is also a good deal that is false in this idea. We cannot sustain the claim that human nature perspicuously grounds a set of moral prescriptions. We cannot claim that it is possible to arrive at any determinate account of human nature at all, prior to, and apart from, the conception of our capacities and limits that emerges over many generations of socially mediated experience of ourselves as creatures acting in the world. Whatever the conception of human nature that emerges in a given society, it will necessarily be a provisional social construct. And while it is possible to ground norms for action in such a conception, we cannot claim that these norms are grounded immediately in human nature, seen as standing over against culture and providing an independent basis for its critique.

Yet having acknowledged that the exigencies of human existence cannot be taken as a basis for moral prescriptions, independently of the particular culture in which those exigencies are construed, we may still grant that they do have a substantive impact on the formation, the specification, and the revision of moral norms. As individuals come to realize that a particular norm is destructive, that it impedes or diminishes human well-being, they may be able to call that norm into question precisely on those grounds. That does not mean that every norm that might be questioned in this way necessarily *will* be so questioned, since many individuals have an enormous capacity for absorbing abuse and diminishment in the name of preserving an established social order. Moreover, a critique along these lines would, in any case, most likely be pursued in conjunction with a critique of the wider ideals in the name of which the organic nature of the self is so abused. There may well be ideals for the sake of which some diminishment and distortion of the self is justifiable; but if an ideal is experienced as calling for some such distortion, then that fact at least counts as a reason why it needs some special justification if it is to be sustained.

THE OTHER-REGARDING VIRTUES

In the traditional ranking of the cardinal virtues, justice occupies the next highest place, after temperance and fortitude
(II–II 58.1, 2). According to Aquinas, this ranking reflects the
fact that justice is a virtue of the will, which is a more com-
prehensive faculty than the passions of desire and aversion
regulated by temperance and fortitude (I–II 60.3). These latter
passions are not naturally directed to the individual's good,
and, therefore, they must be informed by temperance and
fortitude in order to move in a direction that is consonant with
the individual's overall good (I–II 56.6). The will, he goes on to
explain, is naturally directed towards the individual's good,
and for that very reason, it must be informed by the other-
regarding virtue of justice if the individual is to desire and act
in accordance with the good of others and of the community of
which he is a member.

To many of our contemporaries, Aquinas' rationale for the
ranking of the virtues would appear quaint. None the less, the
ranking itself is widely agreed upon. As Pincoffs remarks,
"Justice is, on the present analysis and in agreement with
well-known predecessors, the quintessentially moral virtue – if
justice is understood broadly ..."[9] The priority of justice
reflects a sense that justice, together with other virtues which
concern our relationships with one another, is more significant
morally and also more important to society than the self-
regarding virtues of temperance and fortitude.

Yet the virtue of justice, understood precisely as a virtue,
generates special problems. In the first place, an act of justice,
unlike an act of temperance or fortitude, can be evaluated as
such without any reference to the agent's dispositions, her
passionate reactions, or even her appraisal of a situation. A just
person may well do something unjust, and, conversely, an
unjust person may act justly, and yet in each case what is
relevant to evaluating the particular action (*qua* act of justice)
is simply its conformity to norms of equity and non-
maleficence. In fine, the acts of justice appear to have little or
no organic connection with the agent's character, and that is

why it is so difficult to analyze them as acts *of* a virtue, or to treat justice itself as a virtue in any persuasive way.

Aquinas has an answer to this difficulty, precisely in his claim that justice is a virtue of the will. The concept of the will is difficult, both in Aquinas' own thought and more generally, yet there are certain insights in Aquinas' treatment of the will which are both defensible and illuminating. Aquinas means by the will an enduring natural desire for one's own good (I–II 56.6), which is informed by one's intellectual judgements with respect to that good (I–II 8.1). As such, the will is distinct from the passions, although it can be moved by the passions indirectly, through their effect on the judgement of the individual (I–II 9.2). Moreover, every truly human action proceeds from the will of the agent, on Aquinas' view; that is, he does not allow for the possibility that someone might be moved to act directly by the promptings of passion, without the mediation of the will, as informed by the agent's judgement (I–II 6.1; cf. II–II 156.1).[10]

If the will is understood in this way, as an enduring orientation of the individual towards her overall good, which supervenes on her passions and generates her actions, then it does make sense to speak of justice as a *habitus* qualifying the will so as to bring an enduring orientation towards the common good to the agent's judgements, feelings, and actions. Understood in this way, justice is not expressed directly and immediately in certain kinds of passional dispositions (as temperance and fortitude are), but it is expressed across a range of dispositions and desires, including the passions as those are informed by the agent's judgements and will.

It is true that, on Aquinas' view, the agent's dispositions do not themselves play a constitutive role in determining the norms of justice (as the passions *do* play a constitutive role in determining the mean of temperance and fortitude). For this reason, the actions of the individual can be evaluated from the standpoint of justice, without any reference to the agent's own dispositions and situation. Yet it does not follow that someone could acquire this virtue without some knowledge of the objective norms of justice. Since justice is a virtue of the will, which cannot act except in so far as it is informed by intellectual judgements concerning the nature of the good, it follows that a person must have some knowledge of what justice means, concretely, in order to develop that rationally informed enduring love of justice which is the essence of the virtue.

There is a more serious difficulty in Aquinas' treatment of justice seen in relation to the other virtues, however. In developing his distinction between the virtues of the passions, that is, temperance and fortitude, and justice considered as a virtue of the will, Aquinas treats the former as being primarily self-regarding, whereas justice is seen as being wholly other-regarding. This division makes sense in terms of his account of the passions and the will, and understood in those terms it is cogent. But it creates difficulties for him when he attempts to deal with those virtues (and vices) which are clearly other-regarding, and yet also have a strong passional component, such as mercy and mildness (which he treats together; see II–II 157, especially II–II 157.1, 3), anger (II–II 158, especially II–II 158.1, 2), or patience (II–II 136).

This difficulty is particularly apparent when Aquinas considers the virtues of self-restraint and appropriateness in sexual matters, together with the associated vices (II–II 151–154). He treats the virtue of chastity as if it were primarily a capacity to moderate one's desire and enjoyment of physical pleasure, rather than seeing it as a capacity for appropriate feeling and action with respect to other *people* (II–II 151; especially see II–II 151.3). As a result, the centrally important personal dimensions of sexual desire and pleasure, the complex ways in which sexuality mediates relations between persons, are almost entirely hidden from his view. This helps to explain his notorious ranking of the sins of lust, according to which homosexual intercourse is a graver sin than adultery or rape (at least, considered *qua* sins of lust; II–II 154.12).

The marginal position of other-regarding virtues such as kindness within Aquinas' analysis is partially a reflection of the strictures of his faculty psychology. He finds it difficult to know how to interpret or classify virtues such as mercy or mildness, which appear to straddle a double line, between will and passions, and between what concerns another, and what concerns oneself.

It is also the case that, for Aquinas, the warmer, less determinate capacities for care and responsiveness do not have a central role to play either in the agent's pursuit of her own aims, or in her life in society. Rather, what is central, on Aquinas' view, is the formation of her fundamental capacities for desire and aversion, in such a way that her passions and her will are in accordance with her overall conception of the human good. It is not essential to this process that the person attain some capacities for empathy and felt concern for others, although it would obviously be a good thing if she did. Considered from the standpoint of someone who pursues her own individual aims, the virtuous individual must attain some degree of self-restraint and courage, but a capacity to care for others is not essential to this process. Similarly, considered as a person in community, the individual must orient herself in such a way as to desire, and consistently to seek, the common good; moreover, she must be committed to respecting the general or particular claims of others. Here again, however, it is not necessary that she *feel* particularly kind or merciful or loving or benevolent. It is enough that she consistently *choose* the correct other-regarding course of action.

However, the affective other-regarding capacities for empathy, care, and concern for others cannot be separated so neatly either from the virtues of self-restraint and courage, or from a commitment to justice. In chapter 2, we saw that some degree of empathy for others is a necessary condition for understanding the basic moral notions. Moreover, as Mead argues, the emergence of the individual as a human person, possessed of distinctive capacities for rational action and speech, presupposes some capacities for internalizing the behavior and the reactions of other people.[11] Someone who is incapable of even this minimal degree of empathy for others (as a seriously handicapped child might be) would also be incapable of functioning as a rational agent at all.

It does not follow that an individual must acquire a genuine concern for, and fellow-feeling with, others in order to be capable of action. Unfortunately, we are all too familiar with functioning, rational individuals who are insensitive, boorish, rude, callous, or just plain mean. Furthermore, there do seem to be persons, fortunately not very many of them, who combine a considerable ability to predict others' behavior and reactions, and to control them based on those predictions, with a near-total lack of concern for others as human beings. The so-called psychopath, who combines a capacity for manipulation with murderous indifference to human life, may represent an extreme case of this phenomenon.

None the less, even the boor, the bastard, or the psychopath needs some capacities for empathy for others to function as a human person at all. Just as the individual who is altogether deprived of the capacities for self-restraint and courage crosses the line from vice (or addiction) to outright insanity, so the person who has no capacities at all for fellow-feeling will be incapable of any but the most rudimentary kinds of actions. Thus, while it is not necessary to possess the *virtues* of concern for others, sympathy, kindness, and the like in order to function as an agent, none the less, this family of virtues draws upon, and perfects, qualities which are essential to the functioning of the agent, *qua* agent. It would be reasonable to assume that these sorts of virtues are desirable, are, in a broad sense, beneficial, to the agent herself, as well as to those around her.

Does our experience bear out this assumption? That is, do we find that the callous or cruel or indifferent individual is in some way worse off than the person who is caring about others? The answer to this question is complex, because the virtues of care, like all other virtues, involve intellectual as well as affective components. That is, the caring individual describes the world differently, and desires different things, than does the callous individual. Someone who is really indifferent to the well-being of others may well be perfectly content with her life. She will probably not notice the suffering of others, and, if she does, it will not cause her much distress. So long as her life is filled with her own interests and pursuits, she may not feel the lack of genuine human connections. Like a cat, self-sufficient and complete, she lives her own life, never deliberately injuring others, but never seeking deep involvement in the lives of others, either. If she is missing something, which many of us feel to be profoundly important, she does not feel the lack or suffer on its account. We may not like such a person, but can we honestly pity her?

At this point, the compassionate individual may be driven back to a version of the old rhetorical question: is it better to be Socrates unsatisfied, or a pig satisfied? Is it better to be a caring person, engaged in the joys and sorrows of others, even if that engagement brings some sorrow along with it, or is it better to be self-satisfied, callous, and content? The force of this sort of appeal is not likely to be felt by those who really are thoroughly callous and content, who cannot conceive of what they are missing and therefore do not regret their lack. Rather, this sort of rhetorical appeal depends for its force on the fact that most people are not quite pigs; most people do retain some desire for a dignified human life, which includes some openness to learning and aesthetic experience for their own sakes, and, similarly, most people do care, at least a little, about some other persons, and want to be open to the presence of others in their lives. If someone really does not care about these sorts of goods at all, there is no way to *prove* to her that she is wrong, but it does seem to be the case that most of us would find such a person repugnant or pitiable, and would do what we could to avoid becoming like her. The completely callous person, in particular, would seem to be deprived of any capacity to form bonds of intimate closeness with other persons. And, since intimacy with others seems to be a basic human need, which almost all persons experience to some degree, this fact alone would suffice to give most persons some repugnance for callousness and related vices.

If it is the case that the virtues of care for others are internally connected in some ways to the good of the agent herself, as well as being of benefit to others, then we would not expect to find many people who are really indifferent to others' feelings and needs. Yet surely, it will be said, that is not the case; there are more callous and unfeeling persons than the other kind. Perhaps this is true. Certainly, there are many uncaring people in the world, and even the best of us are subject to fall into callousness or unkindness from time to time. The question that must be asked, however, is why this should be the case. It is impossible to answer this question with any certainty, but it seems at least likely that most persons are not just indifferent to other persons, without qualification or remainder. When we encounter someone who genuinely has no feeling for others, we tend to look back into her childhood, or into her history as an adult, or her circumstances in the present, in search of some trauma, some history of dehumanization inflicted by others, by which we can account for this deformity.[12]

More often, callousness (like other similar vices) is grounded in a failure of the intellect, rather than in a complete lack of feelings for others. In other words, the failing in question is likely to be a failing of the mind and imagination, rather than a defect in sensibility; once again, we find that we cannot fully account for a class of virtues except in terms of their interconnections with prudence. It is all too possible for someone to be kindly and thoughtful in her relations with her family, friends, and colleagues, and yet to be *unaware*, and therefore unfeeling, about the lives of persons who do not come into her direct experience. This unawareness may well extend beyond an indifference to those who are suffering far, far away, to include persons whom she sees every day, but does not think of as each having his or her own inner world of feelings and concerns. It is part of the pathos of the human condition that none of us could function without some degree of this unawareness, to insulate us from the enormous pain and need that is a part of the human condition. It is difficult to preserve this psychic skin without falling into some degree of blameworthy callousness sometimes, so difficult that probably only the greatest saints manage to do so while still retaining their sanity and integrity.

If it is true that the virtues of caring are internally connected to the good of the agent herself, one consequence is that we cannot draw a sharp distinction between self-regarding and other-regarding virtues. This distinction has some merit, in that there are some virtues that do seem to have the agent's own immediate needs and situation as their primary reference, whereas others are intrinsically directed to the good of others. But this distinction should not be interpreted as an absolute line among different sorts of virtues. Even the most basic virtues, without which no one could function at all, are practically inseparable from other-regarding concerns, particularly at the stage of their first inculcation ("Don't be greedy! Share with your sister." "What do you mean, you're scared? Do you want to let down the team?") Similarly, the other-regarding virtues have a self-regarding dimension. It is perfectly reasonable to attempt to be more giving, more attentive to others, more open, because one wants to be a caring person, and wants to avoid becoming calloused.

Someone who is concerned to be a person of this sort may well build this self-regarding concern into her actions and allow it to move her in a direction that she might not otherwise take. For example, a woman might have serious misgivings about the value of giving money to panhandlers, on the grounds, perhaps, that she is thereby participating in their own self-destructive actions. Yet she may still reasonably choose to give to them, because she judges that otherwise she risks becoming a callous person, and that danger seems to her to be more immediate and serious – for her, anyway – than the possible danger that she is enabling someone else's addictions and vices by supporting them. This sort of judgement is not without its own problems, and one could easily imagine someone else coming to an opposite decision of policy, without thereby becoming callous. But, whatever may be said about this woman's choice, surely it would be unfair to charge her with simple indifference to the needs of others, or to a narcissistic preoccupation with herself. It is true that she is concerned about herself, in that she does not want her heart to become hardened by the experience of continually ignoring the needs of others, but that is not quite like a desire to be rich or beautiful, or even to be noble or good in the abstract. Someone who really does not want to be calloused wants, in part, to be the sort of person who cares for other persons, and, if this desire cannot be separated neatly from our desires to behave and to respond in certain ways to others, this is surely because our concepts of self and others are inextricably bound together.

CONSCIENTIOUSNESS, FAIRNESS, AND INTEGRITY

So far, we have focused on what might be called the other-regarding virtues of care for others, which include as one of their components some element of affective concern for others. When we think of justice, however, we are more likely to think of cooler, more impersonal qualities, such as conscientiousness and fairness. How are we to understand these qualities?

Conscientiousness might be described as a settled tendency to attend to, and to respect, the norms, claims, and expectations that are incumbent on the individual as a member of a particular community or association, or as an adherent to a religious or moral framework of beliefs.[13] It would include such qualities as a sense of honor as a member of some valued community, a willingness to "go by the book," to do what is seen as the right thing to do, even when it is inexpedient or even harmful to the agent or others to do so. The contrary vices would include a willingness to cut corners, a tendency to get by with whatever little contrivances suit one's convenience, and the laziness that prevents most of us, some of the time, from doing those things that we are committed to doing, even when we actually want to do them.

As Pincoffs observes, this virtue has taken on enormous importance, so much so that for some moral theorists in the modern period, it has seemed to be the only moral quality, or the most fundamental such quality. He suggests, persuasively, that the reason for this prominence lies chiefly in the growing complexity of modern life, which has made a certain amount of conformity to impersonal and seemingly arbitrary rules more and more important for any kind of social life.[14] At the same time, it should be clear that, if we accept the basic tenets of a socially oriented psychology, there can be no question that some capacity for grasping and obeying rules must be present if any human individual is to make the transition from an organic creature to a fully rational, socialized individual. In order for the individual's identity to emerge, it is necessary for the child to be socialized through participation in a whole series of real and play/assumed roles, which mediate to her her awareness of others' expectations of her and their predictable responses to her. Without this awareness, the most basic capacities for language and thought would be stunted, or, in extreme cases, they would not form at all. If this process is to work successfully, moreover, it is necessary that the child internalize at least some of these roles and begin to behave, on her own accord, in accordance with the expectations that are built into them. In the process of doing so, she must be willing to obey rules, even though the point of those rules may not always be clear to her. She must cultivate conscientiousness, at least to some degree, if she is to function as a human person at all.

At the same time, a willingness to obey rules, simply because they are rules, can very readily become a destructive quality. The same may be said of kindness, sympathy, or of moderation or courage, considered as good tendencies which have not been shaped by the agent's reflective reason. At the same time, it does seem that a readiness to obey rules at all costs is more patent of distortion, and can be taken to a more destructive extreme, than is the case with respect to the good qualities associated with temperance, or the virtues of caring discussed above. (Courage, on the other hand, can be very destructive if it is misdirected.) The parade example of this possibility is provided by the experience of the German people under the Nazi government; this regime could not have functioned except with the cooperation of hundreds of thousands of men and women, military personnel and civilians, at all levels of society, who placed the duty to obey the rules of their government and their particular organizations ahead of every other consideration. It is perhaps unfair to single out the Nazis to provide this sort of bad example, however. Our century alone, to speak of no other, can provide examples from almost every major country at some part of its history in which the foolishness, cowardice, or downright malice of those in high positions was given effect only by the cooperation of men and women determined to do their duty without question.

It should not be surprising that a willingness to follow rules should be so central to human life, and yet so susceptible to deformation in destructive ways. For, given the psychological framework within which we have been working, it is apparent that an ability and willingness to follow rules is one of the most fundamental capacities that a (potentially) rational creature can possess. Without this capacity, persons can neither emerge as fully rational social beings, nor can they act or sustain a course of activity. At the same time, the logical difficulties involved in applying rules to specific cases can make it difficult, and sometimes impossible, to say with certainty whether or not a rule is being followed in a specific case. This ambiguity makes it impossible to rely on rules alone to provide the structure and stability that individuals and communities must have in order to function. Yet security must come to us from some source or other, and, in a complex society, in which implicit shared commitments or a relatively simple economic arrangement cannot provide us with a readily accessible shared form of life, it is very tempting to look to the fiat of some authoritative interpreter of the rules, a father or a judge or a priest, to resolve these ambiguities, on a case-by-case basis if necessary. In these circumstances, it is easy to see how persons might reach maturity without ever developing a capacity to exercise discernment in the following of rules.

If it is easy to see how this sort of capacity can become distorted, it is not so easy to see how a healthy capacity for discernment can be developed. Yet, if we recall what is involved in the process of developing a mature capacity for self-restraint, it becomes apparent that the capacity for exercising discernment with respect to the application of rules develops in somewhat the same way. As we saw, the child who is taught self-restraint (for example) in and through being taught paradigms for desirable behavior will gradually discover, as she matures, that this quality, which was inculcated in her as she was directed by the aims of others, is equally necessary to her as she begins to pursue her own aims. This realization, in turn, can provide her with a basis for critical scrutiny of the forms of self-control that she was originally taught. In the same way, the child who is taught to obey rules will eventually discover that any complex good that she cares about can be pursued and enjoyed only if she is willing to obey rules. At the same time, however, in and through the process of pursuing her own aims, she learns how to exercise discernment with respect to obedience to rules. Finally, if she is able to carry this line of thought forward, her understanding of the rules of her child-hood code is subjected to reformulation in accordance with the same criteria for discernment. Increasingly, she attempts to understand the point behind the rules of this code, to make sense of its inner logic and coherence, and to reformulate her applications of these rules accordingly. If this proves to be impossible, she will begin to form a new code, grounded in whatever she does care about, or whatever other materials are at hand.

MacIntyre's discussion of the relation of the virtues to the pursuit of goods internal to a practice is illuminating in this context.[15] Practices, as MacIntyre understands the term, would include any kind of organized pursuit which is carried out for its own sake, and which offers rewards or benefits that are intrinsic to the activity itself, as, for example, opera singing or football. Practices do not necessarily have any particular moral value, nor is it invariably the case that their prac-titioners are morally good persons. What *is* significant about learning a practice, from our standpoint, is that, in order to do so, it is necessary for the individual to learn how to follow rules that have their point in some sort of intrinsic relation to the goods internal to the practice.[16] In so doing, the individual learns both *how* to apply the rules in question – that is, by reference to the goods at which she aims – and *why* it is important to do so, namely, because this sort of rule-governed behavior is a constitutive component of the attainment of the goods in question. This link is clearest with respect to games and athletic contests, since, in cases such as these, the very existence of the practice in question depends on relatively simple, clearly articulated rules. A practice such as the per-formance of music may provide a still more illuminating example. In order to be a competent performer, an individual must be able to follow a whole series of complex rules involving the use of a musical instrument (or the control of one's own voice), the conventions for musical notation, and, finally, the extended and partially implicit rules by which quality in music is articulated. The difference between a competent performer and a good performer is that the latter, unlike the former, has some "feel" for the relation of the rules of musicianship to what counts as good music, and is able to interpret these complex rules accordingly. The difference between a good performer and a genius, in turn, is that the latter is able to extend the rules in some significant way, even to break rules in order to remake them, in order to extend our sense of the possibilities for goodness that music holds. And, finally, the difference between a genius and a crank is that, in the former case, but usually not in the latter case, other, lesser musicians and connoisseurs can see the point of the innovations of the genius, they can see how these innovations relate to, and extend, goods that they already understood to be goods.

The same sort of internal relation between rule-following and the goods internal to a way of life can be found, in a somewhat more complex way, in the context of those institutionalized ways of life that have the pursuit of some complex good as their point. For example, the academic life, which is institutionalized through colleges and universities and publishing houses and accrediting agencies, exists to promote the pursuit of knowledge and understanding in certain disciplined and self-reflective ways. As such, it is structured through a complex, interlocking array of rules, including some that would be necessary in any institution, and others which safeguard the conditions for, or are even necessary to, the pursuit of the goods of the intellectual life itself. MacIntyre, as was noted above, draws a contrast between norms that are internal to the goods being pursued in a community, which he associates with the virtues proper to that community, and the kinds of failure that would be directly destructive to the community itself, which he associates with the (mostly negative) rules of morality.[17] This dichotomy is too simple, however. Someone who really cares about the academic life will avoid certain behaviors because they would be inimical to the enterprise of intellectual inquiry itself, and not just because they would have the effect of undermining the community. For example, a serious scholar will avoid plagiarism for a number of reasons, including its destructive effects on the community (it undermines trust, and the system of distributive justice proper to the academic community as we know it), but also including its effects on the good in question and her own participation in that good (it circumvents the individual's need to do her own research – which the serious scholar would not want to do).

It is in the context of pursuing goods that she genuinely cares about that the individual develops the skills needed to apply rules in a sound and humane way. This capacity is a central component of prudence, which includes in its functions the application of the basic moral notions to specific instances of choice. Yet the conscientiousness of the committed scholar (for example) will not translate into the prudent conscientiousness of the morally good person automatically. In order for this to happen, the individual must widen the scope of her care. That is, she must come to care for other persons, and for the sustenance of a common life, in the same way that she cares for scholarship (or the arts, or whatever else first awakens her capacities for disinterested love). In the process, her conscientiousness will be reconfigured in the light of a new set of aims, just as the courage of the young man who becomes a pacifist will be reconfigured in the light of his new commitments. Once again, we see that prudence and the moral virtues are ineluctably interconnected, and this interconnection provides the basis for a practical reappraisal and reappropriation of the virtues as they are first inculcated in the individual.

The individual who develops the capacity for a mature and balanced conscientiousness will also thereby develop two other virtues which are essential to justice, namely fairness and its near cousin, integrity. Both of these virtues have in common a willingness, indeed, an insistence, on construing one's own good in the context of some wider good, which is valued more than one's own immediate interests and desires. Fairness and integrity might be described as two forms of an impersonal love for the good, without which a healthy love for oneself and others is impossible. What characterizes the person of integrity, first of all, is her consistent willingness to construe her own good in the context of some greater good (or goods), which she values more than she values her own personal satisfactions, precisely because her participation in this wider good bestows meaning and purpose on her life. The person who attains integrity does not so much move from self-love to altruism, as to a new construal of her own good, which is now seen in relation to a larger good. Because she sees her own good in this way, the person of integrity will not tolerate compromises, on her own part or on the part of others, which would tend to undermine that good or to alienate her from it.

Moreover, because a wider good is also, potentially, a shared good, the person of integrity is open to the participation of others in this good. To some extent, at least, she evaluates her relations with others in the context of that shared participation in some wider good, and that context, in turn, provides an impersonal context for sharing the benefits and burdens intrinsic to any common life. Seen in this context, fairness is nothing other than integrity extended to others. Just as the person of integrity values the good she loves more than she values her personal advantages, so she extends that good to others, provides them access to it, and acknowledges their contributions to it, even when doing so would be contrary to her immediate advantage. In other words, she is fair, that is to say, impartial with respect to participation in a transpersonal good.

So far in our examination of the norms of conscientiousness, fairness and integrity, we have bracketed any consideration of the virtues of caring discussed in the last section. It is necessary at this point to attempt to say something about the relationship between these two sorts of virtues, which must be brought together if one is to live a life that is at once humane and principled.

Since the appearance of Carol Gilligan's *In a Different Voice*, there has been considerable discussion of the supposed differences between masculine and feminine styles of moral reasoning.[18] According to Gilligan, women tend to think in terms of responsibility, interconnectedness, and caring when they reflect on moral dilemmas, whereas men tend to use the Kantian categories of impersonal duty and principle. Since the appearance of her book, it has become impossible to discuss justice without adverting in some way to these supposedly masculine and feminine ways of construing our responsibilities to others; and, to the extent that her work has forced us to take these two different components of the moral life with equal seriousness, it has had a welcome influence on academic discussions of the moral life.

At the same time, Gilligan's argument could well distort our conception of the virtues of caring and conscientiousness, if we concluded from it that there are two distinct styles of moral reasoning which should be embodied in two different classes of persons, namely, men and women.[19] For, as our analysis of these virtues should indicate, neither set of virtues can operate without the other. We have already seen that a determination to obey the rules of one's society without question can be subject to the most hideous distortions, and these are most likely to occur precisely in situations in which a person's sense of connectedness to other persons, which would otherwise deter her from harming them, has remained rudimentary or has been overridden. After two centuries of Kantian moral theory, we need to emphasize again how critically important it is that justice be tempered with mercy, even from the standpoint of justice itself. At the same time, however, a ready concern and empathy for others can also lead to serious distortions in the moral life. A man whose sympathy for the feelings of others prevented him from ever displeasing them would make a bad parent, a bad teacher, a bad employee or boss; in short, he would be a man to avoid.

How are we to balance the competing claims of mercy and justice, caring and conscientiousness? We realize by now that there can be no simple formula for doing so. This balance must be attained through the process of intelligent action in situations of tension among these diverse ideals; this process, in turn, will partially presuppose, and further clarify, some more or less conscious conception of the differing claims of self, others, and the community as a whole, their relative weights, and the correct ordering of priority among them. Once again, we find ourselves at the same conclusion: the person who is able consistently to achieve a felicitous balance between the demands of caring and the demands of conscientiousness will necessarily be a prudent person, whose wisdom is grounded in a sound and reflective conception of the human good.

PRACTICAL WISDOM AND THE VIRTUES AS COMPONENTS OF A HUMANLY GOOD LIFE

In my view, the reformulation of Aquinas' account of the virtues sketched above confirms the central insights of that account, even though it leads us away from his substantive views and the details of his organization at a number of points. What has emerged out of this reformulation, that is to say, is a vindication of his central claims: the traditional cardinal virtues are such because they represent characteristic perfections of human action *per se*, and, correlatively, the cardinal virtues are connected, in such a way that intellectual judgement and passion or sensibility are inseparably linked.

At the same time, this reformulation brings out, perhaps more clearly than does Aquinas' own account, just how much his central insights provide in the way of resources for a critical reappraisal of received notions of the virtues. At the beginning of this chapter, I suggested that a Thomistic account of the virtues, reformulated in the light of a contemporary understanding of the human person, could provide a basis for social critique and reform, as well as individual self-criticism. We are now in a position to see how such a critique might be developed.

Note, first of all, that the connection between the virtues and the notion of goodness in action places constraints on what can plausibly be offered as an account of a given virtue. We have already observed that any cardinal virtue can be conceptualized in a variety of ways, in accordance with different social conditions, different accounts of the good, the worthwhile, or the noble, different expectations for moral behavior, and so on.

Yet these can all be recognized to be analogues of what is plausibly described as being in some sense the same virtue, since all the instances of, for example, courage, will be linked in some plausible way by exhibiting a cluster of shared features; in the case of courage, the virtue will be connected with situations that generate fear or avoidance, it will be characterized by steadfastness in the face of fear, and so forth.

The link between action and the cardinal virtues also places constraints on what can count as an analogue of a virtue in another way: a supposed account of a virtue that does not imply that the subject of the virtue is thereby enabled to act and to sustain action is ruled out as a concept of that virtue. And so, for example, a supposed account of courage which counted the act of tucking tail and running in the face of danger as a *normal* act of courage would simply fail as an account of this virtue. The reason for this failure is not just that this would be a counter-intuitive notion of courage, but, more decisively, it would characterize a person who could not effectively sustain action at all in the face of risk. And yet the whole point of courage, if that term is to have any meaning at all, is to enable us to act in the face of dangers and risks.

It may seem that this observation is so obvious as to be trivial, and, in many cases, it would be. (It would do substantive work in some cases, however, for example, to distinguish praiseworthy forms of temperance and abstinence from self-destructive distortions of sensual desire.) Its significance becomes clearer when we move to the next stage of reflection. For, if a putative account of a virtue can be ruled out on the grounds that it does not allow for the possibility of human action, so an ideal of human flourishing will be ruled out if it implies a social structure, or a pattern of action, that consistently undermines the capacities for human action. To put matters another way, a way of life that produces cowards, sensualists, and frivolous social butterflies, or drudges who live on the basis of mindless obedience, or overwrought violent persons who must be kept in check by their superiors lest they wreak havoc at random, would be ruled out as a false understanding of the human good, of the proper way to arrange a human life.[20]

In the analysis of temperance and fortitude developed above, we noted that it is possible to revise one's ideals of a good human life in such a way as to reappropriate, and then to revise, the conceptions of the most basic virtues that must be possessed in some form if the agent is to act at all. We are now in a better position to appreciate what this process would involve. The individual whose conception of the good life emerges out of practice and reflection, based on the account that is explicitly or implicitly inculcated through her training in the virtues, will necessarily incorporate some elements of the conceptions of those virtues in that account, even as she revises them. Her conception of the human good will include a notion of a human dignity that is grounded in restraint and forthright-ness, a notion of kindliness and decency built up out of the virtues of caring, and a notion of fairness and responsibility that is the basis for justice. Any account of the human good that does not include these components will be truncated and self-defeating, since it will undermine the very qualities that are necessary if it is to be sustained in practice.

Understood in this way, the cardinal virtues do not just set constraints on the conception of the human good that can be sustained in the practices of individuals; they also place constraints on the forms of social life that are consistent with justice in the broadest sense, that is, with a society that enables its members to flourish as individuals and as a community. It is true that the conditions of complex modern societies do not permit them to be structured around a specific, content-rich concept of the human good, both because of the complexity and heterogeneity of modern life, and, even more, because of the possibilities of abuse inherent in the political apparatus of the modern nation-state. None the less, the constraints set by the virtues on particular conceptions of the human good also set constraints on what can count as just social institutions, in that they help to determine what the institutions of society must look like, if individuals and communities are to be able to pursue and sustain lives of real goodness.[21]

To some degree, these constraints are obvious. If a society is to be sustainable, it must encourage its members to develop those same qualities of self-restraint, minimal courage, care and conscientiousness that are necessary for action at the individual level; or, if that proves too formidable a task, it must at least refrain from undermining these qualities. There are two further constraints that a society must respect, if its members are to pursue and live out sustainable conceptions of the human good. First of all, it must allow for what have been described as intermediate institutions, localized communities, since it is only within the parameters of such communities that more fully developed conceptions of the human good can emerge and be sustained.[22] Secondly, as John Stuart Mill pointed out over a century ago, it must sustain the conditions for open enquiry that are necessary for the ongoing pursuit of truth and goodness in all their forms.[23]

Lee Yearley has argued that Aquinas' account of the virtues can be developed still further, into a methodology for approaching the normative traditions of societies other than our own, and arriving at some degree of mutual comprehension. He demonstrates how Aquinas' account of the virtues can function as a medium for comparative study of different normative traditions, by means of a powerful and remarkably convincing comparison between Aquinas' account of courage and the account offered by the Chinese philosopher Mencius.[24] I cannot improve on Yearley's own argument that Aquinas offers resources for rational conversation across cultures, as well as for rational self-scrutiny on the individual and the social level. I would only add that, while Aquinas cannot offer us the basis for certainty that this sort of textured comparison will be fruitful in every case, he does offer us reason to hope that this approach will offer a way of breaking out of the isolation of our separate cultures. If it is the case, as he argues and as this analysis suggests, that the language and practice of the virtues is reflective of the human inclination to act, and to act well, then we do have a reasonable hope of finding common ground between ourselves and others on this basis. Admittedly, this sort of hope is something less than the certainty offered by modern moral theories. Yet it is the most that we can have, and I believe that it will suffice.

It may seem that we have come a long way from the concerns with which this study began. Yet that is not the case. Modern moral theories offered both an account of, and a procedure for implementing, rational moral judgement. Without some such account and procedure, it was felt, morality itself would be threatened, by the pressures of human weakness, human wickedness, and human need. More recently, contemporary work in the philosophy of language and moral philosophy has established that a moral theory in the modern mode is not possible. Aquinas' contribution to this discussion is to show, in considerable textured detail, that a modern moral theory is not necessary either. It is possible to offer an alternative account of moral rationality which does not offer the certainties promised by Kant (for example), but which none the less offers us enough to live by. Although his way of speaking and some of his specific views conceal the fact, Aquinas offers us a profoundly humane and liberating view of the moral life. He indicates that it is possible to live justly and well, even though we must surrender the false security of modern moral theories, with their promise of certainties that we cannot attain.

Notes

INTRODUCTION

1 Joseph Fletcher, *Situation Ethics: The New Morality* (Philadelphia: Westminster Press, 1966).
2 Paul Ramsey, "The Case of the Curious Exception," pp. 67–138 in *Norm and Context in Christian Ethics*, Gene H. Outka and Paul Ramsey, editors (New York: Charles Scribner's Sons, 1968), and Richard A. McCormick, "Ambiguity in Moral Choice," pp. 7–53 in *Doing Evil to Achieve Good: Moral Choice in Conflict Situations*, Richard McCormick and Paul Ramsey, editors (Chicago: Loyola University Press, 1978). Further references on proportionalism will appear in the first chapter.
3 Published in *Origins: CNS Documentary Service*, vol. 23, no.18, October 14, 1993, 297–336.

1 THE MORAL ACT, MORAL THEORY, AND THE LOGICAL
LIMITS OF RULES

1 Immanuel Kant, *Critique of Practical Reason*, Lewis White Beck, translator (Indianapolis: Bobbs Merrill, 1956; originally published, 1788), p. 8.
2 Recently, Robert B. Louden has argued that Kant's view of moral rules is more nuanced and complex than this quotation would suggest in *Morality and Moral Theory: A Reappraisal and Reaffirmation* (Oxford University Press, 1992), pp. 99–124. However, Louden's interpretation should be contrasted with that of Charles E. Larmore in *Patterns of Moral Complexity* (Cambridge University Press, 1987), pp. 1–21.
3 In addition to the second *Critique*, see Immanuel Kant, *Groundwork of the Metaphysics of Morals*, third edition, H. J. Paton, translator (New York: Harper and Row, 1956/1964); see especially chapter 2, "Passage from a Popular Moral Philosophy to a Metaphysics of Morals," pp. 74–113.

4 Jeremy Bentham, *An Introduction to the Principles of Morals and Legislation*, with an introduction by Laurence J. Lafleur (New York: Macmillan, 1948; originally published 1789). See especially 1–7.

5 In particular see Henry Sidgwick, *The Methods of Ethics*, seventh edition (Indianapolis: Hackett, 1891/1907): "I think it fundamentally important to recognize, at the outset of Ethical inquiry, that there is a diversity of methods applied in ordinary practical thought" (p. 6).

6 A. J. Ayer, *Language, Truth and Logic* second edition (New York: Dover Books, 1952/1946); Charles L. Stevenson, *Ethics and Language* (New Haven: Yale University Press, 1944); R. M. Hare, *The Language of Morals* (Oxford University Press, 1952/1964); *Freedom and Reason* (Oxford University Press, 1963/1965); *Moral Thinking: Its Levels, Method and Point* (Oxford University Press, 1981).

7 Bernard Williams, *Ethics and the Limits of Philosophy* (Cambridge, MA: Harvard University Press, 1985).

8 The texts that have given rise to this interpretation are Søren Kierkegaard, *Fear and Trembling*, Walter Lowrie, translator (Princeton University Press, 1941), and Karl Barth, *Church Dogmatics*, II/2, G. W. Bromiley and T. F. Torrance, editors, (Edinburgh: T. & T. Clark, 1957), 37.3, pp. 583–630, and III/4, 55.2, pp. 397–470. My own view, however, is that it is a mistake to read Barth in this way. He defends the view that most of the norms of morality call for application in difficult situations, and there is no guarantee that they may cease to apply in some specific cases; as I argue below, such a position is quite compatible with a belief in the existence and validity of moral rules. With respect to Kierkegaard, the interpretative difficulties surrounding this text are notorious. For an alternative to the usual reading of *Fear and Trembling*, see Ronald M. Green, "Enough Is Enough! *Fear and Trembling* Is *Not* about Ethics," *The Journal of Religious Ethics*, 21, 2 (1993), 191–210.

9 Kenneth E. Kirk, *Conscience and Its Problems: An Introduction to Casuistry* (New York: Longmans, Green and Co. Ltd., 1927), pp. 330–378.

10 Joseph Fletcher, *Situation Ethics: The New Morality* (Philadelphia: Westminster Press, 1966), and "What's in a Rule?: A Situationist's View," pp. 325–350 in *Norm and Context in Christian Ethics*, Gene H. Outka and Paul Ramsey, editors (New York: Charles Scribner's Sons, 1968). It should be noted that Fletcher only declares himself to be unequivocally an act-utilitarian in the latter article.

11 Paul Ramsey, *Deeds and Rules in Christian Ethics* (New York: Charles Scribner's Sons, 1967), pp. 145–225, and "The Case of the Curious Exception," pp. 67–138 in *Norm and Context*. Basil Mitchell takes a similar line in "Ideals, Roles and Rules," 351–365 in *Norm and Context*. Gene Outka points out that, prior to the appearance of Fletcher's book, the Jesuit Thomist, Gerard Gilleman, had also argued that there are certain kinds of actions that are never consistent with Christian love, or charity; see Outka, "Virtue, Principles, and Rules," pp. 37–66 in *Norm and Context*.

12 H. Richard Niebuhr, *The Responsible Self: An Essay in Christian Moral Philosophy* (San Francisco and New York: Harper and Row, 1963); Paul Lehmann, *Ethics in a Christian Context* (New York: Harper and Row, 1963); James Gustafson, *Ethics from a Theocentric Perspective, Volume I: Ethics and Theology* (University of Chicago Press, 1981).

13 The literature generated by this debate is enormous. For a good representative introduction to proportionalism, with an excellent bibliography, see Bernard Hoose, *Proportionalism: The American Debate and Its European Roots* (Washington, DC: Georgetown University Press, 1987). Also see Germain Grisez, *The Way of the Lord Jesus, Volume One: Christian Moral Principles* (Chicago: Franciscan Herald Press, 1983); John Finnis, *Natural Law and Natural Rights* (Oxford: Clarendon Press, 1980), *Fundamentals of Ethics* (Washington DC: Georgetown University Press, 1983), and *Moral Absolutes: Tradition, Revision, and Truth* (Washington, DC: The Catholic University of America Press, 1991); and Germain Grisez, Joseph Boyle, and John Finnis, "Practical Principles, Moral Truth and Ultimate Ends," *American Journal of Jurisprudence*, 32 (1987), 99–151.

14 Stanley Hauerwas, *A Community of Character: Towards a Constructive Christian Social Ethic* (University of Notre Dame Press, 1981) and *The Peaceable Kingdom: A Primer in Christian Ethics* (University of Notre Dame Press, 1983); James Keenan, "Virtue Ethics: Making A Case as It Comes of Age," *Thought*, 67 (1992), 115–127, and "The Casuistry of John Major: Nominalist Professor of Paris (1506–1531)," *The Annual of the Society of Christian Ethics: 1993*, 205–222.

15 Elizabeth (G. E. M.) Anscombe, "Modern Moral Philosophy," originally in *Philosophy*, 33 (1958), reprinted as pp. 26–42 in *Collected Philosophical Papers, Volume III: Ethics, Religion and Politics*, G. E. M. Anscombe, editor (Minneapolis: University of Minnesota Press, 1981).

16 Anscombe, "Modern Moral Philosophy," 26.

17 Ibid., pp. 33–34; emphasis in the original.
18 It is worth noting, however, that, even in 1958, it was not the case that every important English moral philosopher since Sidgwick denied that some kinds of actions are always morally wrong. H. A. Prichard, for one, did not; see "Does Moral Philosophy Rest on a Mistake?" originally published in 1912, reprinted as 1–17 in H. A. Prichard, *Moral Obligation and Duty and Interest: Essays and Lectures,* (Oxford University Press, 1968).
19 See Hare, *Freedom and Reason,* pp. 86–111.
20 Alasdair MacIntyre, *After Virtue,* second edition (University of Notre Dame Press, 1981/1984). MacIntyre acknowledges his debt to Anscombe, without committing himself to defending her thesis as a whole; see *After Virtue,* p. 53.
21 MacIntyre, *After Virtue,* p. 263; in addition to the works of Hauerwas cited above, also see his *After Christendom? How the Church is to Behave if Freedom, Justice, and a Christian Nation Are Bad Ideas* (Nashville: Abingdon Press, 1991).
22 The historical diversity of the Christian moral tradition is richly documented by Ernst Troeltsch in *The Social Teaching of the Christian Churches,* 2 volumes, Olive Wyon, translator (University of Chicago Press, 1931; originally published 1911).
23 MacIntyre himself makes this point with respect to classical Greece; see *After Virtue,* pp. 121–164 and *Whose Justice? Which Rationality?* (University of Notre Dame Press, 1988), pp. 30–68; also see Martha Nussbaum, *The Fragility of Goodness: Luck and Ethics in Greek Tragedy and Philosophy* (Cambridge University Press, 1986). With respect to the biblical tradition, see, for example, Joseph Blenkinsopp, *Prophecy and Canon: A Contribution to the Study of Jewish Origins* (University of Notre Dame Press, 1977); and James Dunn, *Unity and Diversity in the New Testament: An Inquiry into the Character of Earliest Christianity* (Philadelphia: Westminster Press, 1977).
24 MacIntyre, *After Virtue,* p. 222. He subsequently develops this observation into a powerful account of the mode of rationality proper to tradition-guided discourse in *Whose Justice? Which Rationality?* pp. 349–403.
25 Richard McCormick has frequently insisted on the significance of this fact; see, for example, "The Consistent Ethic of Life: Is There a Historical Soft Underbelly?" in his *The Critical Calling: Reflections on Moral Dilemmas Since Vatican II,* (Washington, DC: Georgetown University Press, 1989), pp. 211–232.
26 See, for example, Joseph Fuchs, "The Absoluteness of Moral Terms," originally in the *Gregorianum* 52 (1971), reprinted as

pp. 94–137 in *Readings in Moral Theology No.1: Moral Norms and the Catholic Tradition*, Charles Curran and Richard McCormick, editors (New York: Paulist Press, 1979).

27 Willard van Orman Quine, "Two Dogmas of Empiricism," in *From a Logical Point of View* (New York: Harper and Row, 1961), pp. 20–46.

28 Werner Heisenberg, *Physics and Philosophy: The Revolution in Modern Science* (New York: Harper and Row, 1958), p. 83.

29 Friedrich Waismann, "Verifiability," *Proceedings of the Aristotelian Society*, supplementary volume 19 (1945), pp. 119–150; reprinted as 35–60 in *The Theory of Meaning*, G. H. R. Parkinson, editor, (Oxford University Press, 1968). Subsequent citations refer to the reprint in *The Theory of Meaning*.

30 J. M. Brennan, *The Open-Texture of Moral Concepts* (New York: Barnes and Noble, 1977); Julius Kovesi, *Moral Notions* (London: Routledge, 1967). For an application of Waismann's analysis to legal concepts, see H. L. A. Hart, "Jhering's Heaven of Concepts and Modern Analytic Jurisprudence," originally published in 1970, reprinted as pp. 265–277 in his *Essays in Jurisprudence and Philosophy* (Oxford University Press, 1983). Others who take a similar approach to the understanding of moral (or in Fried's case, legal) judgement developed here include Charles Fried, "The Artificial Reason of Law or: What Lawyers Know," *Texas Law Review*, 60 (1981), 35–58; Charles Larmore, *Patterns of Moral Complexity*, 1987; Garrett Barden, *After Principles* (University of Notre Dame Press, 1990); and Michael Stocker, *Plural and Conflicting Values* (Oxford: Clarendon Press, 1990).

31 Waismann, "Verifiability," 38.

32 Ibid., 39.

33 Ibid., 40.

34 Ibid., 38.

35 Ludwig Wittgenstein, *Philosophical Investigations*, third edition, Elizabeth Anscombe, translator (New York: Macmillan Company, 1958). In particular, I am relying, in what follows, on nos. 185–243, pp. 74–88. I cannot here enter into the extensive and complex debates over the correct interpretation of Wittgenstein's work; my own reading will emerge in what follows. I have been guided in my interpretation by Saul Kripke's *Wittgenstein On Rules and Private Language: An Elementary Exposition* (Cambridge, MA: Harvard University Press, 1982), although I do not follow him at every point.

36 Wittgenstein, *Philosophical Investigations* no. 201, p. 81.

37 Ibid.

38 Ibid., no. 202, p. 81; emphasis in the original.

39 I do not know what Wittgenstein himself would have said on the question of realism. At any rate, he does not seem to believe that the practices of a particular local community are ultimate; see, for example, *Philosophical Investigations* no. 206, p. 82: "The common behavior of mankind is the system of reference by means of which we interpret an unknown language." Note that if Wittgenstein is correct, at stake for the realist is the correct understanding of the thing, or the kind of thing, to which a given concept applies, not the correct understanding of the concept itself; that is to say, the concept is the means through which we understand, not the object of understanding.

40 I first heard the term, "perfected science," from Alasdair MacIntyre, but neither he nor I have been able to determine who first used it. The idea goes back to Aristotle, and more recently, to Gottlob Frege. For MacIntyre's own views on the emergence of a completed intellectual framework, see his *Whose Justice? Which Rationality?*, pp. 349–388.

41 Bernard Williams, for one, appears to accept the possibility that we might someday arrive at something like the ideal of a perfected science in some domains of thought, and yet he argues that ethical concepts could not, even "in principle," be developed to this degree of completeness; see his *Ethics and the Limits of Philosophy*, pp. 148–155. The same conclusion would seem to be implied by Kovesi's analysis of moral concepts; see *Moral Notions*, pp. 147–149.

42 Both Brennan and Kovesi make this point, and in what follows I am greatly in the debt of both. In particular, see Brennan, *The Open-Texture of Moral Concepts*, pp. 15–87, and Kovesi, *Moral Notions*, pp. 144–161.

43 For example, see Hare, *Freedom and Reason*, pp. 1–3.

44 Wittgenstein, *Philosophical Investigations*, no. 198, p. 80. The same point is powerfully argued, from a different philosophical perspective, by Garrett Barden in his *After Principles*.

45 The same point is developed at more length by Eric D'Arcy in his *Human Acts: An Essay in Their Moral Evaluation* (Oxford: Clarendon Press, 1963).

46 R. W. Beardsmore, *Moral Reasoning* (New York: Shocken Books, 1969), p. 76.

47 See Anscombe, "Modern Moral Philosophy," 36–37.

48 See Ramsey, "The Case of the Curious Exception," 74–93.

2 THE MEANING OF MORALITY

1. Hilary Putnam, "Taking Rules Seriously," pp. 193–200 in *Realism with a Human Face*, James Conant, editor (Cambridge, MA: Harvard University Press, 1990), pp. 194–195.
2. Ibid., p. 195.
3. Paul Ramsey, "The Case of the Curious Exception," pp. 67–135 in Gene H. Outka and Paul Ramsey, editors, *Norm and Context in Christian Ethics* (New York: Charles Scribner's Sons, 1968), p. 78; emphasis in the original.
4. Ibid., p. 92.
5. Elizabeth (G. E. M.) Anscombe, "Modern Moral Philosophy," originally in *Philosophy* 33 (1958), reprinted as pp. 26–42 in *Collected Philosophical Papers, Volume III: Ethics, Religion and Politics*, G. E. M. Anscombe, editor (Minneapolis: University of Minnesota Press, 1981).
6. Alasdair MacIntyre, *After Virtue*, second edition (University of Notre Dame Press, 1981/1984).
7. These include, for example, Basil Mitchell, *Morality: Religious and Secular* (Oxford: Clarendon Press, 1980); Jeffrey Stout, *Ethics after Babel: The Languages of Morals and Their Discontents* (Boston: Beacon Press, 1988); and John Casey, *Pagan Virtue* (Oxford: Clarendon Press, 1990). Mitchell, like MacIntyre, regrets the loss of Christianity as a unifying tradition of moral discourse, but the other two emphatically do not. Stout does not view the supposed breakdown of unified moral discourse as a bad thing, and Casey believes that the moral discourse of European societies has been irreducibly pluralistic since the beginning of the Common Era.
8. There are a number of philosophers who take this view, although it should be noted that they differ considerably among themselves in the accounts that they give of the nature and significance of moral, or, more generally, normative, pluralism and diversity. They include Stuart Hampshire, *Morality and Conflict* (Cambridge, MA: Harvard University Press, 1983); Thomas Nagel, *The View from Nowhere* (Oxford University Press, 1986); Edmund L. Pincoffs, *Quandaries and Virtues: Against Reductivism in Ethics* (Lawrence: University Press of Kansas, 1986); Charles E. Larmore, *Patterns of Moral Complexity* (Cambridge University Press, 1987); Michael Stocker, *Plural and Conflicting Values* (Oxford: Clarendon Press, 1990); and Michael Slote, *From Morality to Virtue* (Oxford University Press, 1992).
9. See Bernard Williams, *Ethics and the Limits of Philosophy* (Cambridge, MA: Harvard University Press, 1985), pp. 174–196.

10. Ibid.

11. Anyone who is persuaded that moral or normative considerations are irreducibly diverse, for whatever reason, will not hold out for the possibility of a moral theory in the Kantian or utilitarian sense, but not everyone who argues for the former claim is especially concerned to argue against the cogency or the value of Kantian/utilitarian sorts of moral theories. Those who do make this argument would include, in addition to Williams, Stout and Pincoffs, all cited above, Annette Baier, "Theory and Reflective Practices," and "Doing Without Moral Theory," both in her *Postures of the Mind: Essays on Mind and Morals* (Minneapolis: University of Minnesota Press, 1985), pp. 207–227 and 228–245, respectively; Albert R. Jonsen and Stephen Toulmin, *The Abuse of Casuistry: A History of Moral Reasoning* (Berkeley: University of California Press, 1988); Garrett Barden, *After Principles* (University of Notre Dame Press, 1990); Martha C. Nussbaum, *Love's Knowledge: Essays on Philosophy and Literature* (Oxford University Press, 1990), in particular, pp. 54–105, "The Discernment of Perception: An Aristotelian Conception of Private and Public Rationality;" and Cora Diamond, "Wittgenstein and Metaphysics," "Anything but Argument?" and "Having a Rough Story about What Moral Philosophy Is," all in her *The Realistic Spirit: Wittgenstein, Philosophy and the Mind* (Cambridge, MA: The MIT Press, 1991), pp. 13–38, 291–308, and 367–382, respectively. Robert B. Louden offers a good overview of the anti-theory debate in his *Morality and Moral Theory: A Reappraisal and Reaffirmation* (Oxford University Press, 1992), pp. 85–162.

12. Julius Kovesi, *Moral Notions* (London: Routledge and Kegan Paul, Ltd., 1967), pp. 1–36; this point is developed further at pp. 103–120.

13. Relatively few have been prepared to defend this conclusion, but I believe that it is implied by some of Rorty's remarks; see his "Pragmatism and Philosophy," the introduction to *Consequences of Pragmatism* (Minneapolis: University of Minnesota Press, 1982), xiii- xlvii. It also seems to me that this is essentially Stout's view, in spite of his disclaimers about Rorty's views; see *Ethics After Babel*, pp. 243–265.

14. In what follows, I am indebted to Kovesi, *Moral Notions*, pp. 32–36, and Lee H. Yearley, *Mencius and Aquinas: Theories of Virtue and Conceptions of Courage* (Albany: State University of New York Press, 1990), pp. 182–203.

15. Wittgenstein, *Philosophical Investigations*, no. 198, p. 80; third

edition, Elizabeth Anscombe, translator, (New York: Macmillan Company, 1958).

16. Again, I am following Wittgenstein; see *The Philosophical Investigations*, nos. 195–242, pp. 79–88.

17. The most powerful statement of this view that I have seen is Raimond Gaita's *Good and Evil: An Absolute Conception* (London: Macmillan Press, 1991). Also see P. F. Strawson, *Individuals: An Essay in Descriptive Metaphysics* (London: Methuen Press, 1959); and "Freedom and Resentment," pp. 1–25 in *Freedom and Resentment and Other Essays* (London: Methuen, 1974); Roger Wertheimer, "Understanding the Abortion Argument," pp. 23–51 in *The Rights and Wrongs of Abortion*, Marshall Cohen, Thomas Nagel, and Thomas Scanlon, editors (Princeton University Press, 1974); A. I. Melden, *Rights and Persons* (Berkeley: University of California Press, 1977); Stanley Cavell, *The Claim of Reason: Wittgenstein, Skepticism, Morality and Tragedy* (Oxford University Press, 1979), particularly pp. 247–328; Annette Baier, "Theory and Reflective Practices," and "Doing Without Moral Theory?" both in her *Postures of the Mind: Essays on Mind and Morals*, pp. 207–227 and 228–245, respectively; Cora Diamond, "Anything but Argument?" "Eating Meat and Eating People," and "Having a Rough Story about What Moral Philosophy Is," in her *The Realistic Spirit: Wittgenstein, Philosophy, and the Mind*, pp. 291–308, 319–334, and 367–382, respectively. Others, although they do not express this view directly, do seem to come very near to it; I am thinking in particular of Stanley Hauerwas, in his *Truthfulness and Tragedy*, with Richard Bondi and David B. Burrell (The University of Notre Dame Press, 1977), and *Suffering Presence: Theological Reflections on Medicine, the Mentally Handicapped, and the Church* (The University of Notre Dame Press, 1986), and Judith N. Shklar, *Ordinary Vices* (Cambridge, MA: Harvard University Press, 1984). In this connection, also see Ronald Dworkin, *Life's Dominion: An Argument about Abortion, Euthanasia, and Individual Freedom* (New York: Alfred A. Knopf, 1993), pp. 68–101.

18. For example, Gaita says of a slave owner, who rapes his slave without any sense that he is violating a person who is capable of expressing love through her sexuality: "The slave owner does not fail to see the kinds of things I have been referring to *because* he fails to see her as a human being. To fail to understand (know) such things *is* what it is for him to fail to see her as a human being in the only sense that is relevant, that is, as something more than *homo sapiens*" (*Good and Evil*, p. 161; emphasis in the original). At

the same time, Gaita is aware that this sort of knowledge is culturally conditioned, at least in the sense that a certain matrix of concepts is a necessary condition for attaining it. I believe, but I am not sure, that he would say that the full concept of a human being, as he understands it, is not found in every society.

19. Diamond, "Eating Meat and Eating People," is especially helpful on this point.

20. Oddly enough, Anscombe acknowledges this point, only to retract her acknowledgement a few lines later: "One might be inclined to think that a law conception of ethics could arise only among people who accepted an allegedly divine positive law; that this is not so is shown by the Stoics, who also thought that whatever was involved in conformity to human virtues was required by divine law." Then, two paragraphs later: "Naturally it is not possible to have such a conception [that is, a law conception of ethics] unless you believe in God as a law-giver; *like Jews, Stoics, and Christians*" ("Modern Moral Philosophy," p. 30; emphasis mine).

21. H. A. Prichard, "Does Moral Philosophy Rest on a Mistake?" originally published in 1912, reprinted as pp. 1–17 in H. A. Prichard, *Moral Obligation and Duty and Interest: Essays and Lectures*, (Oxford University Press, 1968).

22. *Summa Contra Gentiles*, iii:ii, chapter 22, Vernon Bourke, translator. Compare *Summa theologiae* i–ii 100.5, where Aquinas claims that the other-regarding norms of the Decalogue can all be derived from a basic prohibition against harming others, together with those special obligations that are appropriate to parents, children, creditors, and the like.

23. None the less, it is possible to understand the concept of morality, and to *argue* that, once we have correctly understood the nature of moral judgement, traditional moral rules are merely presumptive in force. This would be, in effect, an argument that our concept of morality is in some way muddled or inadequate. This, as I understand it, is the line taken by the utilitarians, and, while in my opinion they are wrong, none the less, their position is not incoherent.

24. This observation is central to the work of Casey, Pincoffs, and Slote, all of whom, moreover, tend to equate morality *per se* with non-maleficence.

25. Gaita is right to insist that there is a difference between acknowledging the individuality and humanity of another through respecting fundamental moral boundaries, and *deriving* one's morality from a concept of respect for persons, which starts from

a theoretical account of what it is to be human or rational (*Good and Evil*, 24–41). None the less, there is clearly some affinity between the position taken by Gaita and others, and the views of more traditionally Kantian moral theorists. Among the latter, see in particular R. S. Downie and Elizabeth Telfer, *Respect for Persons: A Philosophical Analysis of the Moral, Political and Religious Idea of the Supreme Worth of the Individual Person* (New York: Shocken Books, 1970); Gene Outka, *Agape: An Ethical Analysis* (New Haven: Yale University Press, 1972); Alan Donagan, *The Theory of Morality* (The University of Chicago Press, 1977); Charles Fried, *Right and Wrong* (Cambridge, MA: Harvard University Press, 1978); and Alan Gewirth, *Reason and Morality* (The University of Chicago Press, 1978).

26. Instances of this sort of argument could be multiplied indefinitely. A famous, or infamous, example, noteworthy for its clarity and straightforwardness, is Michael Tooley's "Abortion and Infanticide," published as pp. 52–81 in Cohen, *et al*, editors, *The Rights and Wrongs of Abortion*.

27. This way of speaking is in homage to Julius Kovesi's *Moral Notions*.

28. I will not attempt the appalling task of surveying the literature that has been generated by recent debates on the morality of killing in various contexts. Ronald Dworkin offers an excellent overview of the issues, together with helpful discussions of many recent cases of importance, in *Life's Dominion*.

29. There has been relatively little discussion of the morality of lying in recent times; Sissela Bok offers a useful history of the discussion of this question, together with her own thorough and illuminating assessments of the issues that this discussion generates, in *Lying: Moral Choice in Public and Private Life* (New York: Pantheon Books, 1978). Thanks to the influence of Hume's discussion of the issue, promising has received more attention; Annette Baier surveys this discussion, and offers her own interpretation and defense of Hume, in "Promises, Promises, Promises," pp. 174–206 in *Postures of the Mind*, 1985. On the more general issues raised by our particular commitments to one another, see Margaret A. Farley's fine discussion in *Personal Commitments: Making, Keeping, Breaking* (San Francisco: Harper and Row, 1986).

30. Lisa Sowle Cahill offers a helpful summary of the relevant literature, together with a defense of this view, in "Human Sexuality," pp. 193–212 in *Moral Theology: Challenges for the Future*, Charles E. Curran, editor (New York: Paulist Press,

1990); also see her *Women and Sexuality*, the 1992 Madeleva Lecture in Spirituality (New York: Paulist Press, 1992).

31. Again, I have made no effort to offer a comprehensive survey of the relevant literature; in my view, the most helpful theoretical discussions are A. I. Melden's *Rights and Persons*, and Ronald Dworkin, *Taking Rights Seriously*, second edition (Cambridge, MA: Harvard University Press, 1977/1978). John Mahoney offers a useful brief survey of the history of the concept of human rights in "The Basis of Human Rights," pp. 313–332 in Curran, editor, *Moral Theology: Challenges for the Future* although he slights the critical contribution of Thomas Hobbes to the development of this concept.

32. This is abundantly clear from an examination of the arguments of the earliest defenders of an account of individual human rights; see Thomas Hobbes, *Leviathan*, C. B. Macpherson, editor (Middlesex: Penguin Books, 1968; originally published, 1651); and John Locke, *Two Treatises of Government*, Peter Laslett, editor (Cambridge University Press, 1960; originally published 1689).

33. On this point, compare J. M. Brennan's account of the procedure for resolving moral disputes; see *The Open-Texture of Moral Concepts* (New York: Barnes and Noble, 1977), pp. 88–149.

34. Alan Donagan offers a very good discussion of these issues in *The Theory of Morality*, pp. 143–171. He argues that the rationality of morality rules out simple moral perplexity, and defends the Pauline principle, but not the doctrine of double effect.

35. Again, see Donagan, *The Theory of Morality*, pp. 157–164. In general, I agree with Oliver O'Donovan that the principle of double effect is more illuminating taken as an expression of our understanding of murder, than as a general norm for judging human acts; see his *Resurrection and Moral Order: An Outline for Evangelical Ethics* (Grand Rapids: Eerdmans, 1986), pp. 192–194. Joseph Mangan gives a good account of the history of the doctrine of double effect among Catholic moral theologians, although he wrongly (as I believe) finds the principle in Aquinas; see his "An Historical Analysis of the Principle of Double Effect," *Theological Studies*, 10 (1949), 41–61. The most influential discussion of the doctrine of double effect among Catholic moral theologians since Vatican II remains Richard McCormick's "Ambiguity in Moral Choice," pp. 7–53 in Richard McCormick and Paul Ramsey, editors, *Doing Evil to Achieve Good: Moral Choice in Conflict Situations* (Chicago: Loyola University Press, 1978). It should be noted that, like Donagan, although for different reasons, McCormick does not defend the doctrine as it is

usually understood. For an example of a more recent defense of the traditional doctrine by a Catholic moral theologian, see Donald F. Montaldi, "A Defense of St. Thomas and the Principle of Double Effect," *Journal of Religious Ethics*, 14 (1986), 296–332. There are also some non-Catholic philosophers who defend this doctrine; see, for example, Thomas Nagel, *The View from Nowhere*, 1986, 175–185.

36. H. L. A. Hart and Tony Honore, *Causation in the Law*, second edition (Oxford University Press, 1959/1985). At the same time, however, they resist the claim that a determination of causation on the part of some agent can always be reduced to a moral judgement on that agent. Jonathan Bennett argues more explicitly that the distinction between direct and indirect causation cannot be sustained in his "Whatever the Consequences," *Analysis*, 26 (1966), 83–102.

37. See Michael Walzer, *Just and Unjust Wars* (New York: Basic Books, 1977), pp. 138–159.

38. Alan Donagan, *The Theory of Morality*, pp. 175–177.

39. Again, see Brennan, *The Open-Texture of Moral Concepts*, pp. 88–149.

40. Gaita, *Good and Evil*, pp. 234–235; emphasis in the original.

41. Bernard Williams, *Ethics and the Limits of Philosophy*, p. 185.

42. This is one of the dominant themes of his *Good and Evil*; the following remarks draw especially on his discussion at pp. 144–190.

43. This is the overall thesis of her *For Your Own Good: Hidden Cruelty in Child-Rearing and the Roots of Violence* (New York: Noonday Press/Farrar Straus and Giroux, 1983/1990).

44. Thomas Nagel, "Moral Luck," pp. 24–38 in *Moral Questions* (Cambridge University Press, 1979), p. 29.

3 MORAL JUDGEMENT IN CONTEXT: THOMAS AQUINAS ON THE MORAL ACT

1 Joel Kupperman, "Character and Ethical Theory," pp. 115–125 in *Midwest Studies in Philosophy, Volume XIII: Ethical Theory: Character and Virtue*, Peter French, Theodore E. Uehling, Jr., and Howard K. Wettstein, editors (The University of Notre Dame Press, 1988), p. 122. The same point is made by Robert Louden in his *Morality and Moral Theory: A Reappraisal and Reaffirmation* (Oxford University Press, 1992), pp. 148–152.

2 Alan Donagan has argued repeatedly for this reading of Aquinas, for example in *The Theory of Morality* (The University of Chicago

Press, 1977), pp. 57–66; "Consistency in Rationalist Moral Systems," *The Journal of Philosophy*, 81,6 (1984), 291–309; and "Teleology and Consistency in Theories of Morality as Natural Law," pp. 91–108 in *The Georgetown Symposium on Ethics: Essays in Honor of Henry Babcock Veatch*, Rocco Porreco, editor (New York: Lanham Press, 1984). Also see Annette Baier, "Doing Without Moral Theory?" pp. 228–245 in *Postures of the Mind: Essays on Mind and Morals* (Minneapolis: The University of Minnesota Press, 1985), p. 223.

3 All subsequent references to Aquinas' work are taken from the *Summa theologiae*, and all translations are my own.

4 As M.-D. Chenu points out, this is what a "summa" is, that is, a systematic exposition of a field of knowledge for the benefit of students; see *Towards Understanding St. Thomas*, translated, with authorized corrections and bibliographical additions, by A.-M. Landry and D. Hughes (Chicago: Henry Regnery Company, 1964), 298–299.

5 The exact interpretation of Aquinas' understanding of sacred doctrine is much disputed. I am here following David Burrell, *Aquinas: God and Action* (The University of Notre Dame Press, 1979), pp. 1–77, and Victor Preller, *Divine Science and the Science of God: A Reformulation of Thomas Aquinas* (Princeton University Press, 1967), pp. 179–265.

6 My interpretation of Aquinas' methodology, and, in particular, the significance of his use of dialectical method, is indebted to Alasdair MacIntyre, *Whose Justice? Which Rationality?* (The University of Notre Dame Press, 1988), pp. 164–208, and Mark D. Jordan, *Ordering Wisdom: the Hierarchy of Philosophical Discourses in Aquinas* (The University of Notre Dame Press, 1986). Chenu offers a very helpful discussion of the general understanding of dialectic and argument among Aquinas' contemporaries in his *Toward Understanding St. Thomas*, pp. 156–202.

7 Not even the famous Five Ways for proving the existence of God should be read in this way. It is important to read this passage (1 2.3) in the context of Aquinas' strictures on the kind of demonstration of God's existence that is possible to us (1 2.2).

8 MacIntyre, *Whose Justice? Which Rationality?*, p. 172.

9 On this point, see Burrell, *Aquinas: God and Action*, pp. 115–118.

10 I have discussed Aquinas' general account of goodness in more detail in *The Recovery of Virtue: The Relevance of Aquinas for Christian Ethics* (Louisville: Westminster/John Knox Press, 1990), pp. 34–68.

11 I have argued for this position at greater length in *The Recovery of*

Virtue, pp. 69–99. For the opposing view, see Anton Pegis, "Nature and Spirit: Some Reflections on the Problem of the End of Man," *Proceedings of the American Catholic Philosophical Association,* 23 (1949), 62–79. Kevin Staley offers a good summary of the issues involved in the debate over whether Aquinas recognizes a natural human end, and defends the view that he does, in "Happiness: The Natural End of Man?" *The Thomist* 53,2 (1989), 215–234.

12 Anthony Kenny offers a helpful discussion of the general problem of the knowledge of particulars in *Aquinas on Mind* (London: Routledge, 1993), pp. 111–118.

13 A full discussion of these issues would require us to compare the distinction between primary and secondary precepts of the natural law, which Aquinas draws in his earlier works, with the distinction among primary principles, proximate conclusions which can be readily drawn, and more remote and difficult applications of these principles to actions. For a helpful discussion of this distinction, see Michael Crowe, *The Changing Profile of the Natural Law* (The Hague: Martinus Nijhoff, 1977), pp. 179–191.

14 This claim is argued in more detail, although not with specific reference to Aquinas' account, by Eric D'Arcy, in his *Human Acts: An Essay in their Moral Evaluation* (Oxford: Clarendon Press, 1963).

15 For a good summary and analysis of the relevant arguments, see Gene Outka, *Agape: An Ethical Analysis* (New Haven: Yale University Press, 1972), pp. 154–168.

16 I have argued for the following interpretation of the significance of the inclinations in more detail in *The Recovery of Virtue,* pp. 82–91.

17 Germain G. Grisez, "The First Principle of Practical Reason: A Commentary on the *Summa Theologiae* 1–2, Question 94, Article 2," *The Natural Law Forum,* 10 (1965), 168–201.

18 John Finnis, *Natural Law and Natural Rights* (Oxford: Clarendon Press, 1980), pp. 94–95.

19 On the ordering of charity, see Stephen Pope, "Expressive Individualism and True Self-Love: A Thomistic Perspective," *Journal of Religion,* 71 (1991), 384–399, and Jean Porter, *"De Ordine Caritatis*: Charity, Friendship and Justice in Thomas Aquinas' *Summa Theologiae,*" *The Thomist,* 53,2 (1989), 197–214.

20 See Ronald Dworkin, *Life's Dominion: An Argument about Abortion, Euthanasia, and Individual Freedom* (New York: Alfred A. Knopf, 1993), pp. 10–15.

21 This position is widely held within the Christian tradition. Paul Ramsey offers an excellent discussion of this view in *The*

Patient as Person (New Haven: Yale University Press, 1970), pp. 113–164.

22 Admittedly, not many Christian theologians have been willing to allow for the legitimacy of suicide under any circumstances; for an example of one who does, see James M. Gustafson, *Ethics From a Theocentric Perspective, Volume Two: Ethics and Theology* (University of Chicago Press, 1984), pp. 187–218.

23 The literature on abortion is enormous. For an excellent summary of the moral and legal debates, see Ronald Dworkin, *Life's Dominion*, pp. 30–178.

24 Joseph F. Donceel, SJ, "Immediate Animation and Delayed Hominization," *Theological Studies*, 31 (1970), 76–105.

25 For a good statement of the objections that a defense of Aquinas' position would need to address, see Kenny, *Aquinas on Mind*, pp. 14–29.

26 Alan Donagan, *The Theory of Morality*, pp. 157–164.

4 MORAL ACTS AND ACTS OF VIRTUE

1. Edmund L. Pincoffs, *Quandaries and Virtues: Against Reductivism in Ethics* (Lawrence: University Press of Kansas, 1986), p. 14.
2. Ibid.
3. The most influential discussion of the relevance of the virtues to contemporary moral thought remains Alasdair MacIntyre's *After Virtue*, second edition (University of Notre Dame Press, 1981/ 1984). In addition to this and Pincoffs' book, other important contributions to the retrieval of the virtues would include James Wallace, *Virtues and Vices* (Ithaca: Cornell University Press, 1978); Stanley Hauerwas, *A Community of Character: Toward a Constructive Social Ethic* (University of Notre Dame Press, 1981); Michael Slote, *Goods and Virtues* (Oxford: Clarendon Press, 1983), and *From Morality to Virtue* (Oxford University Press, 1992); N. J. H. Dent, *The Moral Psychology of the Virtues* (Cambridge University Press, 1984); Gilbert Meilaender, *The Theory and Practice of Virtue* (University of Notre Dame Press, 1984); Judith Shklar, *Ordinary Vices* (Cambridge, MA: Harvard University Press, 1984); John Casey: *Pagan Virtue: An Essay in Ethics* (Oxford University Press, 1990); Stephen Macedo, *Liberal Virtues* (Oxford: Clarendon Press, 1990); Martha Nussbaum, *Love's Knowledge: Essays on Philosophy and Literature* (Oxford University Press, 1990); Michael Stocker, *Plural and Conflicting Values* (Oxford: Clarendon Press, 1990); Lee H. Yearley, *Mencius and Aquinas: Theories of Virtue and Conceptions of Courage* (Albany: State

University of New York Press, 1990). In addition, see Peter A. French, Theodore E. Uehling, and Howard K. Wettstein, editors, *Midwest Studies in Philosophy, Volume XIII: Ethical Theory: Character and Virtue* (University of Notre Dame Press, 1988) for a representative spectrum of opinion on the virtues and their relation to other approaches to moral discourse. Not all of these authors would align themselves with the anti-theory movement, however, and not everyone who distances him or herself from Kantian moral theorizing advocates a return to the virtues. Robert B. Louden offers a good discussion of the relation between anti-theory and virtue ethics in his "Virtue Ethics and Anti-Theory," *Philosophia* 20 (1990), 93–114.

4. In particular, see Pincoffs, *Quandaries and Virtues*, pp. 13–36.
5. Ibid., pp. 76–77.
6. Ibid., p. 77.
7. Ibid., p. 3.
8. Ibid., pp. 21–32; compare the comment on p. 106: "The point to notice is that these principles [i.e., the virtues] are substantive, in the sense that living by them is conceptually tied to being a certain sort of person, where the sort in question is morally significant."
9. Ibid., pp. 133–174.
10. Ibid., p. 142.
11. This parallel is all the more striking, since Pincoffs asserts that a virtue-centered approach to moral training will also provide a concrete content for moral education, whereas the approaches dictated by modern moral theories are too abstract to be of much practical use; see Pincoffs, *Quandaries and Virtues*, p. 171 and following.
12. Pincoffs discusses the indeterminacy of virtue concepts at *Quandaries and Virtues*, pp. 77–78.
13. Ibid., p. 155.
14. Wallace argues in this way; see *Virtues and Vices*, particularly pp. 9–38.
15. This line of argument is frequently offered by religious thinkers who are professedly, even vehemently, anti-liberal; Stanley Hauerwas, cited in note 3 above, is the most influential, but hardly the only one who makes such an argument.
16. Raimond Gaita, *Good and Evil: An Absolute Conception* (London: Macmillan Press, 1991), pp. 83–84.
17. Pincoffs, *Quandaries and Virtues*, p. 77.
18. C. S. Lewis, *The Screwtape Letters* (New York: Macmillan, 1961), pp. 76–79.

19. In this section and the next, I draw on two previously published articles, "The Unity of the Virtues and the Ambiguity of Goodness: A Reappraisal of Aquinas' Theory of the Virtues," *The Journal of Religious Ethics*, 21, 1 (1993), 137–163 and "The Subversion of Virtue: Acquired and Infused Virtue in the *Summa theologiae*," *The Annual of the Society of Christian Ethics 1992*, 19–41. Both articles are used with the kind permission of the editors of the respective journals.

20. In what follows, I follow a line of interpretation suggested by Alasdair MacIntyre, *Whose Justice? Which Rationality?* (University of Notre Dame Press, 1988), pp. 164–182, and especially Lee Yearley, *Mencius and Aquinas*, pp. 170–204.

21. Yearley, *Mencius and Aquinas*, p. 184.

22. Ibid., p. 184.

23. Daniel Mark Nelson, *The Priority of Prudence: Virtue and Natural Law in Thomas Aquinas and the Implications for Modern Ethics* (University Park: The Pennsylvania State University Press, 1992); see in particular pp. 87–104.

24. Giuseppe Abbà, *Lex et Virtus: Studi sull'evoluzione della dottrina morale di san Tommaso d'Aquino* (Rome: Libreria Ateneo Salesiano, 1983); for his discussion of the *Scriptum* in particular, see pp. 9–44. James Keenan falls into the mistake (as I conceive it) of interpreting the relation between prudence and the moral virtues in the *Summa* in this way, which leads him to the conclusion that the moral virtues do not render the agent good in *our* sense of goodness; that is, he takes it that the moral virtues simply produce actions in accordance with a rule of right reason which is antecedently determined by prudence, and, therefore, they bring about "rightness," in our terms, but not real "goodness." See his *Goodness and Rightness in Thomas Aquinas's Summa Theologiae* (Washington, DC: Georgetown University Press, 1992), pp. 92–116.

25. Abbà develops a similar interpretation of Aquinas' account of the virtues and their relation to the passions in *Lex et Virtus*, pp. 174–225. In what follows, I also draw on Mark Jordan, "Aquinas' Construction of a Moral Account of the Passions," *Freiburger Zeitschrift für Philosophie und Theologie*, 33 (1986), 71–97; Servais Pinckaers, "Les Passions et La Morale," *Revue des Sciences Philosophiques et Theologiques*, 74 (1990), 379–391; and Yearley, *Mencius and Aquinas*, pp. 79–112.

26. I take this point from Ronald de Sousa, who argues that the passions set patterns of salience in such a way as to determine both perception and choice in one way rather than another; see

his *The Rationality of Emotion* (Cambridge, MA: The MIT Press, 1987), pp. 171–204. He does not apply this point specifically to the virtues, but, on Aquinas' account, the virtues of the passions *are* materially equivalent to the passions themselves, as qualified by the *habitus* of the virtue to bring one set of saliences rather than another to the individual's perceptions and desires.

27. This is Abbà's conclusion; see *Lex et Virtus*, pp. 265–271.
28. Martha Nussbaum, *Love's Knowledge*, p. 68.
29. Ibid., p. 73.
30. This is the overall argument of *The Priority of Prudence*; in particular, see pp. 69–104. Nelson does not refer specifically to Nussbaum, however.
31. I have only recently come to appreciate this point, as a perusal of my earlier articles, cited above, will indicate.
32. I am grateful to the late Alan Donagan for helping me to see the force of this argument.
33. Compare Pincoffs' defense of perfectionism, *Quandaries and Virtues*, pp. 101–114.
34. I argue this point in more detail in "The Unity of the Virtues and the Ambiguity of Goodness," 154–160.
35. Michael Stocker, *Plural and Conflicting Values*, p. 149. His overall discussion of courage and its relation to judgement concerning incommensurable values and risks is illuminating; see pp. 129–164. Both John Casey and N. J. H. Dent offer a similar argument for the connection of the virtues, although not specifically in reference to Aquinas' thesis; see N. J. H. Dent, *The Moral Psychology of the Virtues*, pp. 96–119, and John Casey, *Pagan Virtue*, pp. 70–78.

5 THE VIRTUES REFORMULATED

1 For a good summary of the difficulties raised by Aquinas' account of the faculties, see Anthony Kenny, *Aquinas on Mind* (London: Routledge, 1993), pp. 145–160.
2 "Virtue ethics" has been widely criticized for its failure to provide adequate resources for social criticism; for a good summary and discussion of the relevant arguments, see Robert B. Louden, *Morality and Moral Theory: A Reappraisal and Reaffirmation* (Oxford University Press, 1992), pp. 148–152. On the other hand, Alasdair MacIntyre offers a powerful defense of the socially critical power of the virtues in "*Sōphrosunē*: How a Virtue Can Become Socially Disruptive," *Midwest Studies in Philosophy, Volume XIII: Ethical Theory: Character and Virtue*, Peter A. French, et al, editors

(University of Notre Dame Press, 1988), pp. 1–11. For a very different, but equally powerful, appeal to the traditional schema of the virtues in the service of social criticism, see Mary Daly, *Pure Lust: Elemental Feminist Philosophy* (Boston: Beacon Press, 1984), pp. 197–316.

3 See George Herbert Mead, *Mind, Self and Society from the Standpoint of a Social Behaviorist*, Charles W. Morris, editor (University of Chicago Press, 1934). Wittgenstein's account of language, which figured so prominently in the first chapter, also implies a social view of the individual mind. There are any number of other psychologists, philosophers, and theologians who take similar views. In what follows, I also draw on the following: Martin Hollis, *Models of Man: Philosophical Thoughts on Social Action* (Cambridge University Press, 1977), pp. 87–142; Alasdair MacIntyre, *After Virtue*, second edition (University of Notre Dame Press, 1981/1984), pp. 88–108; Drew Westin, *Self and Society: Narcissism, Collectivism, and the Development of Morals* (Cambridge University Press, 1985); Ronald de Sousa, *The Rationality of Emotion* (Cambridge, MA: The MIT Press, 1987), pp. 171–204; David B. Wong, "On Flourishing and Finding One's Identity in Community," in *Midwest Studies in Philosophy Volume XIII*, 1988, pp. 324–341; Alistair I. McFadyen, *The Call to Personhood: A Christian Theory of the Individual in Social Relationships* (Cambridge University Press, 1990); and Barbara Rogoff, *Apprenticeship in Thinking: Cognitive Development in Social Context* (Oxford University Press, 1990).

4 Correlatively, it is possible to acknowledge that the human individual is conditioned by his social context, to a far greater degree than Aquinas realized, without implying that the individual lacks a soul, at least in Aquinas' sense of the soul as the form of the living person. Mead himself does not deny the possibility of genuine originality and independence on the part of the individual; see *Mind, Self, and Society*, pp. 186–209.

5 In the *Nicomachean Ethics* III.7, 1115b 8–10; see the translation by W. D. Ross, 928–1112 in *The Basic Works of Aristotle*, Richard McKeon, editor (New York: Random House, 1941), p. 975.

6 For example, this appears to be Ralph McInerny's view; see his *Ethica Thomistica: The Moral Philosophy of Thomas Aquinas* (Washington, DC: The Catholic University of America Press, 1982), pp. 91–104.

7 At this point, I follow Hollis, *Models of Man*, pp. 87–106.

8 Both Michael Stocker and N. J. H. Dent make a similar point; see N. J. H. Dent, *The Moral Psychology of the Virtues* (Cambridge

University Press, 1984), 96–119, and Michael Stocker, *Plural and Conflicting Values* (Oxford: Clarendon Press, 1990), pp. 129–155.

9 Edmund L. Pincoffs, *Quandaries and Virtues: Against Reductivism in Ethics* (Lawrence: The University Press of Kansas, 1986), p. 92. More generally, see his discussion on pp. 89–94. It should be noted that, while he acknowledges the "peculiar importance" of justice (p. 94), he also insists that justice is not the only, or the central, virtue (p. 92).

10 Harry Frankfurt offers a very similar (although not identical) account of the will in his well-known essay, "Freedom of the Will and the Concept of a Person," *The Journal of Philosophy*, 63,1, (1971), 5–20.

11 See Mead, *Mind, Self and Society*, pp. 135–226.

12 On this point, see Leonard Shengold, *Soul Murder: The Effects of Childhood Abuse and Deprivation* (New York: Fawcett Columbine, 1989), pp. 1–31.

13 Both Pincoffs and James Wallace offer illuminating discussions of conscientiousness; see Pincoffs, *Quandaries and Virtues*, pp. 89–94 and Wallace, *Virtues and Vices* (Ithaca: Cornell University Press, 1978), 90–127.

14 Pincoffs, *Quandaries and Virtues*, pp. 28–29.

15 MacIntyre, *After Virtue*, pp. 181–203.

16 This is not quite MacIntyre's own point, although it is consistent with what he says; see in particular MacIntyre, *After Virtue*, pp. 190–194, and compare his remarks at pp. 150–152.

17 MacIntyre, ibid., pp. 150–152.

18 Carol Gilligan, *In a Different Voice: Psychological Theory and Women's Development* (Cambridge, MA: Harvard University Press, 1982). For a good critical discussion of Gilligan's own work, and of the extensive debate that it has generated, see Owen Flanagan, *Varieties of Moral Personality: Ethics and Psychological Realism* (Cambridge, MA: Harvard University Press, 1991), pp. 196–234. For a more recent survey and discussion of this literature, see Cynthia S. W. Crysdale, "Gilligan and the Ethics of Care: An Update," *Religious Studies Review*, 20 (1994), 21–28.

19 However, this does not appear to be Gilligan's own view; see *In a Different Voice*, pp. 151–174.

20 This argument is frequently heard, although it is not always taken beyond the level of sheer rhetoric. Alasdair MacIntyre makes a powerful case for the claim that the virtues cannot readily be sustained in contemporary society in *After Virtue*; see, in particular, pp. 226–278. A similar argument has been a staple of feminist social criticism for some time; see Mary Wollstonecraft, *A*

Vindication of the Rights of Woman, Mirian Brody, editor (London: Penguin Books, 1992; originally published 1792), especially pp. 91–172, and, for a very different, but effective, use of the same argument, Mary Daly, *Pure Lust*, pp. 197–288.

21 This general point is forcefully argued in Stephen Macedo's *Liberal Virtues* (Oxford: Clarendon Press, 1990).

22 Again, MacIntyre makes this point in *After Virtue*, pp. 256–263, although it would not be quite right to say that he sees these localized communities as necessary components of a good society; rather, he sees them as *alternatives* to contemporary society.

23 John Stuart Mill, "On Liberty," 249–360, in *Essential Works of John Stuart Mill*, Max Lerner, editor (London: Bantam Books, 1961; "On Liberty" originally published 1859), pp. 268–304. In my view, the account of rationality as tradition-guided inquiry developed in MacIntyre's writings since 1984 has the same implications; I have argued as much in "Openness and Constraint: Moral Reflection as Tradition-guided Inquiry in Alasdair MacIntyre's Recent Works," *The Journal of Religion*, 73 (1993), 514–536.

24 This is the overall argument of Lee Yearley, *Mencius and Aquinas: Theories of Virtue and Conceptions of Courage* (Albany: State University of New York Press, 1990). See in particular pp. 169–203 for his explicit programmatic statement.

Bibliography

BOOKS

Abbà, Giuseppe. *Lex et Virtus: Studi sull'evoluzione della dottrina morale di san Tommaso d'Aquino* (Rome: Libreria Ateneo Salesiano, 1983).

Ayer, A. J. *Language, Truth, and Logic* (New York: Dover Books, 1952/1946).

Baier, Annette. *Postures of the Mind: Essays on Mind and Morals* (Minneapolis: University of Minnesota Press, 1985).

Barden, Garrett. *After Principles* (University of Notre Dame Press, 1990).

Barth, Karl. *Church Dogmatics* II/2 and III/4. G. W. Bromiley and T. F. Torrence, editors (Edinburgh: T and T. Clark, 1957).

Beardsmore, R. W. *Moral Reasoning* (New York: Shocken Books, 1969).

Bentham, Jeremy. *An Introduction to the Principles of Morals and Legislation*, Introduction by Laurence J. Lafleur (New York: Macmillan, 1948; originally published 1789).

Blenkinsopp, Joseph. *Prophecy and Canon: A Contribution to the Study of Jewish Origins* (University of Notre Dame Press, 1977).

Bok, Sissela. *Lying: Moral Choice in Public and Private Life* (New York: Pantheon Books, 1978).

Brennan, J. M. *The Open-Texture of Moral Concepts* (New York: Barnes and Noble, 1977).

Burrell, David. *Aquinas: God and Action* (The University of Notre Dame Press, 1979).

Cahill, Lisa Sowle. *Women and Sexuality* (New York: Paulist Press, 1992).

Casey, John. *Pagan Virtue: An Essay in Ethics* (Oxford: Clarendon Press, 1990).

Cavell, Stanley. *The Claim of Reason: Wittgenstein, Skepticism, Morality and Tragedy* (Oxford University Press, 1979).

Chenu, M.-D. *Towards Understanding St. Thomas* A.-M. Landry and D. Hughes, translators (Chicago: Henry Regnery Company, 1964).

Crowe, Michael. *The Changing Profile of the Natural Law* (The Hague: Martinus Nijhoff, 1977).

Curran, Charles E., editor. *Moral Theology: Challenges for the Future* (New York: Paulist Press, 1990).

Curran, Charles and Richard McCormick, editors. *Readings in Moral Theology No. 1: Moral Norms and the Catholic Tradition* (New York: Paulist Press, 1979).

D'Arcy, Eric. *Human Acts: An Essay in Their Moral Evaluation* (Oxford: Clarendon Press, 1963).

Daly, Mary. *Pure Lust: Elemental Feminist Philosophy* (Boston: Beacon Press, 1984).

de Sousa, Ronald. *The Rationality of Emotion* (Cambridge, MA: The MIT Press, 1987).

Dent, N. J. H. *The Moral Psychology of the Virtues* (Cambridge University Press, 1984).

Diamond, Cora. *The Realistic Spirit: Wittgenstein, Philosophy and the Mind* (Cambridge, MA: The MIT Press, 1991).

Donagan, Alan. *The Theory of Morality* (The University of Chicago Press, 1977).

Downie, R. S. and Elizabeth Telfer. *Respect for Persons: A Philosophical Analysis of the Moral, Political and Religious Idea of the Supreme Worth of the Individual Person* (New York: Shocken Books, 1970).

Dunn, James. *Unity and Diversity in the New Testament: An Inquiry into the Character of Earliest Christianity* (Philadelphia: Westminster Press, 1977).

Dworkin, Ronald. *Life's Dominion: An Argument about Abortion, Euthanasia, and Individual Freedom* (New York: Alfred A Knopf, 1993).

Taking Rights Seriously, second edition (Cambridge, MA: Harvard University Press, 1977/1978).

Farley, Margaret A. *Personal Commitments: Making, Keeping, Breaking* (San Francisco: Harper and Row, 1986).

Finnis, John. *Moral Absolutes: Tradition, Revision, and Truth* (Washington DC: The Catholic University of America Press, 1991).

Fundamentals of Ethics (Washington DC: Georgetown University Press, 1983).

Natural Law and Natural Rights (Oxford: Clarendon Press, 1980).

Flanagan, Owen. *Varieties of Moral Personality: Ethics and Psychological Realism* (Cambridge, MA: Harvard University Press, 1991).

Fletcher, Joseph. *Situation Ethics: The New Morality* (Philadelphia: Westminster Press, 1966).

French, Peter A., Theodore E. Uehling, Jr., and Howard K. Wettstein, editors. *Midwest Studies in Philosophy, Volume XIII: Ethical Theory; Character and Virtue* (The University of Notre Dame Press, 1988).

Fried, Charles. *Right and Wrong* (Cambridge, MA: Harvard University Press, 1978).

Gaita, Raimond. *Good and Evil: An Absolute Conception* (London: Macmillan Press, 1991).

Gewirth, Alan. *Reason and Morality* (The University of Chicago Press, 1978).

Gilligan, Carol. *In a Different Voice: Psychological Theory and Women's Development* (Cambridge, MA: Harvard University Press, 1982).

Grisez, Germain. *The Way of the Lord Jesus, Volume One: Christian Moral Principles* (Franciscan Herald Press, 1983).

Gustafson, James. *Ethics from a Theocentric Perspective, Volume Two: Ethics and Theology* (University of Chicago Press, 1984).

Hampshire, Stuart. *Morality and Conflict* (Cambridge, MA: Harvard University Press, 1983).

Hare, R. M. *Moral Thinking: Its Levels, Method and Point* (Oxford University Press, 1981).

Freedom and Reason (Oxford University Press, 1963/1965).

The Language of Morals (Oxford University Press, 1952/1964).

Hart, H. L. A. and Tony Honore. *Causation in the Law*, second edition. (Oxford University Press, 1985).

Hauerwas, Stanley. *After Christendom? How the Church is to Behave if Freedom, Justice, and a Christian Nation Are Bad Ideas* (Nashville: Abingdon Press, 1991).

Suffering Presence: Theological Reflections on Medicine, the Mentally Handicapped, and the Church (University of Notre Dame Press, 1986).

The Peaceable Kingdom: A Primer in Christian Ethics (University of Notre Dame Press, 1983).

A Community of Character: Towards a Constructive Christian Social Ethic (University of Notre Dame Press, 1981).

Hauerwas, Stanley, Richard Bondi, and David B. Burrell. *Truthfulness and Tragedy* (University of Notre Dame Press, 1977).

Heisenberg, Werner. *Physics and Philosophy: The Revolution in Modern Science* (New York: Harper and Row, 1958).

Hobbes, Thomas. *Leviathan*, C. B. Macpherson, editor (Middlesex: Penguin Books, 1968; originally published 1651).

Hollis, Martin. *Models of Man: Philosophical Thoughts on Social Action* (Cambridge University Press, 1977).

Hoose, Bernard. *Proportionalism: The American Debate and Its European Roots* (Washington, DC: Georgetown University Press, 1987).

Jonsen, Albert R. and Stephen Toulmin. *The Abuse of Casuistry: A History of Moral Reasoning* (Berkeley: University of California Press, 1988).

Jordan, Mark D. *Ordering Wisdom: The Hierarchy of Philosophical Discourses in Aquinas* (University of Notre Dame Press, 1986).

Kant, Immanuel. *Groundwork of the Metaphysics of Morals*, H. J. Paton, translator (New York: Harper and Row, 1956/1964; originally published 1785).

Critique of Practical Reason, Lewis White Beck, translator (Indianapolis: Bobbs Merrill, 1956; originally published 1788).

Keenan, James. *Goodness and Rightness in Thomas Aquinas's Summa Theologiae* (Washington, DC: Georgetown University Press, 1992).

Kenny, Anthony. *Aquinas on Mind* (London: Routledge, 1993).

Kierkegaard, Søren. *Fear and Trembling*, Walter Lowrie, translator (Princeton University Press, 1941).

Kirk, Kenneth E. *Conscience and its Problems: An Introduction to Casuistry* (New York: Longmans, Green and Co. Ltd., 1927).

Kovesi, Julius. *Moral Notions* (London: Routledge and Kegan Paul, 1967).

Kripke, Saul. *Wittgenstein on Rules and Private Language: An Elementary Exposition* (Cambridge, MA: Harvard University Press, 1982).

Larmore, Charles E. *Patterns of Moral Complexity* (Cambridge University Press, 1987).

Lehman, Paul. *Ethics in a Christian Context* (New York: Harper and Row, 1963).

Lewis, C. S. *The Screwtape Letters* (New York: Macmillan, 1961).

Locke, John. *Two Treatises on Government*, Peter Laslett, editor (Cambridge University Press, 1960; originally published 1689).

Louden, Robert B. *Morality and Moral Theory: A Reappraisal and Reaffirmation* (Oxford University Press, 1992).

Macedo, Stephen. *Liberal Virtues* (Oxford: Clarendon Press, 1990).

MacIntyre, Alasdair. *Whose Justice? Which Rationality?* (University of Notre Dame Press, 1988).

After Virtue, second edition (University of Notre Dame Press, 1981/1984).

McCormick, Richard A. *The Critical Calling: Reflections on Moral Dilemmas Since Vatican II* (Washington, DC: Georgetown University Press, 1989).

McCormick, Richard A. and Paul Ramsey, editors. *Doing Evil to Achieve Good: Moral Choice in Conflict Situations* (Loyola University Press, 1978).

McFayden, Alistair I. *The Call to Personhood: A Christian Theory of the Individual in Social Relationships* (Cambridge University Press, 1990).

McInerny, Ralph. *Ethica Thomistica: The Moral Philosophy of Thomas Aquinas* (Washington, DC: The Catholic University of America Press, 1982).

Mead, George Herbert. *Mind, Self and Society from the Standpoint of a Social Behaviorist*, Charles W. Morris, editor (University of Chicago Press, 1934).

Meilaender, Gilbert. *The Theory and Practice of Virtue* (University of Notre Dame Press, 1984).

Melden, A. I. *Rights and Persons* (Berkeley: University of California Press, 1977).

Mill, John Stuart. *On Liberty*, In *Essential Works of John Stuart Mill*, Max Lerner, editor (London: Bantam Books, 1961; originally published 1859).

Miller, Alice. *For Your Own Good: Hidden Cruelty in Child-Rearing and the Roots of Violence* (New York: Noonday Press/Farrar Straus and Giroux, 1983/1990).

Mitchell, Basil. *Morality: Religious and Secular* (Oxford: Clarendon Press, 1980).

Nagel, Thomas. *The View from Nowhere* (Oxford University Press, 1986).

Moral Questions (Cambridge University Press, 1980).

Nelson, Daniel Mark. *The Priority of Prudence: Virtue and Natural Law in Thomas Aquinas and the Implications for Modern Ethics* (University Park: The Pennsylvania State University Press, 1992).

Niebuhr, Richard H. *The Responsible Self: An Essay in Christian Moral Philosophy* (New York: Harper and Row, 1963).

Nussbaum, Martha C. *Love's Knowledge: Essays on Philosophy and Literature* (Oxford University Press, 1990).

The Fragility of Goodness: Luck and Ethics in Greek Tragedy and Philosophy (Cambridge University Press, 1986).

O'Donovan, Oliver. *Resurrection and Moral Order: An Outline for Evangelical Ethics* (Grand Rapids: Eerdmans, 1986).

Outka, Gene H. *Agape: An Ethical Analysis* (New Haven: Yale University Press, 1972).

Outka, Gene H. and Paul Ramsey, editors. *Norm and Context in Christian Ethics* (New York: Charles Scribner's Sons, 1986).

Pincoffs, Edmund L. *Quandaries and Virtues: Against Reductivism in Ethics* (Lawrence: University Press of Kansas, 1986).

Porter, Jean. *The Recovery of Virtue: The Relevance of Aquinas for Christian Ethics* (Louisville: Westminster/John Knox Press, 1990).

Preller, Victor. *Divine Science and the Science of God: A Reformulation of Thomas Aquinas* (Princeton University Press, 1967).

Prichard, H. A. *Moral Obligation and Duty and Interest: Essays and Lectures* (Oxford University Press, 1968).

Quine, Willard van Orman. *From a Logical Point of View* (New York: Harper and Row, 1961).

Ramsey, Paul. *The Patient as Person* (New Haven: Yale University Press, 1970).

　Deeds and Rules in Christian Ethics (New York: Charles Scribner's Sons, 1967).

Rogoff, Barbara. *Apprenticeship in Thinking: Cognitive Development in Social Context* (Oxford University Press, 1990).

Shengold, Leonard. *Soul Murder: The Effects of Childhood Abuse and Deprivation* (New York: Fawcett Columbine, 1989).

Shklar, Judith N. *Ordinary Vices* (Cambridge, MA: Harvard University Press, 1984).

Sidgwick, Henry. *The Methods of Ethics*, seventh edition (Indianapolis: Hackett, 1891/1907).

Slote, Michael. *From Morality to Virtue* (Oxford University Press, 1992).

　Goods and Virtues (Oxford: Clarendon Press, 1983).

Stevenson, Charles L. *Ethics and Language* (New Haven: Yale University Press, 1944).

Stocker, Michael. *Plural and Conflicting Values* (Oxford: Clarendon Press, 1990).

Stout, Jeffrey. *Ethics after Babel: The Languages of Morals and Their Discontents* (Boston: Beacon Press, 1988).

Strawson, P. F. *Individuals: An Essay in Descriptive Metaphysics* (London: Methuen Press, 1959).

Troeltsch, Ernst. *The Social Teaching of the Christian Churches*, 2 volumes, Olive Wyon, translator (University of Chicago Press, 1931).

Wallace, James. *Virtues and Vices* (Ithaca: Cornell University Press, 1978).

Walzer, Michael. *Just and Unjust Wars* (New York: Basic Books, 1977).

Westin, Drew. *Self and Society; Narcissism, Collectivism, and the Development of Morals* (Cambridge University Press, 1985).

Williams, Bernard. *Ethics and the Limits of Philosophy* (Cambridge, MA: Harvard University Press, 1985).

Wittgenstein, Ludwig. *Philosophical Investigation*, third edition, Elizabeth Anscombe, translator (New York: Macmillan Company, 1958).

Wollstonecraft, Mary. *A Vindication of the Rights of Woman*, Mirian Brody, editor (London: Penguin Books, 1992; originally published 1792).

Yearley, Lee H. *Mencius and Aquinas: Theories of Virtue and Conceptions of Courage* (Albany: State University of New York Press, 1990).

ARTICLES

Anscombe, Elizabeth. "Modern Moral Philosophy," in *Collected Philosophical Papers, Volume III: Ethics, Religion and Politics*, G. E. M. Anscombe, editor (Minneapolis: University of Minnesota Press, 1981), pp. 26–42.

Bennett, Jonathan. "Whatever the Consequences," *Analysis*, 26 (1966), 83–102.

Cahill, Lisa Sowle. "Human Sexuality," in *Moral Theology: Challenges for the Future*, Charles E. Curran, editor (New York: Paulist Press, 1990), pp. 193–212.

Crysdale, Cynthia S. W. "Gilligan and the Ethics of Care: An Update," *Religious Studies Review*, 20 (1994), 21–28.

Donagan, Alan. "Consistency in Rationalist Moral Systems," *The Journal of Philosophy*, 81,6 (1984), 291–309.

"Teleology and Consistency in Theories of Morality as Natural Law," in *The Georgetown Symposium on Ethics: Essays in Honor of Henry Babcock Veatch*, Rocco Porreco, editor (New York: Lanham Press, 1984), pp. 91–108.

Donceel, Joseph F., S-J. "Immediate Animation and Delayed Hominization," *Theological Studies*, 31 (1970), 76–105.

Fletcher, Joseph. "What's in a Rule? A Situationist's View," in *Norm and Context in Christian Ethics*, Gene H. Outka and Paul Ramsey, editors (New York: Charles Scribner's Sons, 1968), pp. 325–350.

Frankfurt, Harry. "Freedom of the Will and the Concept of a Person," *The Journal of Philosophy*, 63,1 (1971), 5–20.

Fried, Charles. "The Artificial Reason of Law or: What Lawyers Know," *Texas Law Review*, 60 (1981), 35–58.

Fuchs, Joseph. "The Absoluteness of Moral Terms," in *Readings in Moral Theology No. 1: Moral Norms and the Catholic Tradition*, Charles Curran and Richard McCormick, editors (New York: Paulist Press, 1979), pp. 94–137.

Green, Ronald M. "Enough is Enough! *Fear and Trembling* Is *Not* about Ethics," *The Journal of Religious Ethics*, 21,2 (1993), 191–210.

Grisez, Germain G. "The First Principle of Practical Reason: A Commentary on the *Summa Theologiae* 1–2, Question 94, Article 2," *The Natural Law Forum*, 10 (1965), 168–201.

Grisez, Germain, with Joseph Boyle and John Finnis. "Practical Principles, Moral Truth and Ultimate Ends," *American Journal of Jurisprudence*, 32 (1987), 99–151.

Hart, H. L. A. "Jhering's Heaven of Concepts and Modern Analytic Jurisprudence," in H. L. A. Hart, *Essays in Jurisprudence and Philosophy* (Oxford University Press, 1983), pp. 265–277.

Jordan, Mark. "Aquinas' Construction of a Moral Account of the Passions," *Freiburger Zeitschrift für Philosophie und Theologie* 33 (1986), 71–97.

Keenan, James. "The Casuistry of John Major: Nominalist Professor of Paris (1506–1531)," in *The Annual of the Society of Christian Ethics: 1993*, 205–222.

"Virtue Ethics: Making a Case as it Comes of Age," *Thought*, 67 (1992), 115–127.

Kupperman, Joel. "Character and Ethical Theory," in *Midwest Studies in Philosophy, Volume XIII: Ethical Theory: Character and Virtue* (1988), 115–125.

MacIntyre, Alasdair. "*Sōphrosunē*: How a Virtue Can Become Socially Disruptive," in *Midwest Studies in Philosophy, Volume XIII: Ethical Theory: Character and Virtue*, 1988, pp. 1–11.

Mahoney, John. "The Basis of Human Rights," in *Moral Theology: Challenges for the Future*, 1990, 313–332.

Mangan, Joseph. "An Historical Analysis of the Principle of Double Effect," *Theological Studies*, 10 (1949), 41–61.

McCormick, Richard A. "Ambiguity in Moral Choice," in *Doing Evil to Achieve Good: Moral Choice in Conflict Situations*, Richard McCormick and Paul Ramsey, editors (Loyola University Press, 1978), pp. 7–53.

Mitchell, Basil. "Ideas, Roles and Rules," in *Norm and Context in Christian Ethics*, 1968, 351–365.

Montaldi, Donald F. "A Defense of St. Thomas and the Principle of Double Effect," *Journal of Religious Ethics*, 14 (1986), 296–332.

Outka, Gene H. "Virtue, Principles, and Rules," in *Norm and Context in Christian Ethics*, 1968, pp. 37–66.

Pegis, Anton. "Nature and Spirit: Some Reflections on the Problem of the End of Man," *Proceedings of the American Catholic Philosophical Association*, 23 (1949), 62–79.

Pinckaers, Servais. "Les Passions et La Morale," *Revue des Sciences Philosophiques et Theologiques*, 74 (1990), 379–391.

Pope, Stephen. "Expressive Individualism and True Self-Love: A Thomistic Perspective," *Journal of Religion*, 71 (1991), 384–399.

Porter, Jean. "Openness and Constraint: Moral Reflection as Tradition-guided Inquiry in Alasdair MacIntyre's Recent Works," *The Journal of Religion*, 73 (1993), 514–536.

"The Unity of the Virtues and the Ambiguity of Goodness: A Reappraisal of Aquinas's Theory of the Virtues," *The Journal of Religious Ethics*, 21 (1993), 137–163.

"The Subversion of Virtue: Acquired and Infused Virtue in the *Summa Theologiae*," in *The Annual of the Society of Christian Ethics: 1992*, 19–41.

"*De Ordine Caritatis*: Charity, Friendship and Justice in Thomas Aquinas' Summa Theologiae," *The Thomist*, 53,2 (1989), 197–214.

Putnam, Hilary. "Taking Rules Seriously," in *Realism with a Human Face*, James Conant, editor (Cambridge, MA: Harvard University Press, 1990), pp. 193–200.

Ramsey, Paul. "The Case of the Curious Exception," in *Norm and Context in Christian Ethics*, 1968, pp. 67–138.

Rorty, Richard. "Pragmatism and Philosophy," in Richard Rorty, *Consequences of Pragmatism* (Minneapolis: University of Minnesota Press, 1982).

Staley, Kevin. "Happiness: The Natural End of Man?" *The Thomist*, 53 (1989), 215–234.

Strawson, P. F. "Freedom and Resentment," in P. F. Strawson, *Freedom and Resentment and Other Essays* (London: Methuen, 1974), pp. 1–25.

Tooley, Michael. "Abortion and Infanticide," in *The Rights and Wrongs of Abortion*, Marshall Cohen, Thomas Nagel, and Thomas Scanlon, editors (Princeton University Press, 1974), pp. 52–81.

Waismann, Friedrich. "Verifiability," in *Proceedings of the Aristotelian Society*, supplementary volume 19 (1945), 119–150.

Wertheimer, Roger. "Understanding the Abortion Argument," in *The Rights and Wrongs of Abortion*, 1974, pp. 23–51.

Wong, David B. "On Flourishing and Finding One's Identity in Community," in *Midwest Studies in Philosophy, Volume XIII: Ethical Theory: Character and Virtue*, 1988, pp. 324–341.

Index

abortion, 62, 119–124
also see murder and killing
Anscombe, Elizabeth, 11–18, 36–40, 44, 51, 210 n.20
anti-theory in ethics
see theory, moral
Aquinas, Thomas, 5–7, 52, 86, 89, 110–112, 114, 116–119, 121–127, 137, 167–174, 180–183, 196–200, 210 n.22, 212 n.35
dialectical methodology of, 89–91, 142–159
on the moral act, 91–102
on reason in morals, 102–110, 150–159
on the virtues, 138–150, 159–166
Aristotle, 6, 91, 92, 95, 105, 141, 149, 150, 159, 155–156, 164–165, 173
autonomy, 55–56, 114–115
Ayer, A. J., 9–10

Baier, Annette, 208 n.11, 209 n.17, 211 n.29, 214 n.2
Barden, Garrett, 205 n.30, 206 n.44, 208 n.11
Barth, Karl, 10, 202 n.8
Bennett, Jonathan, 213 n.36
Bentham, Jeremy, 9, 45
Blenkinsopp, Joseph, 204 n.23
Bok, Sissela, 211 n.29
Brennan, J. M., 22–23, 206 n.42, 212 n.33
Burrell, David, 214 n.5, n.9

Cahill, Lisa Sowle, 211 n.30
Casey, John, 207 n.7, n. 24, 216 n.3, 219 n.35
Cavell, Stanley, 209 n.17
Chenu, M.-D., 214 n.4, n.6
Christian ethics, 1–5, 11, 88

circumstances, 95–98
concepts, 23–31
analogical character, 49–50
concepts, moral, 22–23, 31–40, 46–47
criteria for understanding, 34–36, 49–50, 73–83, 183
and emotions, 78–83
and general concept of morality, 46–47, 58
and non-moral concepts, 101–102
and rules of morality, 58, 100–101
and virtues, 133–138
also see morality, concept of; rules, moral
conflicts of duties, 60, 68–72
consequentialism, 4, 9, 15–16, 37, 63, 110, 210 n.23
conscientiousness, 188–193
courage
see fortitude
Crowe, Michael, 215 n.13
Crysdale, Cynthia S. W., 221 n.18

Daly, Mary, 220 n.2, 222 n.20
D'Arcy, Eric, 206 n.45, 215 n.14
Dent, N. J. H., 216 n.3, 220–221 n.8
de Sousa, Ronald, 218–219 n.26, 220 n.3
Diamond, Cora, 208 n.11, 209 n.17, 210 n.19
Donagan, Alan, 72–73, 124, 211 n.25, 212 n.34, 212 n.35, 213–214 n.2, 219 n.32
Donceel, Joseph, 122
double effect, 69–72
Downie, R. S., 211 n.25
Dunn, James, 204 n.23
Dworkin, Ronald, 113, 209 n.17, 211 n.28, 212 n.31, 216 n.23